MAPPING THE GREAT GAME

Published in Great Britain and the United States of America in 2019 by
CASEMATE PUBLISHERS
The Old Music Hall, 106–108 Cowley Road, Oxford OX4 1JE, UK
and
1950 Lawrence Road, Havertown, PA 19083, USA

Hardcover Edition: ISBN 978-1-61200-8141
Digital Edition: ISBN 978-1-61200-8158

A CIP record for this book is available from the British Library

Printed and bound in the United Kingdom by TJ International

For a complete list of Casemate titles, please contact:

CASEMATE PUBLISHERS (UK)
Telephone (01865) 241249
Email: casemate-uk@casematepublishers.co.uk
www.casematepublishers.co.uk

CASEMATE PUBLISHERS (US)
Telephone (610) 853-9131
Fax (610) 853-9146
Email: casemate@casematepublishers.com
www.casematepublishers.com

All maps created by Roger Smith of Geographx. Maps 3 and 5 based on maps published by Matthew Edney and Geoffrey Wheeler respectively.

MAPPING THE GREAT GAME

Explorers, Spies & Maps in Nineteenth-century Asia

RIAZ DEAN

CASEMATE

Oxford & Philadelphia

For Beth

Contents

Maps

All maps created by Roger Smith of Geographx.
Maps 3 and 5 based on maps published by Matthew Edney and Geoffrey Wheeler respectively.

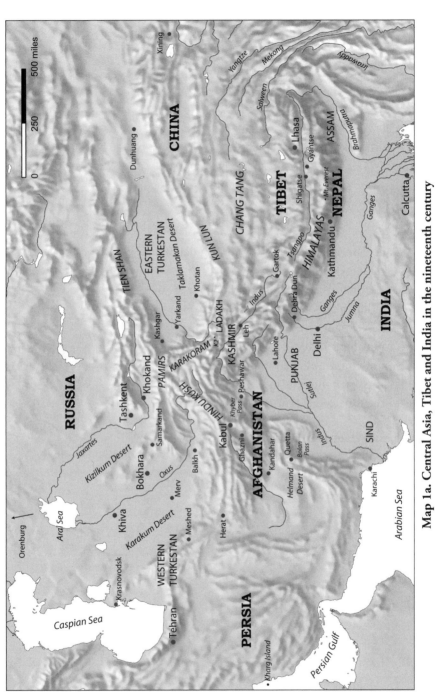

Map 1a. Central Asia, Tibet and India in the nineteenth century

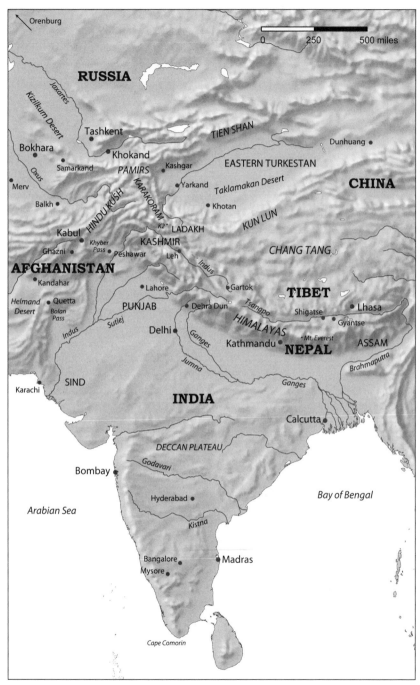

Map 1b. Central Asia, Tibet and India in the nineteenth century

Introduction

The exploration and mapping of Asia and its subsequent carve-up by competing empires make up a fascinating part of its recent history. Most of this activity occurred during the nineteenth century, when large portions of its vast terra incognita previously left blank on maps, or simply marked 'Unexplored', were finally filled in. The continent would reluctantly reveal its mysteries: a myriad of people and cultures; and, inland, an extreme geography and weather, far removed from the moderating effects of any ocean. This was a time when large parts of the world and its people remained little known to Europeans, and the desire for geographical knowledge—translated into books and maps—was an end in itself. The quest for adventure too, even at great personal risk, needed no further explanation or justification.

Although this book is set within Asia, it has a sharper focus. It will zoom in on an arc of countries on India's northern borders. If one were to draw this arc centred on the old Mughal capital of Delhi, it would encompass, starting from the west, Persia (today Iran), then Afghanistan, Western Turkestan (later known as Russian Turkestan), Eastern Turkestan (also known as Chinese Turkestan) and finally Tibet to the east.

For India's neighbours along the arc, this period would have an added twist. It was here that a contest of high stakes and espionage, referred to as 'the Great Game', was played out between two of the most powerful empires of the day—Great Britain and Imperial Russia. Both sides eagerly sought out information about these borderlands, but some countries such as Tibet were closed off to foreigners for the best part of the century. Others such as Afghanistan and Turkestan were off limits too, but in their case this was due to the dangers travellers faced in these often lawless regions infested by bandits. Travel was even more hazardous for Christian Europeans in Muslim lands as local tribesmen considered them non-believers and they ran the real risk of being killed out of hand. Despite these difficulties, there was a desperate need for competing powers to explore and map these regions, both for offensive and defensive purposes. Indeed, the first need of an army in a strange land is a reliable map. They obtained this intelligence by employing explorers and spies, although in many cases the line between the two was blurred, or simply did not exist.

As the Great Game encompasses such a large subject area, this book will limit its scope to the defence of India against the threat of an overland invasion. Within its borders, the British could readily explore and map the entire subcontinent through the Great Trigonometrical Survey of India (the GTS). Outside these borders, they undertook this work primarily with the help of two distinct groups: a band of army officers engaged in playing the Great Game; and an obscure group of natives employed by the GTS, who would come to be known as the Pundits.

Both the Great Game and the Survey of India involved a multitude of players from several countries, from the political and military establishments. To avoid overwhelming the reader with the many names, ranks and titles of the participants involved, as well as the numerous place names and dates, our book will mention just the main ones, as far as possible.

A timeline of the key events covered, highlighting their relationship, is shown at the end of the text. But this book is not meant to be a detailed historical study of these topics—there are specialist texts already available which do this well enough.

Rather, it tells the true story of a group of extraordinary explorers, spies and map-makers, who, though perhaps forgotten today, are its real heroes.

Players who shaped the Great Game—clockwise from top left: Alexander
Burnes, Dost Mohammed, Francis Younghusband and Lord Curzon.

Survey of India employees and equipment—clockwise from top left: William
Lambton, George Everest, the Great Theodolite and the Khalasis.

Pundits of the GTS and their founder—clockwise from top left: Thomas Montgomerie, Nain Singh (and again on Indian postage stamp), Kintup and Kishen Singh.

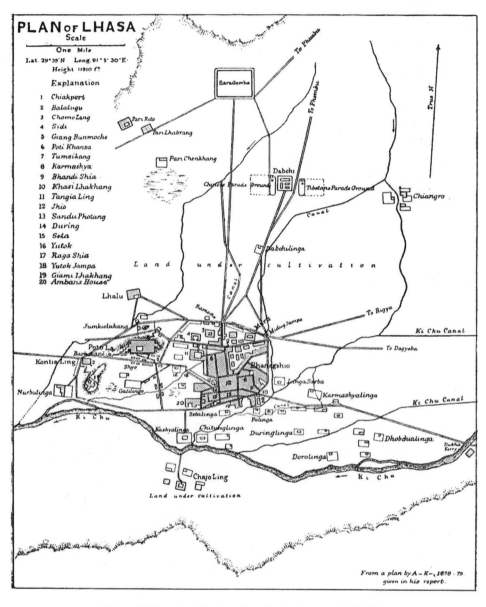

Plan of Lhasa by Kishen Singh (codenamed A-K).

PART ONE

THE GREAT GAME BEGINS

'Now I shall go far and far into the North, playing the Great Game.'

—Rudyard Kipling, *Kim*

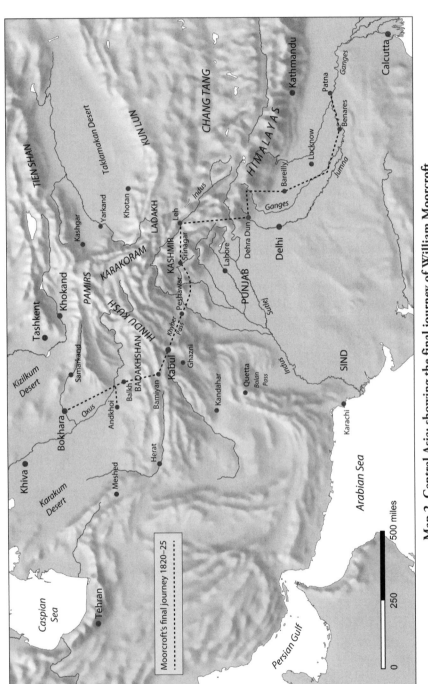

Map 2. Central Asia: showing the final journey of William Moorcroft

Moorcroft's final journey 1820–25 ┈┈┈┈

1

The Early Years

When Captain Arthur Conolly wrote to a friend who had just been posted to Afghanistan in 1840, saying, 'You've a great game, a *noble* game before you . . .', the sentiment he expressed was one of envy—that he too desired such an opportunity. It wasn't long before he would get his wish, but had he known it would lead to a horrible end, perhaps he would have wished differently. Conolly would die under an executioner's sword in the secluded city of Bokhara a mere two years later, trying to save the life of a brother officer beheaded with him. Two words from that line in his letter have lived on though, popularized in the evocative phrase 'the Great Game'. It came to describe the strategic rivalry between Russia and Britain for territory across much of Asia, and their attempts to redraw the lines on this vulnerable region's map.

Rudyard Kipling immortalized this phrase in his masterpiece and surely one of the best-loved English language books, *Kim*.* His portrayal of the Great Game forever touched it with a flavour of imperial romance. The opposing side, Tsarist Russia, had its own term, referring to it as 'a Tournament of Shadows'. Both phrases, though euphemistic and somewhat cynical, proved to be not far off the mark.

---

* Kipling was awarded the Nobel Prize in Literature in 1907 at the age of forty-one, and remains its youngest recipient to date.

The Stakes Involved

These lands in Asia are on a scale incomparable to most countries of Europe. For example, Western Turkestan (then comprising the three Central Asian khanates of Bokhara, Khiva and Khokand) when combined with Eastern Turkestan covered an area of roughly 1,000,000 square miles, twelve times the size of Great Britain.

Prominent in this landscape is the sweep of mountains separating Central Asia and Tibet from the Indian subcontinent. These mountains, which include the mighty Himalayas (Adobe of Snow) and Pamirs, are spectacularly high—parts of which are known as the Roof of the World—and many of their passes are higher than the tallest peaks in most nations. The region's deserts can be brutal too, with overbearing heat and swirling sandstorms which have claimed the lives of many a traveller. They contrast with the hundreds of icy streams hurtling down from snow-capped mountains on to open floodplains, steppe lands, lakes and inland seas.

The timeline for the Great Game—when it started and finally ended—depends on the account one happens to be reading. Some have it beginning early in the eighteenth century, when Russia first failed in its attempt to annex the khanate of Khiva in 1717. At the other end, many saw it as still active after World War I, as the Bolsheviks tried hard to destabilize India, with Lenin exhorting: 'England is our greatest enemy. It is in India that we must strike them hardest.' Others suggest it continued well after this time, that 'the game' was really the Victorian prologue to the cold war years, although the rivalry would now often manifest itself in subtler ways. Taking the broadest view, if the Great Game is seen as a struggle for the control of this region, then clearly it remains alive and well today. For the purposes of this book, however, we will focus mainly on the nineteenth century, for it was during this 100-year period that it intensified and the threat of war between the two empires reached fever pitch. Although the two sides never came to all-out conflict, despite coming close on a few occasions, there was plenty of real and imagined posturing on both sides.

The stakes in this contest were always high. For Britain, the steady expansion of territory by its adversary, as it swallowed up large portions of Central Asia, was deeply disturbing and threatening. It believed Russia had made its ultimate intention clear: to continue advancing into Asia until it wrested control of India. With hindsight, though, many historians believe the British were mistaken in greatly exaggerating this threat. Their mindset and consequent actions largely became a self-defeating one, as this merely provoked the Russians into behaving in a similar manner. As is often the case, suspicion only begat suspicion.

Much has been published about 'the Great Gamers', especially by Britons, describing their daring exploits in detail. Regrettably, the efforts of the native Asians who assisted them are less well acknowledged. And even when they ventured out on their own—as the Pundits did—their activities weren't well publicized.

Unlike their British counterparts, there are fewer accounts of Russian players, and even less translated into English. Also, the secret service records detailing their efforts were, in many cases, lost in the aftermath of the destruction of the Russian archives. Moreover, it wasn't customary for military personnel in Russia to write about their feats as readily as other European officers did. Yet, even the published works of these explorers-cum-spies, from both camps, are too numerous to do them justice in just a few chapters. Some of their adventures will be related, however, to give a sense of what they experienced.

Napoleon, the Tsar and the Shah

In 1801, from his capital in St Petersburg, Tsar Paul I sent Napoleon Bonaparte a secret proposition: a joint invasion of India to drive out the English and their East India Company once and for all, before dividing the rich spoils. The tsar believed a Cossack force of 35,000 together with a similar-sized French army would be ample for victory—perhaps with some help from the fierce Turcoman tribes who may be induced to join their expedition along the way. They would meet the French south of the Caspian Sea, and then cross through Persia and Afghanistan, to be at the gates of India in an ambitious time frame of four months. The young Napoleon was understandably reluctant. He had just been defeated and forced to withdraw from Egypt by Britain and its allies, and was less than convinced of the soundness of the tsar's plan or its promise of success.

Not to be discouraged, the tsar decided Russia could succeed without French support, and take a more direct route to get there, in even less time. He ordered his loyal Cossacks to launch the invasion; even though his army was much depleted, having been able to muster only 22,000 troops, he was not deterred. That this was an ill-conceived undertaking was obvious not only to Bonaparte; it must have further convinced the Russian nobility their manic-depressive tsar was losing his sanity as well.

The Cossack cavalry, renowned for their hardiness and ruthlessness, started out from the frontier town of Orenburg and headed south for Khiva, some 900 miles away across the Kazak Steppe, in the dead of winter. Supported by small amounts of artillery, they each took a spare horse and whatever food they could carry. Even for these tough troops, the conditions would have been bitterly cold and cruel, both for the men and their animals. Only a month out and less than halfway to Khiva, relief came in an unexpected way: Tsar Paul was dead and the mission recalled, averting certain disaster for the Cossacks and sparing Russia an embarrassing humiliation.

In fact, his own court officials had assassinated the old tsar; after trying unsuccessfully to force his abdication, they finally strangled him. His son and heir, Alexander, promptly gave the order to abort the mission, ending the Russian Empire's first attempted invasion of India. It wasn't until later that the British learnt of this threat that had fizzled out—but this would not be Russia's last attempt.

* * *

Around this time events were also starting to stir in Persia, which would soon become embroiled in a three-way struggle between France, Britain and Russia for the riches of the East. Sitting on the overland route from Europe, and as the land bridge to the subcontinent, Persia's strategic importance to India was unquestionable. Napoleon's agents were rumoured to be courting the shah of this ancient kingdom, Fath Ali. In 1800, the British governor-general of India had sent a large and impressive diplomatic mission to Tehran with the key objective of securing a treaty forbidding French troops from entering the country. Additionally, this defensive alliance sought an assurance from the Persians stating they would go to war with their old adversary, the Afghans, should the latter also decide to move against India, as they had done through their infamous raiding for centuries. What Britain promised in return was to come to their aid if either France or Afghanistan were to attack them. Such a treaty would allow it to conveniently fight a French force bound for India on Persian soil and in Persian waters.

A deal was struck but not formally ratified, as it was thought unnecessary following Napoleon's defeat and evacuation from Egypt the following year. In British eyes this oversight meant the treaty was technically not binding. This suited them well as they had extracted the desired commitments from the shah without giving up much in return, except the few lavish gifts they had taken along. Fath Ali and his court liked what they saw laid out before them, but soon discovered just how hollow the treaty accompanying the gifts was.

The following year Russia annexed the small, independent kingdom of Georgia, inflaming the Persians, who regarded it as lying in their own sphere of influence. When, in 1804, Russia continued advancing south and laid siege to the city of Erivan (today the capital of Armenia), which the shah considered his possession, the move brought the two sides to all-out war. However, when he pleaded for Britain's help, in keeping with its end of the bargain, Fath Ali was sorely disappointed. The treaty made no mention of Russia, only France and Afghanistan; hence Britain would not respond to his call, especially since it now needed the tsar as an ally against Bonaparte, who had recently crowned himself emperor. He was threatening Europe again, which meant Britain was not about to alienate Russia. Although they had wriggled out of a tight diplomatic spot, the British lost face with the shah, who felt betrayed and bitter.

That same year, Napoleon approached Fath Ali for safe passage through Persia to invade India. Initially, the shah held out, hoping to maintain ties with his old ally, in spite of his recent experience. But when the assistance he sought to fend off Russia was again not forthcoming, he signed a binding treaty with France in 1807 to wage war against Britain.

As Napoleon's Grande Armée advanced through Europe, it defeated the Russians decisively at the Battle of Friedland, the defenders suffering horrific casualties. In the ensuing peace talks with Tsar Alexander I, the French emperor discussed his grand design of combining their forces to conquer and divide the world between them—the West going to France and the East to Russia. After defeating Turkey, they would march through it, before crossing Persia, whose support was now assured, into India. The tsar was receptive and overheard to say: 'I hate the English as much as you do and am ready to assist you in any undertaking against them.'

Napoleon Bonaparte had dreams of emulating Alexander the Great, believing he could overrun the subcontinent with an army of 50,000 troops. London managed to learn of the secret pact between the countries, by having a spy listen in on the meeting as the two leaders conversed. One report suggested this informant may have been a disaffected Russian nobleman, who hid himself under the river barge on which the leaders met, his legs dangling in the water.

Once the shah was informed of this backroom deal, realizing the French would not help him against the Russians, he made a U-turn and fell back into the arms of his old ally. Fath Ali was known to possess one of the finest diamond collections in the world; so, amongst the other lavish gifts sent by the British monarch, there was an enormous diamond valued at 11,000 rupees that perhaps persuaded him to forget past transgressions. Under the new treaty, he would not allow a foreign army passage across his country bound for India. Britain, in return, would go to his assistance with arms and troops should Persia be attacked, even if the invaders were at peace with the British. This additional clause ensured any future territorial threats from Russia would be covered, should history repeat itself. Other than being more careful about the treaty's wording, the shah demanded, and received, a large annual payment from Britain, together with the services of its officers to help modernize his army.

John Company

These British officers would mostly come from the Honourable East India Company (often referred to simply as 'the Company') and its large standing army in Asia. It was through the Company that Britain had first gained a trading foothold in India. This had come to pass on the last day of the year 1600, when a little over 200 merchants of London were given a royal charter by Queen Elizabeth I to trade in the East Indies, those exotic lands east of the Indus River. From this humble beginning, the Company would grow dramatically, and is still regarded by many today as the greatest commercial enterprise in history.

Initially, it was known to Indians as John Company—a colloquial term its representatives found easier to use rather than explain the structure of one of the world's first chartered companies: one that offered limited liability to its shareholders, after having secured a monopoly to develop commercial interests in distant lands. To defend these interests, and its territory in India, the Company raised its own army of sepoys. They were supplemented by Royal troops shipped out from Britain, but whose numbers were small in comparison: around one British soldier to every five sepoys. The latter were commanded by Royal officers who infused them with high levels of training and discipline.* Together, they soon proved capable

---

* King's Commission was available only to British officers until 1919, when Indians were first included.

of defeating other armies, even when vastly outnumbered, including those fielded by the country's many princely states.* Ironically, Britain would ultimately conquer India using Indian soldiers.

The Company also kept its own navy—over forty warships by the end of its tenure—which patrolled the waters around India and maintained a squadron in the Persian Gulf. By the early nineteenth century, its armed forces had grown to well over 250,000 men, twice the size of Britain's, representing the largest military power in Asia. An old saying from Kashmir reflected its dominance: 'The world is Allah's, the land belongs to the Pashas, but it is the Company that rules.'

The enterprise had expanded to such an extent, both commercially and politically, that in 1784 the British Parliament passed the India Act to enforce a level of oversight on its Court of Directors. By 1818, the Company effectively ruled the subcontinent, after defeating the Marathas on the Deccan Plateau in the Third Anglo-Maratha War. But the British government progressively took control of India's affairs through its successive governor-generals, compelling the Company to wind down all its commercial activities after 1834. No longer could it profit from buying and selling basic commodities such as cotton, silk, salt, spices, opium and tea. From this point on, it was limited to raising revenues through taxes and tariffs, and was required to govern in the interests of Britain and India rather than for its few shareholders.†

The Company had evolved by way of three presidencies: Bengal, Bombay (now Mumbai) and Madras (Chennai). Each had its own government and armed forces, although in due course Bengal—the largest and most important presidency, headquartered in Calcutta

---

* In 1900, there were almost 700 princely states of greatly varying size and population; by 1947 they still numbered over 550.

† Even at its demise, soon after 1857, the Company only had about 1700 stockholders.

(Kolkata)—appointed both the governor-general and commander-in-chief of India. At the time, this presidency was made up of the neighbouring states of Bihar, Orissa (Odissa) and West Bengal, as well as modern Bangladesh; and Calcutta would remain the capital of India until 1911. After 1857, when the Indian Mutiny—or Indian Rebellion, depending on one's viewpoint—was put down, the East India Company was replaced by Crown rule, heralding the birth of the British Raj, which would last until the colony became independent in 1947.

Since its inception, the Company had continued to grow rapidly, driven by the belief that further annexation would lead to increased trade and more effective government. This expansion wasn't always seen as being in the best interests of its shareholders at home, particularly when the extra military and administrative burdens of acquiring new territories cut into their profits. Its Court of Directors in London were regularly at odds with its 'management' in India, who were required to exercise their own judgement. They needed to make decisions on the spot and, once taken, these actions were often irreversible.

The tyranny of distance greatly affected communication time between London and Calcutta, and this delay must be appreciated to understand why events sometimes unfolded as they did. In the early years, a dispatch sent by ship from London took between five to eight months to reach Calcutta and, because the monsoon dictated sailing schedules, there could be up to a two-year wait for a reply. Later, with the opening of the Suez Canal in 1869, and the advent of faster steamers, this time would be cut down to two months, and finally to a few hours with the introduction of a submarine telegraph link the following year.

During its heyday, the Honourable East India Company ruled over nearly one-fifth of the world's population, employing its own armed forces and civil service, and minting its own money. Yet its government in India was owned and operated by a group of businessmen whose shares were bought and sold daily on the stock exchange in London. One prominent historian of the time, Thomas Macaulay, commented on this unique arrangement: 'It is the strangest of all governments, but it is designed for the strangest of all empires.'

Astonishingly, the Company had a revenue larger than Great Britain's. India was vital to its economy, and regarded as 'the jewel in the crown' of the British Empire. But a thing of immense value invariably attracts predators and must be protected, so Britain took any threat of an invasion very seriously, no matter how small. George Curzon, then a member of Parliament (later to become Lord Curzon, and later still viceroy of India), summed up this sentiment: 'Whatever be Russia's designs on India . . . I hold that the first duty of English statesmen is to . . . guard what is without doubt the noblest trophy of British genius and the most splendid appanage of the Imperial Crown.' Not surprisingly then, John Company and its officers were destined to take a lead role in the Great Game.

An Unlikely Explorer

An adventurer who would go on to achieve great note now began his travels from northern India into Central Asia. He is credited with being the first British player of the Great Game, before most of his countrymen even knew the game existed. Furthermore, he was one of the few pioneer explorers of the region who wasn't an army officer or worked for the Survey of India. The other unusual thing about him was his age. Born in 1767, by the time he started his adventuring he was already well over forty, which was considered old for that period, certainly in terms of the life expectancy for Europeans in Asia. His name was William Moorcroft, and he sailed east in 1808 to take up an appointment as Superintendent of the Stud for the Company's large horse-breeding farm located near Patna, upriver from Calcutta.

This was a critical project set up by the Company's Military Department to replenish and build its cavalry stock, which was suffering from much neglect and could produce a mere one-tenth of its needs. Moorcroft was well-qualified for the task, being the first Englishman to graduate as a veterinary surgeon; in the years to come he would be described as 'one of the most important pioneers of modern veterinary medicine'.* After completing his studies, he went on to build a thriving practice in London, and a considerable fortune. Unfortunately, he lost most of it in an attempt to patent and mass-produce horseshoes, using an elaborate machine he had built—in hindsight, a mad scheme that eventually went bust.

Horse breeding seems to have had a chequered past in India, as the legendary Venetian traveller Marco Polo observed after a visit there during the thirteenth century. At the time, fine horses were being imported at great expense from Arabia, Persia and the Turcoman tribes. However, the vast majority of them died, as Marco Polo learnt, unable to adjust to the climate, lacking proper care and medicines, and after being unwittingly fed poorly by their new owners. The merchants wouldn't educate the Indians or provide grooms, thus ensuring that a fresh supply of their mounts was always required, and guaranteeing themselves handsome, ongoing profits.

Around Patna, the 5000-acre stud farm and its associated operations extended over an enormous area, roughly the size of southern England. Moorcroft estimated he would need 3000 breeding mares to produce the 600 cavalry horses the military required every year. Under his charge the stud improved rapidly, no doubt assisted by his instituting equine inoculation and a proper diet—the latter after introducing the cultivation of oats into India on a large scale for the first time. These innovations were characteristic of the many agricultural and commercial ventures he would pioneer in the coming years, even though more than a few would go no further than being just ideas on paper.

---

* A memorial brass plate mounted on the wall of the Royal College of Veterinary Surgeons, almost a century ago, marks his lasting contribution.

After supervising operations for six years, Moorcroft came to the conclusion that he needed better breeding stock, which could only be obtained outside British India's borders, to its north or west. During this time, he was also seized by a realization that would consume his remaining years: that his heart really lay in exploration. Despite sometimes strong objections from the Company, he would make several long journeys into some of Asia's wildest areas, ostensibly seeking better breeding stock, particularly the bloodline of the famed Turcoman horses.

On his initial trip, commencing in early 1811, he pushed past territory controlled by the Company into India's northern plains just south of Nepal, to attend a horse fair held annually in one of its towns. Although disappointed by the quality of horses sold here, he made good contacts amongst the Gurkhas; this would prove invaluable on his next trip, when he would be held in detention in their country. In another town further west, he was successful in acquiring a string of mares and colts, while getting a better sense of where the prime horse-breeding areas lay. Here, for the first time, he heard mention of fine horses being traded in the mysterious desert city of Bokhara, and his desire to go there would soon become an obsession.

* * *

Shortly after his return in 1812, Moorcroft embarked on a second journey through northern India and into forbidden Tibet, skirting along its western edge. Although he did receive permission 'to penetrate into Tartary', this sanction only came from the governor-general's local agent. By the time the governor-general and his government learnt of the plans of their stud superintendent it was too late to stop him, despite being 'strongly disinclined to sanction a project so replete with danger to himself and his companions, and so little likely to be of productive advantage to public service'. This would have mattered little to Moorcroft, who later wrote of himself: 'my obstinacy almost equals my enthusiasm'.

Since he couldn't obtain approval from the Company to hunt for horses this time, Moorcroft switched his attention to bringing back 'shawl goats' from western Tibet, with the hope of starting an industry in this cloth. The soft undercoat of these animals produces the fine *pasham* (wool), which is half the thickness of regular wool and used for making the much-prized Kashmiri (cashmere) shawls. The merchants and weavers of Kashmir and Ladakh jealously guarded their monopoly of this lucrative trade, and Tibetan herdsmen faced the death penalty if caught selling *pashmina* goats to outsiders. Moorcroft, not to be dissuaded, would manage to bring back fifty of these beautiful animals, whose wool would one day become the mainstay of trans-Himalayan trade.

This time he took a travelling companion with him: Captain Hyder Hearsey, a colourful but controversial soldier of fortune.* Born an Anglo-Indian of a native Indian mother, Hearsey's mixed blood initially denied him entry into the Company's army. This prompted him to become a mercenary with one of India's princely states (a common alternative for illegitimate sons of British officers at the time). Later, he joined the Company's ranks to fight against his old employer during the Second Anglo-Maratha War. By the time Moorcroft met Hearsey, he had married a princess: Zuhur-ul-Missa, the adopted daughter of the Mughal emperor.

The pair travelled in disguise as trading pilgrims under the assumed names of Mayapori and Hagiri, staining their skins with lampblack, walnut juice and the ash of burnt cow dung. Included in their caravan of fifty-four persons was a young man named Harkh Dev, who would help them undertake a 'route survey'.

Also known as a route map or compass traverse, this was a rudimentary type of survey made by explorers, or undertaken during military marches, to map new territory with the aid of a compass. A running record was kept of the distances travelled, compass bearings,

---

* Hearsey was accused of claiming a map that detailed the source of the Ganges, supposedly drawn by another officer, as his own work. However, author Charles Allen tries to exonerate him in *A Mountain in Tibet*.

main features of the countryside and, if possible, estimates of latitude and longitude using a sextant and chronometer.

However, a route survey is not a complete map in itself, but helps fill in the details of an area being charted. Being rudimentary, it often has an inherent error of around 10 per cent, even under the most favourable conditions. This is because as the route passes over hills and down through valleys, taking twists and turns, the cumulative distance of all the legs measured between points is further than the true distance as the crow flies. In earlier times, this required overall distances logged to be reduced by a factor (usually between one-tenth and one-seventh), which was done by a cartographer based on experience, when he finally converted the data collected into a map. Route surveys were the prime method for compiling the earliest maps of Indian territories, and it was mandatory for every detachment of the Company's army to complete one during a march.

Harkh Dev was trained to walk consistently while counting out a measured pace to estimate the distances they covered; in this, he would be a forerunner to the Survey of India's Pundits. Although Moorcroft wasn't a surveyor, Hearsey was, and he took compass bearings as Dev kept track of his paces. Hearsey recorded his observations discreetly to avoid arousing the suspicion of locals, at times even writing minuscule notes on his fingernails. He would eventually produce a map of some accuracy, on a scale of 1 inch to 10 miles (1:633,600), and fill in some of the blank spaces and topographical details of northern India and Tibet.

Moorcroft took copious notes wherever he went, while collecting specimens of flora and fauna which he would send back in crates to Calcutta and England; at one time nearly thirty botanical species bore his name. As always, he was coming up with ideas and schemes to lift the living standards of the poor by improving local agriculture and commerce, a passion that drove him throughout his life.*

---

* A later European traveller claimed Moorcroft also took a strong liking to the region's famed nautch girls who were customary entertainment and plentiful, but there is no evidence to substantiate this.

While they were in western Tibet, Moorcroft and Hearsey were taken prisoner by the local authorities, probably because they were European, and held in a fort for a few days. During their custody, they were visited by two young brothers who were Bhotias (Indians of Tibetan origin) from a small village on the Indian side of the Himalayan range, working as traders. These hillmen interceded with the authorities by offering surety, and helped get the pair released. Later, they would again offer Moorcroft assistance during his third journey, this time to act as guides and to supply yaks. The brothers were Bir and Deb Singh, and one day their sons, Nain and Kishen Singh respectively, would go on to become arguably the two greatest Pundits.

During this trip, while they were in Tibet, Moorcroft came across evidence of Russian presence and commercial activity, sharply observing locals using their cloth and other manufactured goods. From then on, he would be constantly alerting British authorities to the dangers of letting Russia get a foothold in the region; but, although his reports were going to the Company's Secret and Political Department in Calcutta, his early warnings fell on deaf ears. And he was the first to voice suspicion of Russian intentions so far as India's northern flank was concerned. He contended that Britain had to choose whether the people of Central Asia and Tibet 'shall be clothed with the broadcloth of Russia or England'. Understandably, the Russians believed he was a spy, and the evidence would suggest they were at least partially right.

Moorcroft and Hearsey were two of the first Europeans to set eyes on Mount Kailas and visit the nearby Lake Manasarowar high in the Himalayas, both of which are extremely sacred to Hindus and Buddhists alike.* Although they did not find the source of the Ganges River as hoped, they did manage to do so for the Sutlej, and were able to draw other correct conclusions about the Indus and Brahmaputra rivers. Sven Hedin, possibly the foremost explorer of this region, described their

---

* Hindus consider Mount Kailas to be the home of their god Shiva, while Buddhists see it as the centre of the universe.

work as 'one of the most brilliant chapters in the history of exploration around the lakes and the sources of the great rivers'.[*]

In December 1812, Moorcroft returned home safely with Hearsey—but not before a narrow escape when fierce Nepalese Gurkhas, armed with their trademark kukris, held them captive for seventeen days on the accusation of spying. They were only released after a farmer, in gratitude for Moorcroft curing his sick son, helped get letters back to the British authorities, who then interceded on their behalf. One interesting aside from Moorcroft's brush with the Gurkhas was his prediction that 'under our government they would make excellent soldiers'.

* * *

Moorcroft's third and longest journey, which he set out on at age fifty-three, would also be his last. He was finally headed for the bazaars of Bokhara, to 'the greatest horse market in the world' as he had been told, searching yet again for the best equine bloodlines in Central Asia. He started out from Patna in 1820 with a large caravan, including a nineteen-year-old Englishman named George Trebeck as his assistant; the pair would soon become as close as father and son. While Harkh Dev once again paced out their route, Trebeck took bearings and astronomical observations, and an Anglo-Indian, George Guthrie, joined them as medical assistant.

Another person in this party, who had already played a crucial role in this venture, was an interpreter named Mir Izzat-Allah.[†] He had previously travelled the caravan route to Bokhara and its horse markets, on Moorcroft's instructions and payroll. Izzat-Allah was an able explorer in his own right, and his reconnaissance trip for Moorcroft, beginning in 1812, took him through Kashmir, Ladakh, Yarkand and

---

[*]   Neither Sven Hedin nor Nikolai Przhevalsky (another notable explorer of the region during this era) is discussed in this book as they weren't quite as prominent within the Great Game.

[†]   Mir was, and is, used as an honorific title in many parts of Asia.

Kashgar, before arriving in Bokhara. He was away for well over a year, during which time he survived illness and imprisonment. Izzat-Allah's journal of his fascinating journey, when it was published in Persian, was an immediate success and later translated into many languages. He would prove himself to be a faithful employee too; and, like Dev, was another forerunner to the Pundits.

Moorcroft took with him many gifts for the local rulers to help smooth the way, and merchandise to trade, all of which, at one time, needed 300 porters. His journey would eventually take three times longer than the two-year estimate he had given to his employer, but exceeding his brief was not unusual for Moorcroft. In another example, he negotiated a commercial treaty with the ruler of Ladakh, even though he had no authority to do so; the Company, having little interest in this far-flung outpost, promptly disclaimed it.

During their two-year stay in Ladakh, the horse doctor endeared himself to the locals through his extensive medical work. With Guthrie's help, he successfully performed many eye operations to remove cataracts, despite his lack of qualifications to treat humans or the availability of proper medical facilities. Nevertheless, this type of humanitarian work would assure Moorcroft a warm welcome wherever he went in the wilds of Central Asia.

In Srinagar, he healed a learned Hindu teacher of a near-incurable disease, and in gratitude was shown a copy of the *Raja Tarangini* (The River of Kings). Written in Sanskrit verse in the twelfth century, this rare manuscript chronicles the history of Kashmir and its kings. Over a period of three months, Moorcroft engaged ten teachers to make him a copy, which he then sent to Calcutta, to be later translated and published in Paris.

After travelling through Kashmir, the party crossed into Afghanistan by way of the legendary Khyber Pass. Further on, as they passed through the valley of Bamiyan, Moorcroft and his companions were the first Europeans to see the now-famous Bamiyan Buddha statues, dating back to the sixth century, which were once painted a dazzling gold and adorned with brilliant gems. The pair was carved into the side of a cliff, the larger one rising to 175 feet. The visitors left behind proof of their presence by writing their names in charcoal in one of the caves.*

Finally, after almost six years spent trekking 5000 miles of mostly uncharted lands, Moorcroft's caravan marched into Bokhara in February 1825. They were the first Englishmen to visit this secluded holy city in over 200 years—a remarkable achievement in itself. But here, he was sorely disappointed to find few fine horses available for purchase. To make matters worse, the best ones departed with the emir's army soon afterwards, as they hurried off to suppress an insurrection nearby. Despite Moorcroft waiting around for five months they did not return, and before long his party had to leave the city. During this wait, he took the initiative to recruit and set up a network of 'newswriters' (a euphemism for local spies working for the British), who would alert Calcutta in coded messages at the first sign of any Russian activity there.

Quite unexpectedly, on their return journey home, while separated from his caravan and alone, Moorcroft died of fever. This tragedy occurred in the small desert town of Andkhoi, near Balkh in northern Afghanistan in August 1825. He had left the bulk of his party behind to make a short detour to this desolate settlement, in a final bid to secure good horses. The circumstances surrounding his death are mysterious, and there is some suggestion he may have been poisoned. Both Trebeck and Guthrie died in Balkh soon afterwards, either from fever, slow poison or perhaps a combination of the two. Fortunately, Moorcroft's copious notes and logbooks were eventually recovered and later published, shedding light on his epic final journey.

---

* Neither statue has survived today after the Taliban blew them up in 2001 as part of their religious iconoclasm, but which was seen across the world as extreme cultural vandalism.

Twenty years later, the locals of Lhasa told a curious story to two Lazarist priests, Huc and Gabet, from a visiting French mission. They maintained Moorcroft had arrived in their city in 1826—a year after his recorded death—and lived amongst them for twelve years, travelling the region extensively and making maps. They ended by telling the two priests how he was finally murdered on his way back to India. It is often said of the east that 'nothing is ever forgotten, but little remembered with accuracy'. So whether this last chapter of Moorcroft's already incredible life is true we will never know; however, his biographer Garry Alder discounts this story.

As to his legacy, Alder points out that it wasn't helped by 'his quite remarkable incapacity for self-advertisement'. And due to the late publication of his diaries, in the intervening decades much of the accolade for penetrating this region went to lesser men. Still, William Moorcroft is remembered by many today as the Father of Modern Exploration of both Central Asia and the Western Himalayas—a fitting epitaph for a true pioneer. Perhaps his wanderlust was best captured in two lines of verse from Kipling's *The Explorer*:

> Something lost behind the Ranges.
> . . . Anybody might have found it but—His Whisper came to Me!

The Russian Bogy

While Moorcroft was completing his first journey, back in Europe the pact between the emperor and the tsar lay defunct, for a number of complex reasons well-documented in history. France now attacked not British India, but Russia, to the latter's astonishment. However, the tsar's troops inflicted a stunning defeat on the French, aided by Russia's greatest natural ally, mother winter. A simple monument in the Baltic town of Vilnius best sums up the French retreat during that terrible winter. The front plaque reads: 'Napoleon

Bonaparte passed this way in 1812 with 400,000 men.' The reverse side, facing Moscow, shows: 'Napoleon Bonaparte passed this way in 1812 with 9000 men.'

For Britain, his capitulation meant that the threat to India had passed for the moment, and the initial phase of the Great Game, influenced by the hand of France, was effectively over. Russia and Britain had emerged triumphant from the Napoleonic Wars. Yet even as French power in Europe waned, a new threat to Britain's jewel emerged—this time from a stronger Russia, now able to act in its own right.

It was no secret that the tsar and his generals harboured a great desire to add the Indian subcontinent to their Asian territories. The early part of the century had already seen a remarkable growth in the size of the 'motherland'. During the first sixteen years of Tsar Alexander's reign, starting in 1801, the Russian empire had already acquired some 200,000 square miles of territory, equivalent to two and a half times the size of Great Britain. The dilemma faced by these two rapidly expanding powers in Central Asia often revolved around where their 'natural' frontiers lay, and what buffer states should separate them. At the beginning of the century, over 2000 miles lay between their borders, but by 1876 this distance had been halved; and before the century was over it would be whittled down to less than 20 miles at its narrowest point deep in the Pamir Mountains.

The Pamirs would come to occupy a special place in the Great Game. Known locally as Bam-i-dunya (Roof of the World), this range has peaks towering well over 20,000 feet; even its valleys average around 13,000 feet. Much of the snow falling on its slopes never melts, instead accumulating to form the largest ice cap on the planet outside of the polar circles. To counteract the cold and rarefied air here, wild animals—bear, yak and sheep—grow extreme in size, and would become much sought-after by big game hunters.

By the end of its thrust into Asia, Russia's territorial gains would come to mark the greatest colonial expansion in history. As Great

Game historian Edward Ingram noted, Britain simply wasn't able to halt its adversary's march into Western Turkestan. All it could do was try to limit the consequences: 'to make sure that a game which could not be won, should not be lost either'. But all that lay in the future.

This was indeed the Age of Imperialism, when the rich and powerful nations of Europe zealously pursued empire building, often under the guise of bringing 'a great civilizing mission' to local tribespeople. They needed little justification as to the moral correctness of absorbing, mostly by force, large swathes of territories or even whole countries. Very different attitudes and values prevailed then about the rights and wrongs of colonialism, and the fair treatment of native people in those lands—it would be difficult to understand this period in history without keeping this reality in perspective. And it can be truthfully said that those colonized *did* benefit in many and significant ways from their interactions with Western empires.

For European monarchs and their subjects, much prestige was to be gained by extending the size of their kingdoms, and admiring the expanse of colour they represented when a world map was rolled out. Great Britain would proudly point out how literally 'the sun never sets on the British Empire'. The Russians proved just as keen on enlarging their territories, and Tsar Nicholas I is said to have decreed: 'Where the imperial flag has once flown, it must never be lowered.'

In Britain, the 'Russian bogy', as it became known, was frequently raised with good effect in response to Russia's territorial advances. This fear was heightened by an impressive growth in the tsar's military machine: in the decade to 1817, it was estimated to have increased from 80,000 to 640,000 strong, excluding his Cossack cavalry, second-line troops and the like. The scale of these figures was misleading, however, as they overestimated Russia's actual military strength, which many historians believe was in a weak state during this period—as the Crimean War would soon prove. Nevertheless, this bogy was menacing and real enough for Britain. It was even whispered that it all had to do with Peter the Great's secret command to his heirs in 1725, as he lay dying in St Petersburg: to conquer the world and fulfil Russia's destiny.*

Unlike its adversary's wider view of expansion into Central Asia, from Britain's perspective, the Great Game had a sharper focus. In a nutshell, it desperately sought ways to defend India as best as possible. Almost as important a consideration was how to achieve this at the least possible cost, since Parliament thoroughly scrutinized and resisted any large expenditures in this regard. Its members were reluctant to spend money on Britain's colonies, which were meant to be a source of revenue, not a cost to taxpayers at home. The Government of India, still in its early years, could ill-afford to spend on defence either. The long voyages required to ship out large numbers of royal troops, and then pay for their upkeep on the subcontinent, added substantially to the costs involved.

Britain was not in a good position to defend India at this time—neither from an invading army, nor from a rebellion within. This had much to do with its reluctance to keep a large standing army at home, which at any rate was still half a world away if troops were suddenly needed in Asia. Moreover, its principal military asset—sea power—was largely irrelevant to military manoeuvres made in the heart of an essentially land-locked Central Asia, and of limited use in defending India.

Within both the British and Russian camps there were conflicting schools of thought on how to best deal with the other side. Each had their hawks and doves: those who favoured aggressive military advances, versus others seeking to avoid conflict and find political solutions instead. In Britain, the hawks' stance was euphemistically referred to as 'forward policy', and they derisively labelled their opponent's position 'masterly inactivity'. The latter conservative approach, the 'close-border policy', argued it would be preferable to

---

*   He supposedly stated this in his last will and testament, although most historians doubt the existence of this document.

fight an intruder once they reached the Indus River, *after* the Afghan tribes had mauled them as they came through the passes.

Between the two main political parties in Britain there were key differences, and they often took opposing views and strategies. The Conservatives tended to be hawkish, while the Liberal Party favoured a policy of masterly inactivity. This led to changing instructions to Calcutta depending on the government of the day in London, much to the frustration of senior political and military figures in India. Whichever side was in power though, public opinion, as always, had a strong influence on both policy and strategy. 'Opinions are stronger than armies' was how one English lord had put it, and this was often the case where India's security and the Great Game were concerned. The British public followed these topics with avid interest, and they became key issues during parliamentary elections.

In Russia, where the tsar had more power invested in him, and without an elected parliament to question his decisions, public opinion didn't influence matters as much: many of his subjects were poor peasants who were far more concerned about overcoming life's daily struggles. This was a tumultuous century in Russian history, when the birthright and absolute power of the tsar was constantly being eroded—and, of course, with the Bolshevik Revolution in 1917 it would be gone.

The British viewed Tsarist Russia with some ambivalence as they considered it to be backward, both culturally and industrially, compared to the enormous strides they credited themselves to have recently made. Unlike its peasants, though, the Russian military hierarchy had a powerful voice, and strongly advocated for advancing and annexing territory. This was understandable, particularly for Russian commanders in faraway Turkestan, where military conquest was far more interesting than defensive policies or being confined to isolated forts. Even junior officers saw military adventure as a way out of the 'prison sentence' of being posted to the wastelands of Central Asia. Britain recognized this motivation driving Russian officers, with Curzon observing: 'Where the ruling class is entirely military and where promotion is slow, it would be strange if war, the sole available avenue to distinction, were not popular.'

Individual British players, too, had their own reasons for entering the Great Game, including a strong attraction for adventure. Some participated on their own time and expense, while on 'shooting leave': combining the hunt for wild game, in inaccessible areas such as the Pamirs, with a hunt of a different sort. But few officers wanted to be labelled a 'spy'; whereas the 'adventurer' tag, in pursuit of trophies such as the rare *Ovis poli* (Marco Polo sheep) or geographical knowledge, suited them well. Often, they took to the field without any official status, which allowed their government to conveniently disown them if caught, thereby avoiding unpleasant diplomatic incidents.

The British were well known for their insatiable thirst for exploration, and few heroes stood taller than explorers during the Victorian era. Here was a chance for adventure in the badlands of Central Asia, engaging in espionage amongst mysterious rulers and kingdoms with romantic names such as Bokhara and Samarkand, in defence of their beloved empire. No surprise then that a British officer in similar circumstances should coin the phrase 'the Great Game'.

This was another reason why the army in India, although it was badly paid compared to the civil service, seemed to attract a good deal of intelligent and ambitious men, excited by the prospect of serving in an expanding empire. The officers who served with the Company often did so without holding hope of ever seeing home again.* Even many of the British foot soldiers, condemned to a lifetime of service in India, looked forward to active duty away from the tedium of their cantonments and the chance to seize booty. A good deal of the early expansion of British India, and the advocacy for a forward policy, can be attributed to the self-interest of officials and officers striving to get

---

* Company estimates made around this time show that only about one in ten officers survived.

ahead. When viewed in this light, they really weren't that different, after all, from their counterparts in the Russian military.

In both camps, these Great Game players were, almost without exception, men of courage who were hardy and resourceful. These traits were a prerequisite, and essential for survival in the hostile environments in which they operated. Most of them also had a military background, since soldiers were able to gain the backing of their governments more readily, by combining their own adventure-seeking expeditions with specific intelligence-gathering activities. They were also more likely to recognize and appreciate the strategic features of a country they passed through, which potentially could be of military importance.

As well as a passion for exploration, many had a head for languages, while others excelled at spying or map-making, and a select few possessed all these skills. The Great Game would provide them a unique opportunity to prove their talents.

2

Britain Attacks to Defend India

The ultimate prize of the Great Game may have been India, but its northern neighbours would experience most of the intrigue and action. The Russian Army had to find a feasible route first, while keeping its supply lines secure, before crossing one of their frontiers and forcing its way in. This was no easy task, as India was and remains well protected by natural borders all the way along its northern arc.

The Door In

From the time of Alexander the Great, Afghanistan has been a staging post for invaders into India, crossing the Hindu Kush and swooping on to the hot plains of the Punjab. These mountains pose a formidable barrier. One interpretation of its name is 'Hindu killer', as explained by the famous fourteenth-century Moroccan traveller Ibn Battuta, who wrote: 'Many of the slaves brought to us from India perish while crossing the high passes on account of the severe cold and great quantities of snow.' In Alexander's first traverse of these peaks, the Persians had left the passes unguarded, believing they were impenetrable in winter—a mistake that cost them dearly. Even then, he is thought to have lost more men and animals during that winter crossing than in all his campaigns in Central Asia.

Nevertheless, London and Calcutta viewed any threat of Russia occupying Afghanistan, or even exerting undue influence in its affairs, as of vital importance to India's defence. This stance resulted in many strategic moves being made on their neighbour's territory. It would eventually lead to their waging war against Afghanistan on more than one occasion, bringing to mind the adage 'Attack is the best form of defence'.

It should be remembered that during this period not all of Afghanistan was united. Cities such as Herat, Kandahar and even the rural areas were mostly independent for long periods, ruled by their own provincial chiefs who did not answer to the emir of Kabul. For that matter, India during the nineteenth century was not a united country either, contrary to many popular histories and images. At the time, British India excluded large territories outside of the presidencies of Bengal, Bombay and Madras.

The need for Britain to fortify Afghanistan against unfriendly powers meant the latter's western neighbour Persia would also be drawn into the conflict at times. The tsar's army needed safe passage through the shah's territory to reach at least one of two key mountain passes into India, the Khyber or the Bolan. The other obvious route, marching along the coastline of the Persian Gulf towards Karachi, was too vulnerable to attack by the Royal Navy. Napoleon had already felt the brunt of its firepower. In 1798, close to his entire fleet had been sunk after he led his so-called Army of the Orient into Egypt, in an attempt to undermine Britain's trade with India. The Russian Army couldn't counter this naval threat to its communication lines by moving further inland, as the Helmand Desert, which separates Afghanistan from Persia, was vast and not easily traversed.

The Great Game now entered a new and dangerous phase, with an expanding Russian Empire becoming a real threat for the khanates of Turkestan, as it edged towards the more elusive prize: India. The intensity of the rhetoric from diplomats on all sides was escalating; and in Britain, a few experienced and knowledgeable professionals were influencing public opinion. Mostly former military men, they were finding a voice through newspapers, pamphlets and some well-researched books. This debate would strongly sway the public, who demanded its government better protect British interests on the subcontinent.

One man in particular was most responsible for creating the Russian bogy: Sir Robert Wilson, a decorated general known for his hot-headedness. He had first-hand experience in dealing with the Russians, as an official observer when Bonaparte's army had attacked Moscow. Disregarding his non-combatant status, he joined the defenders in battle, earning their admiration and receiving a knighthood from the tsar. Wilson was there when Moscow burned, and was the first to relate the news of Napoleon's stunning reversal of fortune following the crushing defeat of his army.

However, when he returned to England, Wilson was blunt about his negative assessment of Russia. He spoke of the many atrocities he had witnessed there, committed by troops and civilians, including the women, against French captives. Four years after his return in 1817, following his election to Parliament, he wrote a bestselling book titled *A Sketch of the Military and Political Power of Russia*. In it, he made scathing attacks on his former comrades, and what he believed was their secret intention: to fulfil Peter the Great's supposed deathbed wish to conquer the world. He highlighted the massive build-up of the tsar's military machine and his recent territorial gains. Wilson pointed out how Russia was pressing ever closer to western European cities, and the seat and jewel of the Ottoman Empire, Constantinople (today Istanbul). It guarded the entrance to the Black Sea, and was also historically significant as once capital of both the Roman and Byzantine empires.

Despite his book containing many false assumptions and flaws, coming from someone with Wilson's experience, the damage was done. Even though most people in Britain remained unsure of the tsar's ill intentions towards them, Wilson succeeded in convincing a good section of the public and the press. Anti-Russian sentiment had been raised, and this topic would remain a hotly debated subject for many years to come, affecting policies from Parliament and directions from the government.

Once the possibility of an invasion had been established by the likes of Wilson and other proficient military analysts, even if the level of risk was debatable, this threat was bound to be taken seriously in Britain and India. The question of *if* had shifted to *when* and *how*. Given the immense distances an army would need to cover, the next vital question became: what was the likely route an invader would take? If this could be established with some confidence, defences could be better organized to meet any threat. Could an army be landed somewhere along India's long and vulnerable coastline? Or would they need to travel overland, crossing somewhere along its northern arc?

British officers serving in the Indian Army carried out a detailed military assessment, and were quick to rule out the sea option. Any foreign fleet would have to first contend with the formidable Royal Navy, which was at the height of its power then and undoubtedly 'ruled the waves'. No, most experts were convinced the threat, when it came, would be by land. This was an easy first conclusion to reach, but the problem became a lot harder from this point on since there were many routes to consider. Much would depend on the reaction of whichever of India's neighbours an invading army happened to pass through. How that nation dealt with foreign troops on its soil would, of course, be influenced by whether they were its ally or not.

At the time, two overland routes seemed most feasible. If an aggressor, akin to a Bonaparte, were starting out from Europe, then the likely path would be directly eastwards, entering Persia at some point before marching on to Kabul. Alternatively, if the invaders originated from Russia, they would probably advance south-eastwards through the khanates of Western Turkestan, before again imposing on the Afghans. Since both roads led to this landlocked country, whether it wished it or not, Afghanistan would soon be sucked into the Great Game. And it would be forced, yet again, to face the most powerful of interlopers, just as it had over the centuries confronted the Greeks under Alexander the Great, the Mongols under Genghis Khan, and the Timurids under Tamerlane.

Once they had crossed the mountain passes, the invaders would find themselves either in the Punjab to the north or Sind to the south, with the Indus River being their last major geographical barrier to overcome. Maharaja Ranjit Singh ruled the independent kingdom of the Sikhs, commanding an 85,000-strong army that was both well-trained and well-equipped. Although blinded in one eye since childhood from smallpox, he was a strongman and known as the Lion of Punjab. His Sikhs were a warrior race, ever-ready for battle, and they controlled the Khyber and the city of Peshawar on the Indian side. Sind, on the other hand, being a collection of smaller independent states, was not as powerful and, as it was accessed from the lesser important Bolan Pass, would play a smaller role as the game unfolded.

Around this time, dramatic events were heightening fears of Russian territorial ambitions. During 1829, they had defeated in swift succession both Persia and Turkey, to rapidly reach the gates of Constantinople, much to the alarm of other European powers. The tsar's armies had demonstrated their capability, and were primed to take the most coveted prize of the Near East and the key to its domination. But, to the intense disappointment of his generals, the tsar held them back, deciding against a final push for the city due to other pressing geopolitical considerations, particularly the risk from the fallout if the Ottoman Empire were to then collapse. Understandably, following this military expedition, the Russian bogy was reignited in Britain, and Anglo-Russian relations consequently plummeted. To add to this fear, a frustration Britain continually faced was that whenever it opposed the tsar in Europe, Russia would in turn threaten India.

At the forefront of renewed anti-Russian attitudes were two more books, both written by another soldier, Colonel George de Lacy Evans, who would go on to become a general and receive a knighthood. They were published in successive years, to a largely receptive British audience. The second, released in 1829, *On the Practicality of an Invasion of British India*, became the virtual handbook for Great Game players, and had a profound influence on policymakers in London and Calcutta. Evans argued that Russia's initial aim would be to destabilize British rule in India, which was the biggest fear of the East India Company, as native Indians vastly outnumbered Britons.

The threat of a rebellion from within was far more alarming to the Company than any invasion, or the danger of bankruptcy for that matter. The worst possible scenario would involve fighting a foreign army *and* an insurrection simultaneously. Enticing the natives to rise up against British rule during an invasion had always been an axiom of Russian strategy; and the Indian Mutiny in 1857 would prove this was not a far-fetched idea.* To fight and win a two-pronged attack would require substantial troop reinforcements from England, and obviously large sums of money, quite possibly bankrupting the Company.

An outspoken Sir Charles Metcalfe, later to become acting governor-general, put it bluntly: 'Our dominion of India is by conquest . . . It is naturally disgusting to the inhabitants and can only be maintained by military force.' There was a deep feeling of isolation within the British community, and the constant fear of rebellion greatly influenced its behaviour in India. One example of this was the Company's attitude to Christian missionaries: since the prospect of religious reform could incite the pious Indians, it resisted attempts to try to convert them, or interfere with their religious practices.

Evans's book carefully considered possible invasion routes, and ruled out an approach through Persia as being the likely one. His research suggested that a force of some 30,000 could be transported from the eastern Caspian shore to Khiva, then sail up the Oxus River (today the Amu Darya), before marching on to Kabul. Although he

---

* Even after the rebellion, amid some 200 million Indians, the British Army on the subcontinent numbered only 60,000. In comparison, the princely states of India could field an estimated 300,000 troops.

made light of the difficulties involved—such as crossing the Karakum Desert where temperatures over 125 degrees Fahrenheit (52 degrees Celsius) have been recorded—with his detractors lacking first-hand experience to challenge the practicality of his theories, they found more favour than they perhaps deserved.

The Need for Information

Edward Law, 1st Earl of Ellenborough, was a member of the British cabinet and had recently been appointed president of the Board of Control for India.* He read Evans's book soon after its release with much interest. Invasion theories and their likelihood were being discussed at the highest levels of government, and he was corresponding regularly with the prime minister, the Duke of Wellington, about his concerns. Ellenborough summed up the dilemma they faced on the subcontinent:

> Upon the subject of the invasion of India my idea was that the thing was not only practical but easy, unless we determine to act as an Asiatic Power . . . It is not on the Indus that an enemy is to be met. If we do not meet him in Kabul, at the foot of the Hindu Kush or in its passes we had better remain on the Sutlej. If the Russians once occupy Kabul they may return there with the Indus in their front, until they have organised insurrection in our rear and completely equipped their army.

Ellenborough believed such a force could be defeated before it reached the mighty river, but was worried about the destabilizing effect it could have on Indians. With the help of his advisers, he produced a 'situation paper', which argued that the Russians would first march to Kabul, before using the city as a base for an all-out

---

* He would hold this position three other times between 1828 and 1858; and serve as governor-general of India between 1842 and 1844.

attack. To get there, this army could come either by way of Persia and the city of Herat or, alternatively, through Western Turkestan across the Oxus.

What worried Ellenborough most was not so much the actual danger of an invasion, but the uncertainty of whether this was possible. 'What we ought to have is *Information*. The first, second and third thing a government ought always to have is *Information*,' he is reported as saying. Yet when he asked for detailed maps of possible incursion routes and reliable intelligence about the region— its geography, its people and their rulers, and the current military and political situation—he was to be disappointed. To his horror, he learnt that few maps existed, and those that did could not be trusted for their accuracy. As for regional intelligence, well, there wasn't a lot of that either, as the necessary spy networks had simply not been built. What they did have was more than a dozen newswriters, based in key centres such as Kabul and Tehran, who sent in periodical letters describing recent developments in these areas. Officers and their staff also gathered information by quizzing traders returning from sensitive frontier zones, but there was no real coordinated effort.

The British could only blame themselves for this situation, and it has been suggested this stemmed from their strong aversion to the use of spies in the first place, as this was alien to the traditions of government they brought to India. Perhaps they had forgotten the age-old saying 'Spying is the world's second oldest profession', which, if anywhere, would surely hold true in Asia.

In fact, the only intelligence readily available had to be gleaned from within Russia, through spies working for London based in St Petersburg, but there were doubts about the worthiness of this information. Ellenborough wanted this gap in their knowledge rectified, and he was able to persuade Wellington of its urgent need: historian Edward Ingram even marks the start of the Great Game from this event, in the last days of 1829 and the deliberations of these two statesmen.

* * *

Ellenborough believed the Russians would utilize a strategy where the trader preceded the soldier, and in a slow but steady way would creep up to within striking distance. Protecting its merchants would be the pretext for the Russian military to follow in their footsteps. In a nutshell, his view was that commerce would prepare the way for conquest—not a new concept, as the British had already demonstrated in India. If this theory was correct, then some important deductions could be made with the right intelligence: by carefully monitoring the progress of Russian trading posts through Central Asia, it should be possible to determine their preferred route *and* rate of encroachment towards India. This implied that another pressing need, in addition to accurate maps, was the establishment of some form of 'listening posts' situated in strategic locations. Those who manned these stations would alert Calcutta to the first signs of Russian moves into the region—just as Moorcroft had attempted to do with his newswriters.

Ellenborough was of the belief that gathering all this information was best achieved by employing their own agents, whose reports could be trusted. Their brief would be to travel through much of Central Asia and engage in espionage: to observe and map likely invasion routes, create alliances with local rulers where possible, and always be looking and listening for any sign of a Russian presence. A few British personnel had already attempted this work, but in an uncoordinated manner and mainly through their own initiative, often driven by the lure of adventure. Now it became official policy, and their work was needed as a matter of urgency, no less than for the defence of India.

At the same time, the Russians were also sending their best men out into this supposed no man's land, as yet unclaimed by either empire, to gather information and advance their national cause. These men, from both sides equally, were destined to become the classic Great Game players, and their time to take the stage had come.

Arthur Conolly

The first of Ellenborough's intrepid spies set out soon afterwards. His name was Arthur Conolly—a quiet and intensely religious man, who would prove himself a brave officer. He had arrived in India in 1823 as a somewhat shy and sensitive sixteen-year-old cadet, to join the Company's army. Now, six years later and a lieutenant in the Bengal Cavalry, he was returning to the subcontinent after a period of sick leave spent at home in England. Rather than take the easier sea route to India, he decided to ride. After making his way to Moscow, he set out on horseback through Russian territory, while observing all he could of the tsar's military machine.

The first part of his journey was not particularly risky as his counterparts were still officially allied with Britain, although this relationship was deteriorating as 'the game' was beginning to take shape. The tsar's officers even provided him with a Cossack escort through the dangerous Caucasus region. From Tabriz in northern Persia, an interpreter named Said Karamut Ali accompanied him, who would later prove to be a faithful friend as well, nursing Conolly when he was stricken by fever.

After Persia, their journey became more perilous, as they attempted a crossing of the Karakum Desert to reach Khiva and observe the strength of Russian presence there. Conolly disguised himself as a merchant, complete with goods to trade in the bazaars, camels, servants and a guide. He knew full well the risk he ran being killed as a 'non-believer', if he was exposed as an Englishman. He would, of course, face almost certain execution as a spy, if it was discovered he was a British officer. His plan was to join a large caravan bound for Khiva but, before he could do this, Turcoman brigands captured his party. They only extracted themselves from the bandits' clutches with difficulty, after handing over most of their money and goods. Conolly had little option at this point but to give up his bid for Khiva, although he had succeeded in securing some intelligence about the region and Russian activity here.

Now he made no attempt to hide his Christian beliefs, and even stood up for his faith despite travelling with strict Muslims. He used whatever disguise suited him, sometimes posing as a *hakeem* (physician), and at times using the name Khan Ali in a wordplay on his true name. First, he headed for Meshed in eastern Persia, and then rode across the border into the closely guarded city of Herat. Afterwards, he went on to Kandahar, then Quetta, and finally re-entered India through the Bolan Pass—completing a gruelling ride of more than 4000 miles lasting over a year.

Conolly had collected valuable information for Ellenborough, having reconnoitred large sections of the route an invading army would most likely use. He described his fascinating journey in a lengthy book published a few years later, which established his reputation as an exceptional traveller and, less publicly, as a first-class intelligence agent.

'Bokhara' Burnes

While Conolly was completing his marathon journey, Ellenborough had been giving his 'commerce prepares the way for conquest' theory more thought. He wanted to expand the idea now, after Wellington gave him a virtual free hand with regard to India. While believing this would be Russia's tactic, Ellenborough wanted to employ a similar approach to achieve further gains in Central Asia. With the offer of superior British goods, in place of what he considered shoddy Russian merchandise, not only could the advance of the tsar's merchants be halted, but Britain's own power and influence in the region would be increased at the same time.

Goods made in England could be transported from the coast deep into Central Asia using the Indus, but it needed surveying first, to determine to what extent it was navigable. Herein lay the next challenge, as the river, from its mouth, initially crossed land belonging to Sind in the south and Punjab in the north. Thus, the first hurdle to overcome was convincing these rulers to allow an exploratory mission to pass through their domains. What better way than to send the maharaja of Punjab a gift from the king of Great Britain? An offering lavish enough to delight him into accepting it, and large enough that it could only be transported by river. A gift of five enormous English dray horses pulling a splendid state coach should do the trick! Some senior officials in India were horrified at the idea, seeing it as devious and unworthy of His Majesty's government. They seriously doubted whether this would fool anyone as to the real purpose of the mission (it didn't); and a parallel to the Greek's Trojan Horse, five in this case, was not too difficult to draw.

To lead this mission, another young and ambitious officer was chosen. He would seize this opportunity to enter the Great Game and soon become one of its most memorable players, achieving fame beyond his dreams. This man was Lieutenant Alexander Burnes, a Scotsman.* He had enlisted with the Bombay Army at age sixteen, but was astute enough to later join the ranks of the 'politicals': within the Company's army, the posts most sought-after by officers were the political and diplomatic appointments, as they offered the best chances for advancement and to wield power. This new breed, who still carried military rank but whose first loyalty lay with the governor-general, came to be known as politicals—officers who exchanged their sword for the pen.

However, this career shift, combined with the drift to the better-paying Indian Civil Service, would have the long-term effect of denuding the Indian Army of its best and brightest. It would leave behind a disproportionate number of the young, aged or those less capable—an outcome that would have grave consequences for both the military and civilians in future conflicts.

Burnes was a brilliant linguist, fluent in Hindi, Arabic and Persian, who was at ease with the flattery and flowery hyperbole of the East. His flotilla of five flat-bottomed native boats had on

---

* Scots were prevalent in the army and its officer ranks, calling themselves English when overseas; the Empire, though, was always referred to as British.

board a doctor, a native surveyor, servants and, of course, the coach and horses. They sailed up the Indus in January 1831, carefully charting the river and sounding its muddy depths. The surveyor worked mostly at night, in order not to arouse the suspicion and ire of the emirs of Sind; nevertheless, the locals were soon on to the expedition. Despite encountering much hostility along the way, including snipers taking potshots from the banks, in five months the mission reached Ranjit Singh's capital, in Lahore. Much to their relief, they were received with pomp and ceremony; and the massive horses caused a sensation, as they were a larger breed than any seen in this part of the world.

Burnes had come through with flying colours, and on his return the governor-general commended him for his 'zeal, diligence and intelligence'. Not only had he demonstrated that he was a man of considerable political ability, his mission had fulfilled its key objective. It had proven the river was navigable, at least as far as the Punjab capital; and he supplemented this finding by preparing a *Map of the Indus and Punjab Rivers from the Sea to Lahore*. With this information in hand, his superiors believed they could soon start shipping British goods into Western Turkestan and compete directly with the Russians, first for trade and then for territory, as Ellenborough had envisaged.

Safely back from his first mission, Burnes quickly moved to build on his success by proposing to the governor-general a second expedition. Although this was a more ambitious undertaking, his timing was impeccable. Despite his relatively junior rank, permission was soon granted and the necessary passports obtained for his party. His aim was to explore the unmapped routes into India that ran north of those already scouted by Conolly the previous year. After this, he planned to continue on to Kabul, to establish friendly links with the emir of Afghanistan, Dost Mohammed Khan, and gauge the strength of his army.

One dissenting voice regarding this expedition was that of Major Claude Wade, the political agent and spymaster based in Ludhiana.

He was now running British intelligence networks across Central Asia from the Company's residency in this cantonment town, a lone outpost on the wild Northwest Frontier. Wade saw Burnes as something of an interfering young upstart, and regarded him as a threat to his own position. The major resented his direct access to the governor-general but was unable to stop the mission, although he would long remain a thorn in Burnes's side.

Burnes's party of five included a native surveyor to assist with map-making. With the aid of a compass, sextant and chronometer, and by timing their rate of travel, they would approximate the positions of key places along the way. First, they carefully measured the rate at which their string of camels marched, and found this to equal 2 miles 300 yards per hour over flat country. Latitude could be determined typically to within a mile using a sextant. This involved observing either the sun by day or certain stars by night, and then looking up this coordinate in a nautical almanac for that particular date. Longitude was calculated by taking the difference between Greenwich time, kept by the chronometer,* and local time, determined using the sextant.†

Burnes had hired a young Kashmiri named Mohan Lal as his munshi (secretary and/or translator); though he would soon prove far more valuable than just a scribe, both to Burnes and his British masters. Mohan Lal deserves to be credited as a Great Game player in his own right—possibly the first notable Indian one.

The travellers reached their destination in the spring of 1832, when Kabul was at its prettiest, and Burnes fell in love with the

---

* A chronometer's superior accuracy allowed it to be used as a portable standard (for Greenwich time), which a pocket watch could not achieve. In those days, even a chronometer had difficulty holding time during long journeys, especially if exposed to jolting or extreme temperatures.

† A difference as little as four seconds of time is equivalent to one mile at the equator. This fact also highlights the sizeable error introduced to longitude measurements if a chronometer fails to hold its time.

capital, describing it as 'paradise'. He got on famously with the Dost (an honorific title meaning friend), and soon came to the important conclusion that this man was British India's best bet as an ally, and should be supported in his continual struggle to retain the Afghan throne.

After leaving Kabul, Burnes and his companions made for Balkh, where in a poignant moment on a moonlit night they located William Moorcroft's rough grave. His decomposing corpse had been moved here for burial soon after his untimely demise. Next to him lay one of his companions, George Guthrie. Both were buried in unmarked graves outside the town walls, since the locals regarded them as infidels—in death as in life. Burnes would later say that Moorcroft had seen the future while others were content with the present, and it was in the hope of completing the latter's work that he had embarked on his own travels.

With high anticipation, after crossing the Oxus, Burnes and his party finally rode into Bokhara at the end of June 1832. A saying in Turkestan about this fabled city maintained: 'In all other parts of the world light descends upon Earth, but from holy Bokhara it ascends.' This may not have reflected reality, though, as according to a scholar writing in the middle of the eighteenth century: 'Drunkenness, gambling, carousing and lewdness are rampant . . .'

This state of affairs hadn't changed much a century later, when the Hungarian traveller and Turkologist Arminius Vambery visited the city. He would later write the *History of Bokhara*, and described it as 'the most shameless sink of iniquity that I know in the East'. Still, it had many redeeming features, as Vambery noted:

Bokhara was not, however, merely a luxurious city . . . it was also the principal emporium for the trade between China and Western Asia, in addition to the vast warehouses for silks, brocades and cotton stuffs, for the finest carpets, and all kinds of gold and silversmiths' work; it boasted a great money-market, being in fact the Exchange of all the population of Eastern and

Western Asia; and there is a proverb current to this day: 'As wide awake as a broker of Bokhara'.

Burnes stayed here for the best part of a month and befriended the grand vizier, although, try as he might, this friendship was not able to gain him an audience with the secretive emir. He was constantly gathering information for Ellenborough and the intelligence arm of the Military Department, commenting later: 'Simple people! They believe a spy must measure their forts and walls; they have no idea of the value of conversation.'

He also visited Bokhara's slave bazaar, and later heard first-hand of the plight of a middle-aged Russian who had been abducted from an outpost as a ten-year-old. The Russian yearned to return home with his wife and child, but Burnes was powerless to help.

A year after starting out, Burnes made his way back to India to a hero's welcome, having visited distant and dangerous places, witnessing exotic sights such as few Europeans had before him. Shortly afterwards, during a visit to London, King William IV gave him a private audience, and he was asked to brief members of the cabinet and the India Board of Control.

Burnes was quick to publish his *Travels into Bokhara*, which extended to three volumes and included a splendid map of Central Asia. The work was an immediate bestseller, although the military intelligence gathered during his travels was, of course, circulated in a secret report to the government. Ironically, it was the French translation of his book that may have first prompted the Russians to take a closer interest in British activities across Central Asia—the very thing Burnes's masters were trying to avoid.

His mission won for him the kind of acclaim it would for Lawrence of Arabia 100 years later, and thereafter the press and public frequently referred to him as 'Bokhara Burnes'. In 1835, the Royal Geographic Society (RGS) in London presented him with the equivalent of its gold medal—an award started three years earlier, following an annual gift of 50 guineas by the British monarch, 'for the encouragement and promotion of geographical science and discovery'.* Receiving this honour was truly the pinnacle for any explorer. During this era, the RGS was the pre-eminent institution in the world as far as exploration and the dissemination of geographical information were concerned. Its famous Map Room was, as the society would later claim, 'the Mecca for all true geographers, the home port of every traveller'.

Burnes returned to Afghanistan in 1836, having convinced the newly appointed governor-general, George Eden, 1st Earl of Auckland, to set up a permanent 'commercial mission' in the capital. Ostensibly to promote the trade of British goods, its real purpose was to closely monitor the political situation there, and especially keep a close eye on the Russians. It was here, in his beloved city of Kabul, that Burnes's final chapter would be written.

Herat

In the meantime, conflict was again erupting between neighbours Persia and Afghanistan, and these long-time rivals would soon become embroiled in another classic Great Game chapter, but, as was often the case, Britain and Russia would enter the fray, pulling strings at the crucial moment to decide the outcome.

Persia had always coveted Herat, and laid claim to it in the past. As one of the great caravan towns of Central Asia, it was vital to the defence of Afghanistan and the Punjab. An aggressor would probably head for this fertile valley first, to re-provision, before choosing either of the key passes to enter India. Known as the granary of Central Asia, it was a prosperous region with a large population of Persian Shiites.

The current shah, who had ascended the throne in 1834, wanted to annex the province as another way of consolidating his rule.

---

*   In 1839, the RGS converted this sum into two gold medals—the Founder's Medal and the Patron's Medal—both of which are awarded annually to this day.

Britain, however, was determined it should not fall into unfriendly hands. By this stage, many believed Persia was in a chronic state of near collapse, and had consequently become a virtual client state of Russia. The tsar was encouraging the shah to take over this province as a way to compensate Persia for recent territorial losses to Russia in the Caucasus. Herat would quickly become yet another bone of contention between the two empires, but neither had an appetite for all-out conflict, as Lord Palmerston (then foreign secretary, later serving twice as prime minister) reflected in 1835: 'We are just as we were, snarling at each other, hating each other, but neither wishing for war.'

Two years later, Persia made its move, attacking and laying siege to the city, with the help of Russian military advisers led by Count Simonich and a contingent of soldiers masquerading as refugees. Their hopes for a quick victory were utterly frustrated, though, as the citizens found an 'accidental hero' who came to the fore: Lieutenant Eldred Pottinger had been gathering routine intelligence in the area, and quickly offered his services to the local ruler. He then began tirelessly helping the Heratis to better organize their defences against an army numbering over 30,000. The torturous siege dragged on for many months, well into the following year. Count Simonich took charge of the offensive, and finally launched a full-blown attack, trying to find a breach in the defences. When all looked lost, at the critical hour, Pottinger rallied the local troops and helped save the city. His actions wrote him into folklore, and a best-selling book was published later describing what had transpired, titled *The Hero of Herat*.

At this point Britain intervened in a roundabout but most effective way, literally with 'gunboat diplomacy'. Rather than send a relief force to Herat, it played to its strength and dispatched a naval task force to the Persian Gulf, to threaten the shah's western cities across the other side of his kingdom. Once their troops had landed at Kharg Island, Britain bluntly informed the shah that any further action on its part would depend on his own actions in Herat. The shah knew he was on dangerous ground, and immediately withdrew his army. This brought the siege to an end, leaving the city's inhabitants jubilant and the Russians indirectly defeated, with Count Simonich having to shoulder the blame back home.

The Dost

Like the shah of Persia, the emir of Afghanistan had designs on reclaiming territory he believed was rightly his. Dost Mohammed had pledged to wrest back the rich and fertile province of Peshawar—which Afghans still regarded as their second capital—from his long-standing rival Maharaja Ranjit Singh, who had annexed it some years earlier. Back in 1837, led by his eldest son Akbar Khan, they had defeated the Sikhs resoundingly in a major battle near Peshawar, but had fallen short of retaking the province.

Now Dost Mohammed needed help in dealing with the Sikhs again, so he first turned to the British in India, preferring them as a partner over the Russians. Burnes, who was stationed in Kabul at this stage, explained to his good friend the emir why this would be impossible: Britain already had a treaty with Ranjit Singh and wasn't about to offend him, or risk a frontier war under any circumstances. The Sikhs represented the last native force on the subcontinent capable of challenging British might, prompting the Company to station almost one-half of its Bengal Army along the Punjab frontier as a precaution. Since the Sikhs and Afghans were historical enemies, it put Britain in an impossible position of trying to form close alliances with both rulers.

Burnes did point out to his superiors that Ranjit Singh was now old and frail, and there was no guarantee his successor would remain friendly towards Britain, but still the politicals would not risk upsetting the Sikhs. Actually, an alliance with Dost Mohammed would have made sense *if* the Punjab had already been subsumed, as this would have taken British India's frontier all the way up to Afghanistan (which did occur, but only later in 1849). For now, London and

Calcutta preferred the status quo, and they tried unsuccessfully to get the emir to give up the idea of recovering Peshawar.

Finally, in early 1838 the governor-general, Lord Auckland, told Dost Mohammed as much again, this time in a blunt and uncompromising manner, in writing. He advised the emir that should he turn to the Russians for support, Britain would not feel obliged to restrain any incursions made into his country by Ranjit Singh's army. Burnes was instructed to spell out Britain's message, and warn him that should he choose to ally with the Russians he would be ousted as the Afghan ruler.

This was a far cry from Auckland's initial assurance to Dost Mohammed upon his arrival in India, when his words were: 'My friend, you are aware that it is not the practice of the British government to interfere in the affairs of other independent states . . .' Now he needed a compliant ruler on the Afghan throne, and was determined to have one. Understandably, this ultimatum infuriated the emir and he felt deeply insulted. The seeds had been sown for the First Afghan War,* which would set the course of Central Asian and Indian history for the next 100 years.

* * *

Dost Mohammed, like many Asiatic rulers, was well versed in the craft of political double-dealing, and had been hedging his position for a while in case no help was forthcoming from Britain. As it happened, another player from the opposing side had been waiting in the shadows during this time, and had brought with him rare and precious gifts to impress the emir. He was Burnes's political equivalent, and they were well matched in many respects. Of similar age, both were brave and ambitious; and although unconnected to the ruling elite, both had risen to prominence through sheer merit, especially their talent for languages and first-hand knowledge of

---

* Today, the Afghan Wars are also referred to as the Anglo-Afghan Wars.

the region. When they had shared a Christmas dinner in Kabul the previous winter, theirs was the first such meeting in the history of the Great Game.

Burnes's nemesis was Captain Yan Vitkevich. Born of an aristocratic Lithuanian family, he had once been arrested as a dissident in Poland but had escaped execution due to his youth, having just turned fourteen. Instead, he was exiled to Siberia where, three years later, he was conscripted into the Russian Army. Here, he made the best of his bad situation, learning Kazak and other languages of the steppe, becoming an interpreter, and memorizing the Koran by heart. Slowly, he clawed his way up the ranks, volunteering for lone and dangerous missions across Central Asia. Often he went disguised as a Kazak Muslim, undertaking espionage activities for Russia, and becoming one of the first players in its Tournament of Shadows.

Now he was in Kabul as the tsar's envoy, trying to convince the emir an alliance with Russia would better serve Afghanistan. Of course, it would serve the tsar's purposes too, as one of his high officials, the governor of Orenburg, noted: 'If the patronage of Russia can support Dost Mohammed on the throne, he will undoubtedly, in gratitude, remain a good friend of ours and an enemy of the English; he will cut them off from Central Asia, will place a barrier to their beloved trading power.' At the time, Kabul was at the height of its prosperity, and well placed as the centre of the region's lucrative caravan trade. The city, with its 70,000 citizens, was seen as a fabulous prize in its own right.

Although Dost Mohammed would not initially deal with Vitkevich, after being rejected by Calcutta he warmly received the envoy as a friend. The emir's only motive had been to use him as a means to put pressure on Britain, but it would backfire badly. His action turned out to be the point of no return in this saga, and the war that was to follow.

Burnes had repeatedly tried to get his superiors to recognize Dost Mohammed's value, even breaching the chain of command

and writing to Auckland directly. Later, he would tell the governor-general the emir was 'a man of undoubted ability: and if half you must do for others were done for him . . . he would abandon Persia and Russia tomorrow'. With Vitkevich's ascendancy, Burnes had no option but to leave the capital. In April 1838, after a stay of seven months, he returned to India, despondent and frustrated at Calcutta's refusal to heed his advice. In this at least, Burnes would soon be proved right.

As it turned out, things didn't go well for Vitkevich either. Although he did succeed in winning over the emir for Russia, the accolades he deserved never materialized. Nor was his aristocratic title restored, as he had dearly hoped. After strong diplomatic pressure was applied from London, the tsar recalled him from Kabul; and back in St Petersburg, much to his surprise and for reasons that aren't clear, his superiors disowned him. In a state of utter dejection, after locking himself in the room of a boarding house, Vitkevich ended his life with a bullet to the head; the note he left behind was silent as to his reason why.

Dost Mohammed, meanwhile, sat at home waiting for events to unfold, perhaps knowing full well this was the calm before the storm.

The First Afghan War

As far as the Afghan question was concerned, London and Calcutta had three options to choose from. The first was to leave the country to Russia, which meant admitting defeat, and so was quickly rejected. The second was to take Burnes's advice and support the emir; but such a move could destabilize the frontier, given his bitter enmity with the Sikhs. The third option was to replace him with another ruler—one ready to do Britain's bidding.

By receiving Vitkevich, Dost Mohammed had signalled, inadvertently, that he had chosen Russia as his ally going forward. For Britain this was intolerable, and settled the question of whether it should oust the emir—but who to replace him with? After lengthy discussions, Sir William Macnaghten's candidate, an exiled Afghan leader named Shah Shujah, whom Claude Wade also favoured, was accepted. Macnaghten was then secretary to the Secret and Political Department in Calcutta, a brilliant orientalist but a 'desk jockey' nonetheless, who was inclined to be pompous and vain. He believed the throne legitimately belonged to Shujah, who had ruled from 1803 for six years, before being forced into exile for almost three decades. During this period, he failed in three separate attempts to regain his crown from Dost Mohammed's clan.

This wasn't Shujah's only loss. To his lasting regret, he had been stripped of his most prized possession by Ranjit Singh while seeking refuge in the Sikh court. The item in question was the world's largest diamond at the time, the Koh-i-Nur (Mountain of Light). The maharajah had revealed it to Burnes during their first encounter, after he had navigated the Indus to Lahore; he would later describe that moment:

> Nothing can be imagined more superb than this stone; it is of the finest water, about half the size of an egg. Its weight amounts to 3½ rupees, and if such a jewel is to be valued, I am informed it is worth 3½ millions of money; but this is a gross exaggeration.*

Macnaghten's plan entailed using the Sikh Army to do most of the frontline work necessary to invade Afghanistan and place Shujah on the throne, even as Burnes continued making friendly overtures in Dost Mohammed's court. Other than this duplicitous scheming, the obvious dangers of an enemy *imposing* a ruler on the Afghan people seem to have been overlooked as well.

A secret agreement was signed in June 1838 between the three parties: Maharajah Ranjit Singh, Great Britain and Shah Shujah.

---

* More likely an underestimate. Its market value has forever been debated; often, it is simply tagged 'priceless'.

The first would supply the troops; the second would put up the money and advisers; and the third would, in effect, be the puppet ruler (who, to no one's surprise, had been ignored during the lead-up negotiations). This deal was soon followed up with Lord Auckland's Simla Manifesto,* justifying their removal of Dost Mohammed. Despite denying they were *invading* Afghanistan, or their dubious claim of merely supporting the legitimate ruler 'against foreign interference and factious opposition', the manifesto was essentially a call to arms and a declaration of war. Although it gave the impression that British troops would merely be used to support Shah Shujah's small army, it fooled no one. As the time for action drew closer, the wily Ranjit Singh, not wanting to risk his army, wriggled out of committing any troops at all. Besides, Shujah baulked at the idea of entering his country with the help of his traditional enemy, the Sikhs. He did manage to raise a smaller army of his own, although still trained and paid by the British. His 6000 men were mostly Indian irregulars, with only a few Afghan fighters. This turn of events eventually compelled Britain to get its hands dirty and provide the bulk of the invading force.

Before this army started its fateful march, an event occurred that gave Britain one last chance to pause and reconsider. It learnt that the Russian-backed siege of Herat, thanks to Pottinger's heroics to some degree, had failed and been called off. This meant a prime reason for removing Dost Mohammed no longer existed, since the danger to India had significantly receded. Here was an opportunity to stay the army, but for Auckland and others, who were firmly committed to seeing their plan through, there would be no turning back from war.

The Army of the Indus, as it was officially labelled, was commanded by General John Keane. Comprising some 15,000 British and Indian troops, it was assembled on the banks of the river. For the majority of the Indians, who were Hindus, this was a difficult

---

* Simla, then a hill station, became the summer capital of British India from 1864.

moment as it would mean breaking their religious taboo by venturing beyond the Indus River. When he returned to India, Mohan Lal would lament: 'I was very coolly received by my countrymen at Dihli [Delhi], who . . . considered me a Mussalman in consequence of crossing the Indus, or forbidden river.'

As with all armies in India, this one marched with a considerable train of camp followers—in this case numbering over 30,000. They were supported by a similar number of camels to carry baggage and supplies, with several herds of cattle in tow for food. Such a large camp, which included bearers, prostitutes and even foxhounds, was clearly excessive; but as one general remarked: 'Many young officers would as soon have thought of leaving behind their swords and double-barrelled pistols as march without their dressing cases, their perfumes, Windsor soap, and eau de colognes.' A senior officer used eighty camels to transport his own personal belongings, and one regiment needed another two beasts just to carry its cigars.

This mass of marching humanity, resembling a slow-moving tented city, was mobilized from various cantonments in early 1839. To add to its difficulties, the army was forced to enter Afghanistan through a longer route, after being compelled to detour south via the Bolan Pass. This problem arose after Ranjit Singh changed his mind about permitting access through the Punjab and Khyber Pass. One look at a map will highlight the extra distance and effort this would have required from an already lumbering army which, much to its disappointment, had no choice but to shed its many luxuries along the way.

Another problem centred on the issue of overall command, which was blurred from the outset. Other than on military matters, it really lay with Macnaghten, now holding the impressive title 'Envoy and Minister on the part of the Government of India at the Court of Shah Shujah'. However, one of the consequences of this impending war would be the significant curbing of the power wielded by the politicals in India, for reasons which would soon become evident.

Alexander Burnes, flushed by his recent success, made up the forward party. He had been promoted again, this time to the rank of lieutenant colonel. And to his amazement, at just thirty-three years of age, awarded a knighthood—his star was clearly on the rise. Although he had vigorously opposed the ousting of his friend Dost Mohammed, his silence and support had seemingly been bought by his appointment as deputy envoy, and the promise of a baronetcy.

Sir Alexander and his men rode ahead of the army, to ease the way with the chieftains of the smaller kingdoms in Sind. Unlike Ranjit Singh, they weren't given any choice in allowing troops passage through their lands, despite this being contrary to a treaty signed just a few years earlier.

To sustain the 50,000-odd column as they trudged through a parched land, Burnes's team helped procure desperately needed water and food supplies—but from a reluctant local population who had already borne the brunt of a failed harvest and had little to share. The circuitous route to Kabul, exacerbated by the approaching heat of summer, meant many died from thirst and exhaustion, despite marching at night. One infantryman, suffocating in his tight-fitting woollen uniform, painted a grim picture: 'I cannot describe our sufferings from the heat, the dust, the desert wind, the myriad of flies. The whole camp smelled like a charnel house. No person could take three steps in camp, anywhere, without seeing a dead or dying man or animal.' All the while, straggling camp followers were regularly set upon by brigands and murdered.

After passing through Quetta, the column negotiated the steep and narrow Bolan Pass, before the army readied itself for its first battle, to neutralize Kandahar. To the troops' immense relief, they met no armed resistance here, and were able to enter and occupy this southern city without a shot being fired. But the first signs of mistrust by Afghans were beginning to emerge, as one sepoy would relate: 'Although they were repeatedly told that the British had not come to take their country away from them, they could not forget the history of Hindustan.'

The Army of the Indus wasn't so fortunate at the next town, Ghazni, 200 miles north-east as the crow flies, which was renowned for its fighters. It was from within these walls, almost 1000 years earlier, that Mahmud of Ghazni had led his warriors through the Khyber and on to the plains of India, to plunder regularly and with impunity. Now, a hard-fought battle ensued to capture its fortress, which was said to be impregnable. It was finally overrun using a technique the British would employ against other fortifications in the future: blowing open a gate with explosives and storming the breach.

It was Burnes's young protégé Mohan Lal who had helped bring about this bold action. He obtained a critical piece of information from one of the defenders, identifying one of the gates that had not been reinforced, thus making it vulnerable to gunpowder. Despite the sappers coming under heavy fire, they managed to place their charge; and after the ensuing explosion, the storming party overcame huge odds in the hand-to-hand fighting that followed.

Their heroic action would win more than just Ghazni: on hearing of its loss, the emir fled, leaving Kabul to surrender without a fight. The maharaja, too, had departed a few weeks earlier, although in Ranjit Singh's case he died in his bed, just hours after supposedly donating his ill-gotten Koh-i-Nur to a holy Hindu temple. (It never got there after his heirs reneged, unable to bring themselves to part with this priceless jewel.)

Some months later Dost Mohammed gave himself up, and Macnaghten, who received him with full honours, admitted to the unfairness of their actions, writing: 'we ejected the Dost, who never offended us, in support of our policy, of which he was a victim'. In spite of Shujah's call to 'hang him like a dog', the fallen ruler, together with his nine wives, was granted exile in India—which was fortuitous as the British would need him again, and sooner than anyone imagined.

In a twist of irony, during his exile Dost Mohammed would occupy Shah Shujah's old house. On seeing the riches of British

India, he mused: 'I cannot understand why the rulers of so great an empire should have gone across the Indus to deprive me of my poor and barren country.' Perhaps he needed to be reminded of an old Indian saying: 'When two elephants fight, the grass beneath them is crushed.'

After an absence of thirty years, Shah Shujah entered Kabul at the head of the Army of the Indus, as the new ruler of Afghanistan. It seemed to confirm, at least initially, that British strategy had been executed flawlessly, leading to much self-congratulations, and titles were duly conferred from London. Auckland was made an earl, Macnaghten a baronet, and the general became Lord Keane of Ghazni. Yet Shujah failed to receive the welcome he might have expected from the tribal chiefs or the common people, which was an early and ominous sign of things to come.

The Afghans were sullen from the start, and before long the British were receiving disturbing reports of widespread trouble brewing. For one thing, it was clear the shah could not maintain his position without constant support from locally garrisoned British troops; otherwise the populace was likely to revolt.

After securing Kabul, the bulk of the army departed with General Keane. For the remaining troops, this expedition was starting to look more like a permanent occupation, especially after the wives and children of soldiers began to join them from India. This was in direct contravention to the Simla Manifesto, which had clearly stated the army would be withdrawn when Shujah was installed in Kabul.

The Afghans' deep-seated desire to be free, and their abhorrence of foreign troops on their soil, has since been demonstrated time and again to Western powers. Added to this, their list of grievances was growing. The presence of this additional mass of people was increasing the demand for basic foodstuff, leading to prices being driven up by as much as 500 per cent for ordinary Afghans, and driving the poor to near-starvation. Another consequence of such a large presence of single men was their fraternization with Afghan women. This enraged locals; even more so when it was conducted openly by the commanding officers, and Burnes with his easy charm was a notorious offender.

The honour of their women, and their strong religious view against the consumption of alcohol, gave the fanatical mullahs further reason to preach jihad across the country. They whipped up rebellion against an army that was led by Christians and comprised mainly Hindu troops—an occupying power alien in both race and religion.

The seriousness of the unrest was neither well-understood nor fully appreciated by the British command during their two-year occupation. It did not help matters that the relationship between Burnes and Macnaghten, who had diametrically opposite personalities, was steadily deteriorating during this time. Macnaghten was anxious to return to India and the promotion that awaited him, having recently been named the next governor of Bombay, the second-highest post in India. Later, it was suggested that he was reluctant to acknowledge the increasing ferment for fear of being asked to stay on longer and help suppress it.

Burnes, his replacement, was simply marking time waiting for Macnaghten to depart, but keeping himself entertained—although his blatant womanizing was making him many influential enemies. To make matters worse, he was seen by many Afghans as the initiator of this occupation. They thought of him as a *namak haram* (impure salt, implying a deceiver) who had acted as a spy during his initial stay in Kabul, when he had befriended Dost Mohammed.

Mohan Lal had warned Burnes of the impending danger to his life, which included a threat by a clan chief to slay him in revenge for seducing his slave girl, then mocking him when he tried to fetch her back. The munshi always had his ear close to the ground amongst the locals and in the bazaars, gathering vital intelligence for the British and ever alert for any signs of an uprising. He urged Burnes to at least move from his isolated house, located in the old part of the city, back to the safety of the cantonment less than two miles away. Burnes chose to ignore his advice, and on the first night of November 1841 he found his enemies gathered at his door. The screaming mob soon swelled to hundreds, and after setting fire to the house they forced him to come out.

A little earlier, his servants had suggested he escape by being wrapped up in a tent and carried off on their shoulders disguised as booty, but Burnes wouldn't abandon the other two officers in his household. Now, he pleaded to his attackers for his life, even offering them a large amount of ransom money—but to no avail.

Mohan Lal witnessed the incident from a nearby rooftop, and later described what happened next: '. . . he opened up his black neckcloth and tied it on his eyes, that he should not see from what direction the blow of death strikes him. Having done this, he stepped out of the door, and in one minute he was cut to pieces by the furious mob.' The torso of Burnes's headless body was discarded in the street for dogs to devour, and it was almost a week before any rotting remains were gathered and buried in the garden of his house.

With Burnes died his younger brother, Charles, who had recently arrived in Kabul, and another officer, as well as some thirty sepoy guards and servants. They had held off their attackers for several hours before finally succumbing. Earlier, Burnes had sent messages beseeching help from the British garrison, but none of the 4500 stationed there came to his aid. Only Shujah sent a force to assist, despite intense animosity existing between the two, but the rioters outnumbered his troops and some 200 of the shah's men were also killed.

The penultimate entry in Burnes's journal, recovered later by his munshi, reads: 'Ay! what will this day bring forth? . . . It will make or mar me, I suppose. Before the sun sets I shall know . . .'

News of the slaughter made it abundantly clear to the British command that something altogether bigger was afoot, which now posed a threat not only to Shujah's rule but to them all. Through their own inaction, however, the first fatal error had already been made: 'When 300 men would have been sufficient in the morning to have quelled the disturbance, 3000 would not have been adequate in the afternoon,' was how one British officer described the debacle in his journal.

At this point, the army realized they had made another crucial mistake by previously relocating from the better fortified Bala Hissar (royal citadel) to a hastily built cantonment, where they now barricaded themselves. This move had come about after a request from Shah Shujah, who had needed more room for his large entourage, including his harem of several hundred women. Worse still, the camp had been badly sited, lying as it did on low, swampy ground, commanded on all sides by hills and Afghan forts. Another British officer later wrote: 'Our cantonment at Kabul, whether we look to its situation or its construction, must ever be spoken of as a disgrace to our military skill and judgement.'

To add to their growing problems, the commissariat, with its food stores and other supplies, had been placed in a small fort *outside* the campsite. Yet the leaders would not countenance making a dash back to the well-stocked Bala Hissar, saying: 'How can we abandon the cantonments when they have cost us so much money?' Soon, their most essential item had virtually run out, as one officer described: '. . . water was served out to the fighting men only, about half a tea cup full to each man, and much of this was mere mud . . . Many sucked raw [sheep's] flesh to assuage their thirst.' Their position now seemed untenable and ripe for disaster.

* * *

Disaster did follow, as tens of thousands of enraged Afghans assailed the cantonment. They were led by Akbar Khan, Dost Mohammed's favourite son, who had ridden in from Turkestan vowing to restore his father to the throne. His numbers had quickly swollen to 30,000-odd as more and more tribesmen joined in. After some sporadic but intense fighting, the British believed their situation to be hopeless. At this point they started negotiating with Akbar Khan and the other chieftains, desperate to buy a truce and safe passage out of Kabul, and ready to desert Shah Shujah in the process. But, as one military historian remarked: 'The jingling of the coin could not drown the voice of an outraged and incensed people.'*

Their cause wasn't helped by the bitter internal quarrelling between the politicals, headed by Macnaghten, and senior army officers, led by Major General Elphinstone (the new commander who had arrived some months earlier). As the situation rapidly deteriorated for the troops, their families and camp followers, the response of their leaders is a classic case study of indecision and ineffective command. The subsequent capitulation and retreat of the British Army from Kabul in the dead of winter, followed by the massacre of 4500 troops and around 12,000 camp followers, have already been well-documented and need not be repeated here, except in brief.

Much of the blame would fall on the elderly and bedridden Elphinstone, and Macnaghten. In fact, the breakdown in command went right through the ranks, and there were cases during the initial fighting when both British and Indian soldiers refused to obey orders, and other times when they simply broke ranks and ran. General Charles Napier, then stationed in England but soon to be celebrated as the conqueror of Sind, wrote of this debacle: 'Jesus of Nazareth, what disgusting stuff is this. With the exception of the women you were all a set of sons of bitches.'†

Unlike the British, Shah Shujah had managed to keep his enemies at bay, holed up in the Bala Hissar with his troops. He met his end soon afterwards, though, when his own godson lured him out of the fortress and hacked him down mercilessly.

Macnaghten had been killed earlier in the siege, while trying to negotiate a way out of the mess he had helped create. He asked Mohan

---

*   Sir John Kaye wrote the *History of the War in Afghanistan* in two volumes in 1851.
†   Revered by his men, the inscription on Napier's statue in London's Trafalgar Square reads: 'Erected by public subscription. The most numerous contributors being private soldiers.'

Lal to act as a go-between and arrange talks with the Afghan chiefs, but they would only agree to meet *outside* the cantonment. Here, in the process of attempting some double-dealing, Macnaghten himself was double-crossed by Akbar Khan. His mutilated body, minus its head and limbs, was displayed later in the Kabul bazaar. His demise would require a sick and wounded Eldred Pottinger, once the 'Hero of Herat' and now a political officer, to attempt the impossible task of negotiating with the besiegers, ultimately for the garrison's surrender and its safe passage back to India.

Amongst its mistakes, one proved decisive for the retreating army. This was an earlier decision to slash payments to the powerful Ghilzai tribe of eastern Afghanistan, who guarded the crucial passes out of Kabul. London had forced this action upon the politicals, in an effort to save the Company money. It proved to be a premature and fatal error, as these fierce tribesmen joined the insurrection and moved in for the kill.

As the Army of the Indus fought its way through the passes, the troops came to realize first-hand the advantages held by the opposing tribesmen. Probably the best marksmen in the world at the time, the Afghani snipers picked them off with their slow-firing, homemade *jezails*. These long-barrelled, smoothbore muzzleloaders were accurate at 800 yards compared to the shorter British muskets, which had not changed since Waterloo and were only effective to about 150 yards. In addition to this, two of the British Army's renowned military strengths, its artillery and cavalry, were next to useless in these steep mountain passes.

What the jezails didn't finish off, the Khyber knives did. Five days after abandoning the cantonment, around 12,000 of the British camp were dead—most falling during skirmishes, and the remainder from sickness or cold. In the end, all but a handful of the 16,000-odd who had retreated from Kabul perished. Other than the hostages still being held in the city, the survivors included sepoys who had deserted, and any who managed to escape or remain in hiding. The rest lay where they had fallen in the passes, their frozen corpses stripped for clothing, first by their own, as those who were still alive tried to keep warm.

The wholesale retreat of the British Army, once seen as unrivalled in Asia, beggared belief; it was perhaps the redcoats' worst defeat to date. The political fallout would be costly too, and in the coming years Britain's loss of face here is believed to have contributed to two wars with the Sikhs, as well as the Indian Mutiny: sepoy regiments who served in Afghanistan and were deserted by their officers, were among the first to rebel.

Politicians at home were quick to blame Elphinstone and Auckland. The major general was derided for his indecisive command from the outset of the uprising. On the night Burnes was killed, after hearing of the incident, he had written to Macnaghten: 'We must see what morning brings and then think what can be done.' The governor-general, for his part, was held accountable for initiating this misguided political and military action in the first place; henceforth this war would often be referred to as Auckland's Folly. News of the calamity was said to have aged him ten years in as many hours, and left him partially paralysed. He was recalled home and would leave in disgrace, to be replaced by the experienced but newly arrived Lord Ellenborough (credited with initiating the Great Game thirteen years earlier). He only learnt of the mess he had inherited on disembarking in India.

It fell to the incoming governor-general to give the order for troops from garrisons in Peshawar and Kandahar to march on Kabul and retake the city. The returning army was charged with freeing the hostages, thought to number around 100, including women and children, and salvaging what they could of Britain's reputation in Asia. Then, they were to most definitely leave.

The Aftermath of Defeat

Within months, a so-called Army of Retribution set out to avenge the defeat in Kabul. The columns of British and Indian troops who proceeded back up the passes from Peshawar acutely felt the fate of their fallen comrades, as the bones of the unburied dead crunched under their feet, hooves and wheels. Regrettably, their return was accompanied by many vengeful actions, and some massacre of the villagers along the passes.

By the time the troops entered the capital, they found Akbar Khan and his troops had fled. The hostages were quickly located and their freedom purchased from their captors—again, with Mohan Lal acting as a go-between and raising the ransom money. Many of the Afghan civilians weren't so lucky, as some troops went on a rampage, raping and killing in a frenzy of revenge. One officer, writing about what ensued, ended by saying: 'In fact we are nothing but hired assassins.'

All that remained to complete Britain's exit was to seek official retribution in some public way. This was extracted by laying waste to Kabul's magnificent covered bazaar, the Char Chatta, until then a cultural icon—an action later described as 'vindictive vandalism' by one of its own generals. It was blown up with explosives, and took army engineers two full days to bring down.

This was the spark for a final round of revenge—the unofficial retribution—as troops ignored orders and, together with their camp followers, violated the womenfolk, looted shops and torched houses, including those of the Hindu and Persian trading communities who were innocent bystanders. As a result, thousands of displaced citizens of Kabul, particularly the poorer ones, would perish from cold and hunger in the mountains.

The army now departed, after executing what could well be described as a 'butcher and bolt' operation, despite many of its sepoys still being held prisoner. One disgusted officer wrote: 'We ought to have remained longer to recover more of our captive people . . . hundreds were left in slavery.'

At a cost of maybe 40,000 lives and an estimated 15,000,000 pounds which near-bankrupted the Government of India, it was an inglorious end to the Afghan War—although only the first, as two more Anglo-Afghan wars would be fought in the coming years.

The redcoats, despite their pretence at being victors, were clearly the losers, as summed up by author Peter Hopkirk: 'A mob of mere heathen savages, armed with homemade weapons, had succeeded in routing the greatest power on earth. It was a devastating blow to British prestige and pride.'

The futility of the whole episode was soon revealed when Shujah's son, who had been installed as the next compliant ruler, was overthrown shortly afterwards. At this point, Dost Mohammed returned to Kabul and reclaimed his throne, without objection from London or Calcutta. This time Ellenborough's Simla Proclamation read very differently to Auckland's initial Simla Manifesto, stating: 'To force a sovereign upon a reluctant people would be as inconsistent with the policy as it is with the principles of the British government... The Governor-General will willingly recognise any government approved by the Afghans themselves . . .' Dost Mohammed would continue his rule uninterrupted for almost another twenty years, until his death in 1863.

Mohan Lal did not fare as well. After the British retreat, he was uncovered as their spy in Kabul and severely tortured. His pleas to his masters to pay the ransom demanded by his captors went unanswered. Although he was eventually released, it was only after being forcibly converted to Islam. He retired in his early thirties into obscurity, disappointed at not receiving due reward from those he had served loyally, and finding himself ostracized at home by his own people.

During the siege, Mohan Lal had taken out large loans in his own name to assist Macnaghten, and again, later, to secure the release of the hostages. By his estimation, this sum amounted to almost 80,000 rupees but, despite his strident requests, it was never repaid, leaving him in severe financial hardship for the remainder of his life. He had rescued Burnes's letters and journals after that fateful night, and returned them to his family during a trip to Britain, when he was presented to Queen Victoria. Later, he would write Dost Mohammed's biography, as well as several other books, proving yet again that he was much more than Burnes's munshi.

Perhaps had Burnes survived, things would have turned out differently for him. Fittingly though, he did receive further recognition, albeit indirectly after his death, when Jawaharlal Nehru wrote: 'In a free India, a man like Mohan Lal would have risen to the topmost rungs of the political ladder. Under early British rule, whatever he might be or whatever he might do, he could not rise higher than the position of a *Mir Munshi* . . .'

* * *

There was one other tragedy resulting indirectly from the events in Kabul, as two more lives were lost across the border in Bokhara. Captain Arthur Conolly had travelled to the city in an attempt to free Colonel Charles Stoddart, who had arrived there three years earlier. The colonel's mission required him to explain Britain's move against Kabul, and allay any fears the emir might have. Additionally, Stoddart was given the task of seeking the release of any Russian slaves held in Bokhara, which might have taken away the pretext for a Russian invasion of the khanate.

Slavery was repugnant to the British, who were leading the charge all around the world to abolish it. For Conolly this was a hazardous mission, yet one he had readily volunteered for. He saw it as his gallant duty as an Englishman to champion Christianity and fight slavery in the badlands of Turkestan, and here was a chance to do just that while assisting a brother officer in dire need.

A few months after arriving in Bokhara in late 1838, Stoddart was held captive by the volatile and cruel emir, Nasrullah Khan. He had been displeased when the colonel had initially failed to dismount from his horse while in his presence, and later came to suspect he was a spy. For much of the three years he spent there, Stoddart was in and out of prison, at times in the infamous Siah Chah (black well). This was a deep 'bug-pit' where the worst prisoners were kept, filled with indescribable filth and vermin, with a rope being the only means in and out. As Stoddart's captivity dragged on, his situation had become increasingly desperate. Inevitably there came a day when, with his grave dug before him, to save his own life Stoddart had to forcibly convert to Islam and be publicly circumcised.

Soon after Conolly arrived in Bokhara in late 1841, he was thrown into prison with Stoddart. This time the pair was kept in a small, unheated cell, in filthy conditions, for many months.* On hearing of the rout of the Army of the Indus, the emboldened emir, believing he now had little to fear from Britain, had both Stoddart and Conolly beheaded in the main square on charges of spying. At the last moment, Conolly was offered a chance to save his own life if he chose to convert but, pointing out how such an act hadn't saved his companion, the deeply religious officer accepted his end instead.

When news of their demise reached London, it was decided that no retaliatory action would be taken. The last thing their government wanted was to be dragged into yet another conflict, and so these deaths were conveniently ignored. Like Burnes, Macnaghten and Vitkevich before them, Stoddart and Connolly died horribly, all victims of the Great Game they were so eager to play.

Prophetically, only weeks before he met his end, Burnes had written to a friend, saying: 'England and Russia will divide Asia between them, and the two empires will enlarge like the circles in the water until they are lost in nothing, and future generations will search for both in these regions as we now seek the remains of Alexander and his Greeks.'

---

* Conolly's little prayer book, with details of their captivity and notes of despair scribbled in the margins, was retrieved by a Russian prisoner. It was eventually posted to his sister in London twenty years later.

PART TWO

THE GTS OF INDIA

'So far as Kim could gather, he was to be diligent and enter the Survey of India as a chain-man.'

—Rudyard Kipling, *Kim*

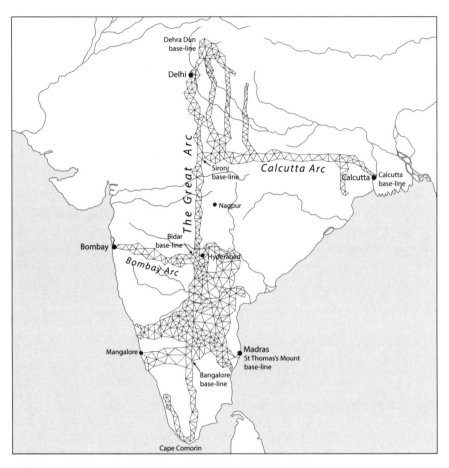

Map 3. The Triangulation of India to 1843. Everest's gridiron system in the north can be contrasted with Lambton's web of triangles across the southern peninsula.

3

Lambton Starts the GTS

At the turn of the nineteenth century, an unusual proposal was put forward to the British authorities in India, which neither they nor anyone else on the subcontinent were capable of fully comprehending. In spite of this, the plan was approved, and in time its far-reaching consequences would be felt not only in India but right across the world. The proposal set out to measure the shape of the earth, while intricately mapping India—a scientific project on a scale not previously attempted anywhere on the planet. The idea's originator was William Lambton, and the venture he began would be completed one day by his successor George Everest. It would then be justly lauded as 'one of the most stupendous works in the whole history of science'.*

Lambton Arrives

Lambton was an officer in the East India Company's army, like Everest, but both were first and foremost cartographers, who would make the mapping of India their life's work. In its pursuit, they would travel over much of the subcontinent, including many of its lesser known and threatening regions, which would turn them

---

* As described by Clements Markham, then secretary and later long-time president of the RGS.

into hardy explorers as well. While surveying in these remote areas, they were expected to gather intelligence about the people they encountered and their rulers. This included noting important commercial and military details, as their employer, the Survey of India, was administered by the Military Department. If need be, they could be recalled for soldiering at any time, as Lambton was on at least one occasion.

Little is known about William Lambton's early years. Even the year of his birth, although recorded as either 1753 or 1756, may have occurred a decade or more later.* Born on a struggling and debt-ridden farm in England, he was given the chance to study in a grammar school through the patronage of some parish gentlemen on account of his parents' poverty, and because of his early proficiency in mathematics. At age twenty-eight if one assumes he was born in 1753 (although 1763 would seem more realistic), he signed up with His Majesty's 33rd Foot Regiment as an ensign. Before long, he was shipped across the Atlantic to fight in America's War of Independence, but was taken prisoner.

After the war, on his release, Lambton was posted to New Brunswick, on the northeastern coast of the continent, where he first began surveying. This often meant working in wild, uncharted terrain, as was the case when delineating the border between British Canada and the United States. During this time, he continued his self-study in astronomy, higher mathematics and especially geodesy (the study of the earth's shape and size). Lambton was a man of simple habits, shy and awkward in society. Tall and well-built, he had a cast to his left eye, caused by incorrectly observing a solar eclipse through a common theodolite, which had rendered the eye partially blind.

---

*   Recently, historian John Keay discovered Lambton's forgotten grave, encased in mortar amid a squatter colony near Nagpur. Scrawled on it was a barely decipherable year of birth with only the first three numerals legible: 1-7-6-, 'at which point the mortar had broken away'.

Soon after this accident, through the help of friends, Lambton procured an additional appointment as a civilian barrack master with an annual salary of 400 pounds, much of which went into supporting his impoverished parents at home. Without the means to purchase a rank, which was the prevalent custom in the British Army at the time, Lambton languished as an ensign, giving up all hopes of advancement.* His luck finally changed in 1793 with the arrival of a new commander, none other than Colonel Arthur Wellesley (later the Duke of Wellington, who would defeat Napoleon at Waterloo in 1815). As the records show, Wellesley, on 'seeing an officer of so many years stationary . . . without knowing anything of him, gave in his name for promotion, and to his astonishment he (Lambton) found himself a Lieutenant'.

In 1796, now forty-three years old, Lambton sailed with his regiment to India. Three years later, he would fight with distinction during the final assault in the Siege of Seringapatam against the armies of Tipu Sultan, ruler of the kingdom of Mysore. He was now at an age when most Englishmen in Asia would already be considered past their prime, yet it would mark the start of the most important phase of his life.

Colonel Reginald Phillimore wrote the definitive *Historical Records of the Survey of India* after having worked with the survey for thirty-one years, including as its acting surveyor general for a short period. On his retirement in 1934, he researched its history over the next thirty years and recorded it in five volumes.† He explains why Lambton's late arrival in India turned out to be a good thing:

---

*   Promotion within the Company's army, in comparison, was determined strictly by seniority.
†   Volume V was withdrawn by the Government of India soon after its release due to the strategic sensitivity around some of its subject matter, and only a few copies are known to exist today.

Officers of the East India Company's service, who came to India before they were twenty years of age, were hardly likely to have the necessary knowledge and training, let alone the conviction and force of purpose, to carry through so great an innovation. The presence in India of a man of Lambton's genius and character, knowledge of mathematics and interest in geodesy, was entirely fortuitous.

The Survey of India

Map-making was integral to the Age of Imperialism, as a territory could only be acquired and governed when it was known. Although maps would add legitimacy to colonial rule, natives often treated the surveying that preceded it with a good deal of suspicion and hostility. In fact, this was true for most of the continent and for good reason, as one European envoy explained: 'to the Asiatic mind a survey is only preliminary to the advance of an army'. They regarded land as largely communal, whereas Europeans had an individual and possessive view, formalized through land titles and maps.

Maps would transform newly won territories—and finally the whole continent—from the unknown to the known. It was essential for British rule to acquire this knowledge for both military and administrative purposes, including the all-important task of collecting revenue. As in other new colonies, the accurate surveying of land quickly became a prerequisite for developing it.

James Rennell, the country's first surveyor general and considered the 'Father of Indian Geography', provided the first definitive image of the subcontinent in 1782 through his *Map of Hindoostan.*[*] He compiled it from route surveys: distances were

---

[*]   Hindoostan was a common nineteenth-century name for India. Rennell's map was produced on a relatively small scale of 1 inch to 1 equatorial degree (1:4,377,600).

measured using the perambulator, directions taken by compass bearing, and positions checked at intervals through astronomical observation. This was an era when maps were still being copied out by hand and, particularly after Napoleon's invasion threat, were jealously guarded by the Company, who only shared the art of surveying with its trusted servants.

By the end of the nineteenth century, less than one-eighth of the world had been accurately surveyed. In contrast, during that time, cartography in India would become one of the most advanced in the world, and few countries could claim to be mapped to the same extent. In describing the work of the Survey of India by the century's end, geographer and astronomer Arthur Hinks—secretary of the RGS for thirty years, from 1915 onwards—would write: 'no country in the world has contributed more to the advancement of geodesy, the thorough organisation of topographical survey, or the methods of work in difficult frontier country'.

Around the year 1800, three large and distinct surveys were started concurrently in India: Revenue, Topographical and Trigonometrical. In 1878, they were finally amalgamated into one entity known as the Survey of India. It remains a thriving organization today with its headquarters at Dehra Dun (today Dehradun), roughly 125 miles north-east of New Delhi. In addition to these three major surveys, others were being undertaken as the need arose, such as the geological, archaeological and marine surveys of India.

Of the large surveys, the first and in many ways the most important, both for the ruler and the ruled, was the Revenue Survey. It was the foundation on which the entire fiscal administration of British India rested. Its prime objective was to raise revenue for the Company by taxing landholders, after having fairly assessed the productive value of their cultivable lands. This work was done out in the plantations and rice fields by small groups of workers supervised by a British officer. Each team was typically headed by a surveyor, sometimes referred to as a 'chain-man', many of whom were still young boys trained at the native surveying school.

They were assisted by a number of *khalasis* (native survey helpers), dressed in turban and dhoti, drawing wages of between 4 and 6 rupees a month.* The khalasis came armed with their twenty-two-yard iron-linked chain, which was the standard British measurement for survey work. They also carried a long, calibrated stave measuring one-quarter of a chain, allowing them to readily step out distances along the ground. When required, one of the group would hold up a flagpole to mark out points their surveyor would sight with his theodolite.†

There were no major technical problems to overcome in land revenue surveying, but it was hard and monotonous work. The survey teams were always at the mercy of the heat, dust, insects and monsoons; nevertheless this was work that had to be done. It was slow and expensive too, to the consternation of the Company and its tax collectors, who were responsible for revenue assessment and soil classification. Much of the delay resulted from surveyors having to spend time resolving boundary disputes.

There was wide recognition that, through want of surveying and proper recordkeeping, the Company was not collecting all the revenue it was due. Of course, there was also much corruption and secrecy at work, as zamindars tried to hide their actual crop yields in an effort to pay less taxes. Another peculiar issue surveyors had to contend with was described by a surveyor general: 'It is strange, but true, that the more ignorant classes actually and sincerely regard all classes of surveyors as *criminals*, sentenced by government to

---

* As a comparison, sepoys were paid 7 rupees, while an agricultural worker earned around 3 rupees a month. At the time, approximately 8 rupees equalled 1 pound.

† A theodolite is essentially a powerful telescope mounted on two circular rings, allowing it to pivot in both the horizontal and vertical planes. As it does this, it can accurately measure angles between distant objects, which is fundamental to surveying.

measure the ground on account of their offences, such being a Hindoo penance.'

Although revenue surveys worked at the lowest and most detailed level, by individual land holdings, they required the least degree of accuracy compared to the other two surveys. At some later stage, they would have to be reconciled with a topographical survey, if a consistent map of a district was to be produced.

At the next level up, therefore, sat the Topographical Survey, which plotted the geographical details of a region: its rivers, hills, settlements, connecting tracks and roads. The standard tools required for this type of surveying were theodolites for triangulation work, plane tables for filling in geographical details, and perambulators and steel chains for measuring ground distances. However, a basic principle of surveying is that direct measurement of distance along the ground should be avoided whenever possible. Physically stepping out measurements, using devices such as perambulators or chains, is tedious and prone to error—hence the need for theodolites and plane tables.

Amongst survey instruments, the plane table is unique. It allows a surveyor to draw a reasonably accurate map while still out in the field, without doing any numerical work or measuring angles (except when drawing contour lines to show elevation). For this reason, it is well-suited for carrying out a rapid survey, for example in uncharted territory during military operations or exploration, and is superior to sketching a map using only a compass. Nevertheless, a compass is inconspicuous, allowing bearings to be logged secretly—something that Moorcroft, Burnes and the Pundits had all relied on.

Other than plane tables, topographical surveying employs triangulation: A slow and painstaking method in comparison, which relies on trigonometry (the mathematics of triangles), as explained in a simplified manner below.

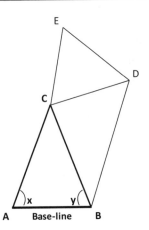

Basic Triangulation

First, the distance of a base-line (AB) is carefully measured out—
the only time a measurement along the ground is necessary.
Next, the internal angles (x and y) from its two endpoints (A and
B) are determined to a third visible point (C), such as a hilltop
or a building. Then, the two unknown distances (AC and BC)
that make up the other two sides of the triangle (ABC) can be
readily calculated using basic trigonometry. Once these two sides
(AC and BC) are known, they can each be used as theoretical
base-lines for creating other triangles (e.g. BCD and CDE); and
the process is continued, until an uninterrupted web is created to
cover an entire region. As work proceeds, if a second base-line is
physically measured out some distance away, it provides a check
on the accuracy of the triangulation between base-lines.

The size of each triangle is limited only by the line of sight
from the two endpoints of a known side to a new apex point. These
lengths depend on the power of the theodolite and visibility afforded
by the topography (e.g., if hills or buildings stand in the way). The
sides do not have to be of equal length, although a triangle should
be made as symmetrical as possible to improve overall accuracy.

The Topographical Survey was manned in much the same way as the Revenue Survey, by small teams of khalasis and surveyors, with a British officer in charge. Additionally, an armed escort usually accompanied them, to protect the surveyors from any violent zamindars and guard the camp's money box and survey instruments. Their presence was also essential for dealing with bandits and wild beasts, when the camp had to travel further afield to survey between towns and villages.

When required, the khalasis took turns at pushing the perambulator, stopping periodically to reset its distance counter. Often, they would build stone cairns to mark out survey points, for when they would be needed again. The surveyor made measurements with his theodolite or alternatively took compass bearings, while logging all the physical features necessary to make a map in his field book. In the early 1800s, the Company was paying its military officers an allowance of 100 rupees per month for plotting route maps as they marched through new territory, but only after field books were approved for their quality of work.

The Topographical Survey was led by a Scottish officer named Colin Mackenzie, who would go on to hold the post of surveyor general of India. He started out from Mysore, with the aim of surveying the Indian peninsula. This was the country's first large-scale survey of this type; and by the time it was finished nine years later, the Mysore Survey would cover 40,000 square miles.

As he surveyed and explored new districts, Mackenzie spent his spare time on his other passion, the study of Indian antiquities. Over a period approaching four decades, and at his own considerable expense, he built up the largest and most important collection of oriental historical materials amassed during the century, totalling many thousands of items. It included ancient manuscripts in various languages, old coins, and drawings of sculptures and monuments. The Mackenzie Collections would keep curators busy 100 years later, as the bulk of his treasure found its way into museums in Britain and India. He would never return to his homeland after setting foot on what would become his adopted country. But without Mackenzie's presence and perseverance, much of Hindoostan's heritage would have surely perished.

The third major survey, and the last of the three to get underway, was Lambton's Trigonometrical Survey (which would come to be named the Great Trigonometrical Survey).* Earlier, as the eighteenth century had drawn to a close, James Rennell's work marked the end of an era in surveying a country. He had utilized route surveying, which was far simpler to conduct and less expensive, but correspondingly less accurate. By the turn of the century, based on recent mapping experience in France and Britain, the scientific men in Europe universally regarded a trigonometrical survey as the only trustworthy basis for an extensive national survey.

Like the Topographical Survey, it was grounded on the principles of trigonometry, except that the primary triangulation it employed required a framework of as few triangles as possible. These had to be extremely accurate, and were plotted on a larger scale using a more powerful theodolite by necessity. The sides of these triangles could measure over 50 miles in length, but were typically around 30 miles when a luminous signal could be sighted at night (although luminous aids were developed only later by Everest). As long as signals were sighted, the theodolite could take a measurement to any distant 'trig point' (triangulation corner or station).

Ideally, a trigonometrical survey should be completed before a topographical one is started. This exercise would definitively fix key points on a regional map and, in the process, create a web-like pattern of large triangles. Then, a topographical survey could construct smaller secondary triangles within the primary ones, usually with less expensive instrumentation, and fill in the local geographical features using plane tables. In the early part of the century, however, the Company could not afford such luxury. Less

---

* After the creation of the Survey of India, sixty years later, it would revert to being called the Trigonometrical Survey. For simplicity, it is referred to as the GTS throughout this book.

than efficient though it certainly was, work on both surveys had to be advanced simultaneously and independently, as administrators demanded more information about their territories in order to raise higher revenues. At the same time, though, they wanted survey costs to be reduced, which constantly put unwelcome pressure on the surveyors as they went about their work far away from the government's Finance Committee. Britain had a growing colony to define, defend and exploit, and for this it desperately needed accurate maps.

The Trigonometrical Survey

In December 1799, Lambton put forward his big proposal for a 'Plan of a Mathematical and Geographical Survey' of the Indian peninsula by 'ascertaining the great geographical features of a country upon correct mathematical principles'. It would accurately determine the position of all its principal points, and measure the peninsula's precise width. What Lambton was asking for essentially amounted to a large-scale trigonometrical survey, with the hope that in time his network of triangles could be extended 'to an almost unlimited extent in every other direction'. And a web of this nature would allow the details of any district or region to be readily filled in afterwards through topographical surveying.

The results of such a survey would be of lasting and practical benefit, and his superiors had little difficulty in appreciating this fact. What Lambton didn't dwell on when discussing his proposal, due to its inherent complexity and scientific aspect, was another expected outcome that he quietly yet passionately desired: to determine the actual shape of the earth in this part of the world (rather than approximate it as a sphere, as is generally done). Of his hopes for this grand plan, touched with some rare emotion but still unable to shake off his formal style, Lambton would write: 'I shall rejoice indeed if it should come within my province to make observations tending to elucidate so sublime a subject.'

Until then, the only real method of accurately determining a location on the earth's surface was by making astronomical observations; but such measurements, especially for longitude, were famously uncertain and could take months, if not years, to complete. Precise observations at a given location required the construction and operation of an observatory, together with expensive instrumentation and highly skilled staff. Although a few of these structures could and would be built, it was near impossible to build and staff the large number that would be required to cover the entire peninsula, leave alone the whole subcontinent. And in any case, mapping a country by astronomical observation had already been shown to be inferior, compared to trigonometrical survey, by the experts in Europe.

Lambton knew this, and he concluded that employing triangulation was the only practical and sensible way to map India. However, this method was not any faster, as his Trigonometrical Survey would ultimately take over eighty years to complete. It would be expensive, too, both in monetary terms and human lives lost: by the time it was completed, it would cost more, on both counts, than many contemporary Indian wars.

To get his proposal accepted, Lambton first sought the backing of his superior, Arthur Wellesley; and on the third day of 1800, to his immense satisfaction and no doubt some degree of surprise, the government approved his plan. So, with the coming of the new century, the way was opened for a mainly self-educated and ageing geodesist to begin his life's most important work.

Lambton's first challenge was to acquire suitable instrumentation capable of the exactness his work would entail. This task alone took him the best part of two years, and it was April 1802 before any surveying could be started. His first purchase was a 100-foot steel chain, required for measuring out a base-line; and a 5-foot zenith sector* to determine latitude. Some years earlier, a visiting British

---

* A telescope designed to point upwards and precisely measure latitude, by observing the vertical angles of overhead stars. This one had a 9-degree coverage either side of zenith.

mission had taken the chain and other English-made celestial instruments as a gift to China, but they had not interested the emperor and were politely returned. This was just as well for Lambton, and he happily acquired the chain together with the zenith sector and some other instruments, even though the instruments arrived in a wretched state and he had to overhaul them to good working order.

The chain was made up of forty bars of blistered steel, each 2½ feet long, linked together with brass hinges, all soundly packed in a teak carriage chest weighing over 100 pounds. With this in hand, Lambton was ready to start work on his all-important base-line, even as he waited for his most significant purchase to arrive from England, a powerful theodolite.

Before laying out the base-line, he needed to carefully establish its height above sea level, as all other heights determined during the course of his surveying would be referenced to this standard. The site Lambton had chosen was a flat plain in Madras, 4 miles from the coast and right next to the city's racecourse. By observing the flagpole above its grandstand and another planted on the beach, while employing a specialized levelling instrument, he meticulously measured the height of the two flags over several days. From this work, he deduced the final height of the northern end of his intended base-line to three decimal places: 15.753 feet above sea level. Lambton would proudly report: 'I may venture to consider it as perfect a thing of the kind as has yet been executed.'

The other crucial information he required was the precise geographical position of the base-line's northern tip in terms of its latitude and longitude, and this was duly determined by the Madras Observatory which stood nearby.

Lambton now began the demanding work of laying out his base-line and measuring its length. It was started from St Thomas Mount, along ground his team had cleared and levelled, to a hill 7½ miles to its south. He began by setting out the 100-foot steel chain, tensioned by a weight at one end while being supported on five 20-foot-long wooden coffers. They were placed on tripods fitted with levelling screws, so the whole chain could be perfectly flat. Each coffer had a thermometer attached to it, allowing measurements to be adjusted for any expansion or contraction of the chain. Such minute changes were caused by fluctuating daytime temperatures, which could vary anywhere from 80 to 120 degrees Fahrenheit (27 to 49 degrees Celsius). In this case, Lambton concluded that a 1-degree variation in ambient temperature would increase the overall length of his chain by 7½ thousandths of an inch. Infinitesimal as this may seem, it highlighted the continuous struggle he faced to account for all sorts of variations inherent in his measurements—and it would remain a constant focus and source of worry (just as it is in any scientific experiment conducted today). Such vigilance was critical to the final accuracy of the base-line, as any error here, no matter how small, would be reflected throughout the rest of the survey *and* in all the years to come.

The base-line took a full forty-two days to measure out, as a team of twenty men moved the chain close to 400 times to cover the 7½ miles involved.* The completion of this task was a major milestone with regard to his original proposal, and marked the first successful field operation by Lambton's Trigonometrical Survey.

Meanwhile, Lambton anxiously awaited the arrival of his large theodolite, which was a true marvel of workmanship in its day and worth a small fortune, being valued at 650 pounds. Its powerful telescope was mounted on a horizontal 'circle' (metal ring) 36 inches in diameter, as well as a vertical circle of 18 inches, each with its own microscope to allow angles to be finely measured. This was a precision instrument of the highest order, and there were only a handful in existence anywhere in the world that would have served his purpose.

------

* As the chain was progressively moved, the small rise and fall of the ground was measured with the levelling instrument, and the overall length of the base-line adjusted accordingly.

It had been shipped out from England months earlier, together with some other instruments, including a smaller theodolite.* However the cargo was still nowhere to be seen, and this was causing Lambton a good deal of anxiety. Finally, when it arrived in September the delay was explained, and he realized just how close his entire plan had come to being wrecked but for some old-fashioned chivalry. The ship had been captured on its way to India by a French frigate. When it docked in Mauritius, the French governor there, upon realizing the instruments were to be used in the pursuit of science, forwarded the package on to the governor of Madras with a complimentary letter.

Geodesy and the Great Theodolite

The science of geodesy may be difficult for the average person to fully appreciate, but we can again look to Arthur Hinks for an eloquent summary of its importance: 'And equally a nation is judged, though by a smaller circle of judges, for the contributions it can make to pure knowledge. An exquisite piece of Geodesy may give as real a pleasure and be as genuine a source of pride, as the masterpieces of art and literature.'

Now, nothing stood in Lambton's way: he could embark on his cartographical adventure, and attempt to solve a key question of geodesy he had pondered for many years. It originated from a knotty problem known as 'spherical excess', which arises because the earth is essentially a sphere. In effect this means the angles of a triangle, rather than adding up to 180 degrees as they would on a flat surface, actually exceed this figure, albeit ever so slightly. If the triangles being marked out are relatively small, then this impact is minor and can be ignored, as Mackenzie was doing in his Topographical Survey. Conversely, as the land area being surveyed becomes larger than 10 square miles, the mathematics of trigonometry must be adjusted for this effect. Thus,

---

* A second steel chain was also procured, never to be used out in the field but kept instead as a measurement standard for the 100-foot chain.

a survey across the whole peninsula would obviously need to take spherical excess into account. But this was only the first part of the conundrum, and actually the simpler of two problems concerning the earth's shape.

The second and more complex problem arises from the well-understood fact that the earth isn't a true sphere, but is flatter at the poles as it spins on this axis.* Isaac Newton had postulated this in the late seventeenth century, as a natural consequence to his theory of gravitation. It had been proven in the 1730s, by two separate expeditions sent out from France—at great expense—to measure one degree of latitude at two different points on the earth's surface. This exercise, which took a number of years to complete and involved much hardship, determined a degree to equal 68.7 miles close to the equator, whereas near the Arctic Circle it measured 69.6 miles. This difference proved beyond doubt that the effect was significant, and must be corrected for if a large-scale survey was to be credible.

The geodetic problem for Lambton boiled down to a similar question: what was the length of one degree of latitude around the tropics where Madras lay? If he knew this, he would have the information needed to determine the extent of spherical excess in this part of the world. Such a discovery would not only improve the accuracy of his own survey, but also, as he put it, 'determine by actual measurement the magnitude and figure of the earth'. It wouldn't be just an academic exercise either, as ascertaining this dimension would have immense practical value: for example, it would improve the compilation of navigation tables and sea charts. Moreover, by measuring the actual shape of the earth on the subcontinent, the true positions and heights of all its places, including its towering mountains, could be fixed.

Once he had acquired his precious instruments and measured out the base-line, this question was finally answered in 1802, although

---

* Earth's diameter at the equator is 27 miles larger than its pole-to-pole diameter, thus making it an oblate spheroid.

it would require a year of painstaking work. First, he triangulated a short arc* just over 100 miles long, equivalent to almost 1½ degrees of latitude. Working down the south coast from Madras, this exercise gave him the arc's precise ground distance, measured in miles. Next, he determined the latitude of both its extremities through astronomical observations and, by subtracting one from the other, determined the arc's span in degrees. Since these two values were determined independently of each other, by dividing the length of the arc in miles by its span in degrees, he was able to deduce the precise length of one degree of latitude. In this way, he was able to finally determine the spherical excess figure that had eluded him for so long.

* * *

Armed with this knowledge, at the end of the following year, Lambton would start triangulating towards Bangalore and the west coast. The Great Theodolite, as it was now being called, began its long journey around India with him. Everest would later note the special significance local Indians attached to it: 'The faith placed in the healing powers of the great theodolite and other instruments employed at any time in observing stars were such that I have had people come many miles to entreat permission to bow down before the lower telescope of this imposing instrument . . .'

When boxed up, it weighed half a ton, and required two relay teams of twelve porters each to carry it. And carry it on foot they must, rather than use a bullock cart, to prevent any jarring of this delicate instrument on the rutted paths they travelled. Interestingly, their efforts illustrated a general principle of surveying in those early days: the accuracy of a survey was limited by the weight one was prepared to carry. Twenty years later, a new theodolite would be

---

*   In this context, arc reflects the earth's curvature.

developed by the physicist Henry Kater.* He had once worked as Lambton's survey assistant for over two years until his health had broken down, forcing him to return home. His theodolite was just as accurate, yet only a fraction of the size and could be carried by one person. It would not be available in Lambton's lifetime, however, which was unfortunate as it could have made a vital difference, as events would soon prove.

It was during his work in southern Tamil Nadu, a few years later, that disaster nearly overtook Lambton's surveying efforts. In the flat delta regions, there are no hills to allow trig points to be established and easily sighted. This compelled Lambton to look for other ways of getting a clear line of sight for his theodolite, through the sea of coconut palms that were the tallest feature around. He hit on the idea of using the many temples dotting the area, which have high sculptured towers standing well above the treeline. They would make ideal trig points—of course, only after the priests had given their permission, probably following a small donation for the temple's upkeep.

One day, while using ropes and pulleys to haul the instrument on to the main tower of the magnificent Birhadeshwara Temple in Tanjore, over 200 feet high, the guy rope suddenly snapped. The Great Theodolite, still in its box, swung uncontrollably and smashed on to the stonework, causing it to be severely damaged. Lambton didn't report this accident to his government; accepting full responsibility, he chose instead to order a replacement from England at his own expense (just as he had previously purchased other instrumentation privately and used them for public survey work).†

He then set to work on the Great Theodolite, to recover what looked to be an instrument damaged beyond repair. For six weeks

---

* He also invented the prismatic compass, which greatly improved the accuracy of route surveys.

† This theodolite was only half the size in terms of its horizontal circle and cost Lambton 230 pounds. Once available, both instruments would be put to good use by the survey.

Lambton shut himself up in a tent with the completely dismantled theodolite, refusing entry to all but the few workmen who assisted him. While the rest of his team anxiously waited outside, he worked tirelessly through the heat of summer and on most nights, until he finally returned it to good working order. This was a remarkable feat, which Everest would later praise: 'Any person but my predecessor would . . . have given the matter up as utterly desperate; but Colonel Lambton was not a man to be overawed by trifles, or to yield up his point in hopeless despondency without a struggle.'

Today, the Great Theodolite, along with the 100-foot steel chain, can still be viewed at the Survey of India's headquarters.

The Khalasis

As they took to the road, Lambton's survey camp was a large one, sometimes comprising as many as eighty men. Other than his staff and camp minders, there were khalasis, porters, water carriers and, more often than not, a military escort of up to two dozen sepoys. Lambton regarded his camp followers as members of his own household. Numbers would swell even further at times when they were joined by their families, especially if the survey stopped for a long period in one location—for example during the measurement of a new base-line. At day's end the campsite was a hive of activity. The armed escort was not idle either, as there were times when suspicious locals would strongly object to survey flags being planted on their land, and were prepared to defend their patch with homemade weapons. Local villagers were understandably ignorant of the importance of map-making and the instruments employed. It is not difficult to see why they would object to the large 'spyglass' these strangers used, which in their minds could look into houses and disrespect their womenfolk. At times like this, the survey team needed to be tactful and flexible. Sometimes small presents such as turbans and cloth pieces, or bottles of liquor, helped ease the situation. In other instances, the team found it expedient to realign its survey and move a trig station, rather than risk an unnecessary confrontation.

Later, when they were surveying in the jungles, it could take a few weeks before the surveyor and his khalasis were able to trek through the undergrowth to reach a distant hilltop. Here, they would have to regularly chop down many trees, hacking out a sufficient clearing to work within. This felling could only start once permission from the zamindars had been secured, after first agreeing on any compensation payments, which could take many days to negotiate. Then, and only then, would land be cleared and the signal post raised, before it was sighted from the previous trig point. Communication between survey parties was usually by runners and, depending on the distances involved and the difficulty of the terrain, it could take anywhere from three to six days just to get a message across stations.

Lambton, being economical with words in his official reports, rarely wrote of the challenges faced by his teams, but we get a good description from Everest later:

> [When I] saw the dreadful wilderness by which I was surrounded; when I saw how, by means of conciliating treatment and prompt payment, my people had managed to collect a sufficient body of hatchet-men to clear away every tree which in the least obstructed the horizon over a surface of nearly a square mile; . . . then I learned to appreciate the excellent management of Colonel Lambton, who had been enabled to train up so faithful a body of men . . .

These men were employed directly by the British surveyors, who paid them wages from their own *batta*—regular military allowances and expenses. Whilst out in the field, surveyors sometimes had to pay for the whole camp's upkeep from their own pocket and seek reimbursement on return, which could be months later. Everest described the somewhat loose hiring arrangement in place, based on trust established between the parties: 'unconnected with and unknown by the Government they served, without provision for themselves in case of being crippled by sickness, accident, or age, or for their families in the event of their death . . .'

Most of the permanently employed men were allowed to go home on half pay during the recess season and, when asked to, would often bring back their brethren to work alongside them. A later surveyor general described their character: 'Patient and long-suffering, inured from infancy to hardships of all kinds, frugal in their habits, and subsisting . . . on a diet of cereals which would be starvation to most Europeans, they are ready to obey all reasonable orders . . .'

The khalasis made up a big part of the survey camp, and were a special breed. Their life was far from an easy one, and much depended on the terrain where the survey was being conducted. Some years later, when the GTS began surveying in the Himalayas, a khalasi would often be required to scale the peak concerned carrying his signal post. In fact, the world's altitude record was held by a khalasi for some twenty years, when he raised his flag on a mountain over 20,000 feet high in 1860. His name was not recorded, but we do know he was being paid 6 rupees per month.

The Trans-Peninsula Survey

When Lambton's survey reached Bangalore, a second base-line was laid out using the trusty steel chain, this time taking forty-nine days to complete. Now, its 7-mile length could be compared with the value predicted by the triangulation network brought up from the Madras base-line, some 200 miles to the east. To the delight and credit of Lambton and his team, a difference of less than 4 inches separated the two measurements, proving beyond doubt the quality of their survey work. The exact position of this new base-line, in terms of its latitude and longitude, was determined by astronomical observations; and it was critical the survey be continually anchored in this manner, limiting any accumulation of errors. Similarly, the precise coordinates of all other future base-lines, plus the more important trig points, would be determined by astronomy.

Latitude, in relation to the equator (the zero for latitude), was pinpointed using the zenith sector, which was even more demanding than triangulation work. It required making multiple measurements over many nights, before an average value could be determined to the required level of confidence. At one base-line, Lambton made more than 200 zenith observations over twenty-seven consecutive nights, from a specially constructed observatory tent he carted around for this purpose.

Longitude was determined by calculating the distance of the trig points from the Madras Observatory. It had been set up in 1786 as a secondary line of north–south longitude or meridian, thus becoming a substitute for the prime meridian at the Greenwich Observatory (the zero for longitude). In fact, the precise position of the Madras Observatory would be the ultimate anchor for the entire survey of the subcontinent. This meant that as the measurement of its longitude was refined over the years, every other location had to be adjusted accordingly. The science behind determining this coordinate was itself undergoing development and, as late as the 1870s, the Indian Atlas, the Survey Department and the Admiralty were all using a slightly different longitude for Madras.[*]

Lambton's unrelenting pursuit of accuracy would be the hallmark of his survey work; for example, he would measure each angle with his theodolite at least four times. Then, he would measure all three angles of his triangles separately, even though, mathematically speaking, only two angles were required, as the third could be readily calculated by subtracting from the 180-degree total—adjusting, of course, for spherical excess. But Lambton would not countenance any such shortcut, and would religiously get his team to break camp, relocate to the third trig point, and make the necessary measurement.

---

[*]   It would be revised again in 1905 by 2 minutes and 27 seconds—equivalent to almost 37 miles.

By taking this rigorous approach, he believed the smallest variations in spherical excess would be detected.

Similarly, Lambton never shrank from the tedious work of recalculating his results when better measurements came to hand, which they frequently did. This was the case with the first spherical excess figure he had determined, based on his early work covering 1½ degrees of latitude at Madras. Once he had measured a longer arc of meridian spanning many more degrees, his initial spherical excess value could be refined, which meant readjusting all of his previous work. The eminent Scottish scientist John Playfair would say of him: 'Lambton has no appearance of a person who would save labour at the expense of accuracy.'

From Bangalore, Lambton triangulated to the Western Ghats mountain range, and then down to Mangalore. During this time there was some healthy competition with Mackenzie, and between their teams. Mackenzie's Topographical Survey, having started out two years earlier, was eager to reach the west coast before Lambton and claim the prize of having completed the first trans-peninsula survey. He couldn't match the speed of advance of Lambton's survey, though, which was governed mainly by the sides of the giant triangles it created, reaching over 60 miles under ideal conditions. In the process Lambton overtook Mackenzie, who could only plod along in comparison, as his men pushed their perambulators and stopped to plot geographical features using plane tables.

Reaching the west coast first had one downside, however, as Lambton had the unenviable task of informing his superiors that Britain had lost some 10,000 square miles of its Indian territory overnight. This fact became apparent when his primary triangulation proved the peninsula at Madras was only 360 miles wide, and not 404 miles as shown on Rennell's map.

The Great Arc Commences

Having completed his first arc, east to west across the peninsula, Lambton was ready to start measuring a second. This time he decided to go in the other direction, south to north across the subcontinent, along a meridian on the 78-degree mark. Although he didn't know it at the time, it would one day become a scientific wonder, stretching across the length of India as the Great Arc of the Meridian or, simply, the Great Arc.

As the first step in this undertaking, Lambton triangulated southwards in 1806, after laying out a new base-line near Coimbatore, 135 miles south of Bangalore. Over the next three years he worked his way down to India's southern tip. As well as working on the Great Arc, at the urging of the government, Lambton began surveying the entire peninsula, covering it with a network of primary and secondary triangles. This had the added benefit of allowing other local surveys to simply adopt the sides of his well-established triangles, rather than tediously measure out separate base-lines.

During this lengthy exercise, he fixed the geographical position of several thousand prominent points, and by the end of 1810 Lambton produced a general map of the *Southern Provinces of the Peninsula*. This was the first map drawn of any part of India based on the sound principles of triangulation; and yet he seemed almost reluctant to acknowledge the significance of his work: '. . . I shall feel peculiar satisfaction if, while my labours are directed to the advancement of science in general, they may at the same time contribute to the more immediate benefit of my country'.

Lambton completed the southern portion of the Great Arc in 1811, from Bangalore to Cape Comorin (Kanyakumari) on the southern tip of India. Achieving this milestone meant he could now refocus his survey and lead the arc north, towards the Himalayas.

Three years earlier, Lambton had purchased his rank of major.* Now, as his regiment made preparations to return home, he applied to remain in India and be allowed to devote himself entirely to surveying and geodesy. The Company not only approved this

---

* His majority cost 5000 pounds, though he offset part of this sum by selling his captaincy for 2000 pounds.

request, but also promoted him to the rank of lieutenant colonel, citing 'the national importance' of his work.

During these early years, however, Lambton received no word of encouragement from the scientific bodies in Europe, including his own, the Royal Society (not to be confused with the RGS). He had received one letter of support back in 1806 from the Astronomer Royal in London, Nevil Maskelyne, which cheered him greatly. It had come at a time when he was facing many difficulties, while trying hard to impress upon his government the value of this survey. Then in 1813, Professor Playfair favourably reviewed his pioneering work, which Lambton had begun publishing in a series of papers.* When wider recognition finally came, it was first bestowed on him by a foreign nation, France, who led the world in the science of geodesy. This spurred the Royal Society into action, and it elected him a Fellow the next year.

All the while, Lambton worked on a shoestring budget, starved of funds by the Finance Committee of the Madras Presidency which controlled the purse strings. Its members had real difficulty appreciating the value of his endeavours, especially its scientific aspect, since it generated no profits, and they plagued him with endless absurd questions and comments. The Court of Directors in London, too, had wavered in its support, and had written to him on more than one occasion: 'We feel that we should hardly be justified in sanctioning the continuance of so large an expenditure . . . unless we have information before us to show that the objects are of adequate utility.' Although money had been initially forthcoming to purchase his vital instruments—the theodolite, zenith sector and steel chain— the same could not be said for the survey's ongoing upkeep, and living conditions in the camps were spartan at best.

Surveying during the monsoon, and straight after it, afforded the best visibility for the theodolite, as it dampened the dust and

---

*   In all, six volumes covering Lambton's work in India would be published, starting from 1802.

heat haze in the air, but with it came the inherent risk of disease and discomfort. Clements Markham, who wrote *A Memoir on the Indian Surveys*, summed up the conditions under which survey teams worked: 'The danger of service in the jungles and swamps of India, with the attendant anxiety and incessant work, is greater than that encountered on a battle field; the percentage of deaths is larger; while the sort of courage that is required is of a far higher order.' And yet, year after year, Lambton's team stayed out in the field, advancing the Great Arc northwards, ever faithful to a leader whom they revered.

By the end of 1811, despite his pleading, Lambton lost the last of the capable British military surveyors he had been assigned as assistants, due to the government adamantly imposing cost cuts.* This meant having to make do with sub-assistants from the Surveying School, set up at the Madras Observatory in 1794. Lambton had four sub-assistants—Joshua de Penning, William Rossenrode, Joseph Olliver and Peter Lawrence—who had all joined him as apprentices many years before, and made the survey camp their home. These boys, and other apprentices and sub-assistants like them, were all Anglo-Indians, otherwise referred to as Eurasians. They were invariably descended from Indian mothers and European fathers—soldiers, traders and the like. Many of the lads came from the Madras orphanage and had worked their way up, but were socially stigmatized in many British eyes by virtue of their mixed blood; in his book Markham describes de Penning, without malice, as 'a half-caste from Madras'.

Lambton didn't see locals in the same light, and indeed he would have three children from two partners in India, one a Muslim and the other an Anglo-Indian. However, they mixed little with other Europeans; moreover, Company rules prohibited Indian wives from

---

* At the time, native Indians were thought unsuitable to be trained as surveyors by the British, other than for the simpler work of land measurement undertaken by the Revenue Survey.

attending government social functions. During his lifetime, Lambton acknowledged his children and provided well for his family. In his will, other than the money he would leave his two surviving children, he left both his partners a monthly pension.

The whole survey team, including camp servants, looked upon him affectionately as a father figure, and they must have seemed as one big family. He had always encouraged his staff to bring their families along, and they formed a little colony of their own. He employed his son on the survey, and several sons of his sub-assistants. Many of the younger lads had been born amongst them, and at one time three generations could be counted residing in his camp.

Lambton took the Great Arc further north into the Nizam of Hyderabad's territory next, with the ruler's approval, and reached the capital in 1815. The survey set up its new headquarters there; and in the process corrected the city's geographical position from what was then shown on the map of India, adjusting both its latitude and longitude.

One special effect Lambton had to account for during surveying was refraction, a phenomenon causing sight lines from a theodolite to become bowed by the earth's atmosphere. It varies not only with temperature and humidity, but even with the time of day. Another significant and complicating effect, only just being understood by geodesists when using the zenith sector, was the problem of plumb lines.* Lambton was finding his plumb bobs being deflected at times due to the presence of a nearby mass such as a hill. Although this effect was already well-understood by scientists, when they deflected at other times without being in the vicinity of hills, he correctly attributed this to the presence of 'a vein of dense ore' under the earth's surface.

By this stage he was being overwhelmed with the work required in calculating and collating the survey's results, as well as

---

* This effect was critical as the zenith sector relies on knowing the true vertical from the earth's centre, determined by suspending a plumb bob.

writing up its detailed reports, all of which took him away from fieldwork. Fortunately, Lambton had nurtured and trained his local sub-assistants thoroughly over the years, and they were able to take over most of the primary triangulation work. In time, some of them would go on to make their mark in surveying, and be rewarded with long careers within the GTS. Now, Lambton spent most of his time measuring out new base-lines, making the vital astronomical observations, and preparing the survey's results.

The mathematics involved in this work was extremely complex, with figures needing adjustment for geodetic and other special effects, which only he was capable of completing. One writer later estimated that during the full course of the survey, these calculations involved over 9000 mathematical unknowns and some of the most intricate equations known pre-computer age. As new discoveries were made or estimates such as spherical excess refined, a lot of the previous work needed to be updated and corrected. He undertook these computations himself, with some help from his assistants, which consumed around two months of his time for every month he devoted to fieldwork.

By 1815, the Great Arc had been extended some 700 miles, from India's southern-most tip to the 18-degree parallel—a distance equivalent to nearly 10 degrees of latitude. This effort surpassed any other meridian arc measured in the world, both in terms of its length and accuracy; and it made geographers and scientists in Europe sit up and take notice of the arc and its originator. Lambton's reputation was steadily growing internationally, as a cartographer and geodesist of note.

Lambton's Final Years

After his survey had worked its way beyond the Madras Presidency, it was placed under the national government. Here, it would start to come under closer scrutiny, particularly due to its ever-increasing cost, which was substantial: about 6000 pounds per year, and over

100,000 pounds in total expenditure during Lambton's tenure. This cost blowout was driven by its ever-growing scope, leading to its projected end date moving further and further out. Nevertheless, at least its work was better understood and appreciated now. In 1818, it officially became known as the Great Trigonometrical Survey of India, reflecting its importance not only to the subcontinent, but for the world's scientific community as a whole.

Lambton, a full colonel by this stage, was appointed its first superintendent. A young captain of artillery, George Everest was named as his assistant, and would be the first officer of any education to join Lambton in six years. Everest's early impression of his ageing superior is telling: '. . . when he aroused himself for the purpose of adjusting the great theodolite, he seemed like a Ulysses shaking off his rags; his native energy appeared to rise superior to all infirmities, his eyes shone with the lustre, his limbs moved with the full vigour of manhood . . .'

In the 1820s, the monumental *Atlas of India* was being created to provide the definitive cartographic image of the country. The Court of Directors were increasing pressure on the GTS to ensure its work would form the basis of this important project.* Its benefits were obvious and tangible: as well as helping shape British presence and rule, it would remain the standard map of India for the next eighty years.

More and more, in his remaining years, as the Great Arc inexorably advanced further north, Lambton stepped back from fieldwork. He spent the bulk of his time directing the GTS, writing up its survey reports, and performing the calculations and recalculations so critical to maintaining the arc's accuracy.

Lambton worked on, seemingly indestructible, rarely laid low by the sicknesses and diseases to which most Europeans typically succumbed in Asia. But the years of suffering from tuberculosis

---

* The atlas was produced on a medium scale of 1 inch to 4 miles (1:253,440).

would eventually catch up with him, and he died on 20 January 1823, aged seventy.ᐧ He had been on the road heading to his camp south of Nagpur—still at his post, doing what he loved best. A portrait of him painted the previous year shows a mild and unassuming man; and from the picture he presents, it isn't difficult to believe accounts of his even temper and benevolence towards his staff and camp followers.

Phillimore wrote of his contribution: 'The debt that Indian geography owes to William Lambton can hardly be adequately expressed, for without him it is difficult to see how the boon of a great trigonometrical survey would have reached India . . .' Under his leadership, the GTS had surveyed an area extending 165,000 square miles, more than twice the size of Great Britain. He had fulfilled his promise to determine the shape of the earth, and proven beyond all doubt that he was a true pioneer of this science; a later surveyor general, Andrew Waugh, would describe him as the 'Father of Indian Geodesy'.

Author Showell Styles has pointed out how there was an element of 'greatness' about Lambton, reflected by how others referred to the things he worked on: the Great Theodolite, the Great Arc and the Great Trigonometrical Survey. Yet today his name is largely forgotten, both in Britain and India. His efforts and accomplishments, though, which formed the bedrock of the GTS, live on through the work of the Survey of India. For many years, his name even appeared on its logo, and a commemorative bust sits today on St Thomas Mount, Chennai, looking out from where he launched his grand project.

All this fuss would have probably humbled Lambton. He had always preferred to throw himself into his work, well away from city and society, surrounded by the local people he best loved and trusted. This had been the happiest time in his life, as he gratefully

---

ᐧ   The *Government Gazette* stated that he died at age seventy-five.

acknowledged shortly before his death, and the last words of this chapter fittingly belong to him:

> These years . . . have been devoted with unremitting zeal to the cause of science, and, if the learned world should be satisfied that I have been successful in promoting its interests, *that* will constitute my greatest reward . . . If such should be my lot, I shall close my career with heartfelt satisfaction and look back with unceasing delight on the years I have passed in India.

4

Everest Completes the Great Arc

A photograph of George Everest taken late in life shows a serious and frowning man, who radiates purpose and achievement. With strong facial features, a full head of roughly brushed, greying hair and a large beard to match, he truly looks the lion of a man he has often been described as. Other choice words such as pig-headed, brilliant-minded and short-tempered could have been equally used. His name, incidentally, was pronounced *Eve–rest*, not *Ever–est*, as George was quick to point out, and always insisted on. He also vehemently objected to being called a *kumpass wallah*—a common Anglo-Indian term for a surveyor—as one fellow officer quickly found out and was forced to retract with an apology.

His roar was legendary within the GTS, and even better known by his staff which felt the brunt of his relentless drive. But his purpose was undoubtedly steadfast: to complete the immense task he had accepted after the death of his leader. In concluding his final report, Lambton had penned: 'I sincerely hope that, after I relinquish the work, somebody will be found possessing zeal, constitution and attainments wherewith to prosecute it . . .' Everest was not one to disappoint, at least not where his life's work was concerned.

Jungle Fever

Born in Greenwich in 1790, George Everest was one of five sons of a London solicitor. He was known to do brilliantly at school, and after choosing a military career as a youngster of fourteen, he sailed for India two years later to join the Company's army. In 1818, by now a captain in the Bengal Artillery, he came to the GTS as Lambton's chief assistant.

Following some brief fieldwork together, which gave the ageing colonel a chance to critically observe his assistant's talents, Everest was given his first assignment involving some secondary triangulation. This should have been a relatively easy task, as it didn't require base-line work or making astronomical observations, but it was more than offset by the unforgiving conditions he encountered.

Everest was surveying between the Kistna (Krishna) and Godavari rivers, on the east coast of the peninsula with two other staff: his sub-assistant Joseph Olliver and a British doctor-cum-geologist named Henry Voysey. Their support team of 150-odd was made up of the usual khalasis, porters, military escort and runners; plus mahouts for handling the elephants they were using to plunge through the dense undergrowth. Wild beasts were an ever-present problem too; and Dr Voysey had earlier witnessed his groom killed by a tiger known to have carried off at least five other villagers. Everest was lucky to have never encountered one, or lost any of his men in this way; the natives believed this was due to his possession of magical powers.

Conditions were trying for everyone, as they laboured through the thick jungle infested with predators and boa constrictors, during the height of the rainy season. At times, they needed to fell trees as high as 100 feet to establish a sight line, and then clear forest up to a mile square, to be able to build visible trig stations. Everest was coming to respect the efforts of his khalasis: '. . . how my unfortunate flag-men . . . without water or provisions, and with the jungle fever staring them in the face, they could have wandered through such a wilderness until they selected the most commanding points for a station, utterly, I confess, surpasses my comprehension'. Everest did much to foster the esprit de corps Lambton had engendered, and he later expressly forbade use of 'the foul name of coolies when referring to regular servants of the department', insisting they be called khalasis (or lascars), to acknowledge that, although uneducated, they were not unskilled.

At an earlier stage, however, conditions had reached breaking point in the jungle and, as one thing led to another, it resulted in a minor mutiny by the workmen, some of whom drew swords. Everest hadn't hesitated to assert his authority then, by ordering his troops to disarm them, before having the ringleaders publicly flogged and dismissed.

For most Europeans, spending the monsoon season working in the jungle would have been suicidal, and the unhealthy conditions finally caught up with Everest as his first surveying season came to an abrupt end. His whole survey team succumbed to jungle fever,* and had to be carried out by nearby townsfolk. Of the 150 men in his camp, one in ten died; and although Everest and Voysey managed to pull through, both would suffer recurrences of the sickness for years to come.

Next year, Everest did go back to finish the job but was again beaten back by a violent attack of fever, and it was left to the dependable Olliver to complete the survey. Everest's condition deteriorated to such an extent that he was finally forced away on sick leave for a whole year. He sailed to the Cape of Good Hope to recuperate, but severe complications would dog him for the remainder of his life.

On his return, starting in late 1822, Everest was charged with triangulating a new east–west arc terminating in Bombay, as the GTS continued to grow its web of triangles. This arc would start from Hyderabad, link up to Poona (now Pune), and ultimately fix the geographical position of Bombay. The surveying here was less strenuous, as there were no jungles, fevers or wild beasts to contend with; and the Maratha people of the region were, according to Everest, 'the best natured and kindest of all the natives of India'.

---

* A remittent tropical fever, like malaria, which never entirely leaves the sufferer.

Unlike Lambton, Everest would make no major contribution to the science of geodesy, but he would prove to be a skilful and practical geodesist. The better conditions on the Deccan Plateau gave him time to innovate, and he soon implemented many new practices which would dramatically alter the way the GTS conducted its future surveys.

While convalescing in South Africa, Everest had learnt of surveys carried out there at night, using lights. This led him to develop and use luminous signals, which made it possible to work outside daylight hours. A disadvantage of using opaque signals such as flagpoles during the day was that they could only be observed from distances of less than 10 miles, because the haze in the air obliterated the contrast between the slender post and its surroundings. Night signals could increase this distance to nearly 50 miles in clear weather, and take advantage of the increased refraction experienced after daylight, as sight lines became further bowed by the earth's atmosphere. This was the same special effect that had caused Lambton problems years earlier, but which Everest now made good use of to see many extra miles out.

The shift to night surveying would be the most far-reaching of all of Everest's improvements. Although it would require his whole camp to completely alter its hours, work could now be moved away from the hazardous monsoon months when the rains and fever were at their worst. It would also save his surveyors many wasted days, waiting for the atmosphere to clear sufficiently to sight their distant trig stations. There was a practical advantage for the men too: in the rainy season, the khalasis and other camp workers wanted to be at home cultivating their fields, whereas in the hot weather they were happy to seek employment with the GTS.

Everest was delighted with the success of this new practice, reporting it 'has changed the whole face of the Indian operations'. Markham later applauded it as saving the 'reckless waste of life and health, besides much suffering and discomfort'. But just as Everest was starting to make big strides with night surveying, he learnt of his superior's death and had to hurry back from his Bombay Arc.

Everest Takes Charge

With Lambton's passing, Everest was promoted to superintendent, being the only assistant of rank left in the GTS. A year earlier, Lambton had tried to also have Voysey promoted to assistant surveyor. When this wasn't approved, the doctor resigned from the GTS, although recurring jungle fever claimed his life before he could sail back to England.*

After taking charge, Everest realized he needed to quickly build his department back to full strength, or face a serious setback. The long-serving khalasis and other camp workers were reluctant to venture too far from their homes, as the survey pushed on further afield. Everest's bigger problem, though, was that his trained sub-assistants were reluctant to follow a leader who was overly demanding, vicious in his criticism, and generally unpopular. Of course, his task was all the more difficult as they had served under the calm and father-like figure of Lambton. Everest's own prejudices concerning the mixed blood of his senior staff, despite these feelings being the norm among Europeans in India at that time, could not have helped the situation either; at times, when frustrated, he would call them Lambton's mestizos.

The new superintendent was quick to pick a fight with just about anyone, including senior British staff, who had the temerity to cross him or interfere with his survey. He was also critical of any work by fellow surveyors that did not measure up to his high standards, and would say so plainly. While Everest could be obnoxious at times (as he himself acknowledged), his motto in life was simple: 'Serve God and fear no man.'

Fortunately for the GTS, he managed to convince Olliver, de Penning and others to stay on, and in time his staff and camp learnt to live with his roar, realizing a mauling didn't always follow.

---

* James Rennell estimated the high mortality rate amongst Englishmen in India at the time as: 'scarce one out of 70 men return to his native country'.

Eventually they came to understand what mattered to Everest, above all else, was the progress of his beloved Great Arc.

With his team back on board, Everest took personal charge of the arc and its extension northwards, crossing the Deccan Plateau and central India towards Nagpur. But here, he was struck down by another bout of illness, which threatened his life. Saturated with fever, his limbs paralysed, Everest was carried around in a palanquin, and had to be physically supported by others before he could operate the theodolite or zenith sector. This was a critical time for the survey, as it was in danger of stalling. Everest was painfully aware his leadership was needed to rally the men, who might otherwise disband and leave. Despite being so debilitated, he ignored doctor's orders to recuperate by the sea. Instead, he soldiered on for over six months, ensuring the Great Arc crossed the Narmada River and pushed past the peninsula into northern India in 1824.

By this stage de Penning had retired, leaving Everest to rely heavily on Olliver, whom he referred to as his right arm. There had been an incident earlier, however, when Everest's temper got the better of him, and he had had his assistant placed under arrest for insubordination. This situation arose when Olliver couldn't attend to his request for immediate assistance after Everest experienced a sharp attack of fever; it took the surveyor general's intervention before Everest was finally placated. Both Olliver and Rossenrode had come a long way since their apprentice days with Lambton, and were now experienced surveyors (but their other colleague Peter Lawrence had been discharged earlier for excessive drinking).

Everest drove his staff hard, berating and cajoling in his usual manner, and just occasionally offering praise. Yet he drove himself harder, even to the point, it is suspected, of partial mental breakdown. Finally, his failing health overtook him, and in November 1825 he was forced to return to England for five years to fully recover. Olliver was given charge of the GTS during these years, but the governor-general held that Company rules forbade his appointment to this covenanted position because he was an Anglo-Indian.*

During this long absence, Everest retained his post as superintendent of the GTS, although reduced to half pay as Company rules prescribed, much to his annoyance. Later that year, the GTS was placed under the surveyor general of India, who also controlled both the Revenue Survey and the Topographical Survey. While he was still in England, this post became vacant; and Everest so impressed the Court of Directors with his tremendous energy that he secured this seat, thus becoming the first officer to hold both positions simultaneously.

He would use this promotion to relentlessly advance the GTS, especially the Great Arc, even at the expense of the other two surveys. He convinced his superiors that trigonometrical surveying should take priority over all other surveys being conducted in India. Later, Everest would not allow new topographical surveys to be organized until a framework of primary triangles was first laid out. Nor would he permit any future work to rely solely on route surveys or astronomical control, except for military or trans-frontier surveys; and he also chose not to use the 'rough and ready' plane tables in his programme. Around this time, the international scientific community had begun recognizing Everest's work, resulting in his election to Fellowships of both the Royal Society and the Royal Astronomical Society.

He used his years back home to catch up with much useful work. As soon as he was able, Everest was writing reports detailing the recent achievements of the GTS, and investigating new survey instrumentation. He eagerly visited a number of instrument makers to place orders for the latest equipment available, and then fussed over the various design modifications he required. Amongst his list of items was another 36-inch theodolite to replace the Great

---

* Covenanted officials were those granted sole authority for managing an agency within the government. The Company barred Indians from holding high office, until a new charter in 1834 changed this rule.

Theodolite, which had suffered further damage the previous year, after being blown over when the survey camp was hit by high winds.

His most important purchase was a set of compensation bars, to further improve the accuracy of base-lines being laid out as the various arcs were extended across India. They would replace the steel chain that had become worn with use, and had always been susceptible to temperature variations. These new bars were twin rods—one iron and the other brass—bolted together in a such a way that led to their different rates of expansion cancelling out the effects of temperature altogether. Each bar was 10 feet long, and six sets were purchased, together with accompanying microscopes to allow precise readings to be taken.

Everest tested his compensation bars first at the Lords Cricket Ground before leaving London, then again when he returned to Calcutta, and was delighted with the improvement in accuracy compared to the old steel chain. The bars would be prone to rust, though, and require meticulous care, including regular coating with mercurial ointment, hog's lard or mutton fat. Yet they would come close to being rendered useless some years later, when left in the care of a young survey assistant. Under the strain of solitary camp life, ill and overcome by religious mania, apart from scratching the bars, he reportedly 'burned off all his toes and several fingers in the slow fire of a candle'. Fortunately, the bars escaped any permanent damage from his tampering.

When Everest had departed for England in 1825, the Great Arc had progressed as far as Sironj, 200 miles south of Agra, where a base camp had been set up and another base-line measured. However, he would not entrust its extension north to his sub-assistants during his lengthy absence. Instead, Everest put Olliver and Rossenrode to work on a new arc series, starting from the Sironj base and moving eastwards to Calcutta. This was a long arc measuring almost 700 miles, and the terrain along it proved to be challenging. Once again, many of the survey team had to be evacuated following an outbreak of jungle fever, and yet again many died, this time including one of Rossenrode's sons.

By the time Everest returned to India in 1830, only 70 miles remained to complete the Calcutta Arc. But Olliver and Rossenrode had encountered a major obstacle that both Lambton and Everest had anticipated years before—something that made the delta along the Ganges River near impossible to triangulate (and finding a solution here would reveal the key to completing the Great Arc itself). The challenge was to survey in a flat and heavily populated area, covered by a perpetual haze, much of it emanating from millions of households and their cooking fires. By using Everest's luminous signals at night, the survey team could overcome the haze, but how to establish sight lines across the densely packed buildings and innumerable trees?

Trials were conducted erecting tall scaffolding towers, but these proved too flimsy to take precise measurements from, as the platform they worked on would shift with the wind. The clue to finding a workable solution came from a nearby line of masonry towers, which were all that remained of a primitive visual telegraphic system. Built a few decades earlier, it employed signallers to manually flash short messages from tower to tower; Everest himself had worked on them before joining the GTS. He discovered these old structures were still stable enough to take measurements from, and could be modified at a reasonable cost. To complete the Calcutta Arc, though, a further eleven towers would have to be specially built at a considerable cost. Everest experimented with the design of the structures and devised a solution that would work not only for this arc, but later become a prototype for the Great Arc as well.

To close off the Calcutta Arc, a new base-line was required, and duly laid out over 6½ miles using Everest's new compensation bars. He chose a straight, level road in the city by the Hooghli River, running from Government House along the Barrackpur Trunk Road. As this stretch of road was a busy one, many restrictions on traffic, pedestrians and their domesticated animals had to be imposed during the two months the team took to complete the measurements. At either end, two masonry towers, each 75 feet high, were erected as trig stations, to allow incoming triangulations to be closed off and reconciled with the base-line. This final exercise, in July 1832, gave Everest the opportunity to showcase the activities of the GTS to the many dignitaries and officials in Calcutta. They came to see for themselves what this mysterious venture was all about, and get a sense of how a significant portion of the Company's funds was being consumed year after year.

Transforming the GTS

With the Calcutta Arc completed, and while he was still based at his headquarters there, Everest turned his focus to reorganizing the GTS and drawing up a blueprint for the coming years. The government subsequently approved his plan, despite the larger budget it demanded, as Britain needed its growing territories—and indeed the rest of India—to be mapped as quickly as possible. Everest set as his priorities two big tasks: the first was to complete the Great Arc, and the second called for a gridiron system of arcs stretching from Calcutta to Delhi.

The adoption of the gridiron would become another of Everest's lasting achievements. It would reshape the GTS's approach to mapping India, while greatly speeding up its work. This system was a major departure from Lambton's initial idea of throwing an intensive web of primary triangles across the country. Everest realized a grid of well-spaced arcs, centred on the Great Arc, would suffice. Then, at some later date, the area in between these arcs could be filled in by less expensive topographical surveying, analogous to the method used by the French and Russians to map their countries. Everest's gridiron called for the triangulation of a set of vertical arcs roughly 1 degree of longitude apart, criss-crossed by horizontal arcs spaced at intervals of about 6 degrees of latitude, to form a virtual grid.

To reduce costs, the government instructed the distance between vertical arcs should be doubled to 2 degrees, but Everest baulked at this, arguing that a higher level of accuracy was required, and convinced his superiors he was right. Like Lambton, he was unrelenting in his quest for accuracy. A few years earlier, for example, when the triangulation of the Bombay Presidency by another British officer was brought under his charge, after carefully enquiring into the survey methods used, Everest deemed the work unfit for incorporation into his Trigonometrical Survey, despite the officer's acrimonious protests. Everest was often at odds with administrators as well over such issues, as Phillimore notes:

> His undaunted force of character prevailed repeatedly against the impatience of a local Government that could hardly follow his lengthy dissertations. Government was all for speed and economy, Everest for the highest accuracy, having to justify one change of programme after another. Though his forceful language was occasionally resented, his professional knowledge commanded respect at all times, though he sometimes only prevailed by an appeal to London.

To carry out his ambitious two-pronged programme, Everest planned to put six surveys teams in the field simultaneously. Two would work on the Great Arc, while the other four advanced the vertical arcs of the gridiron, working off the recently completed Calcutta Arc. The costs involved would increase significantly, as many more men would need to be recruited and trained at all levels, and new observation towers built. Everest estimated this programme of work would cost a hefty 77,000 pounds and take many thousands of workers some five years to complete.

A highly skilled instrument maker, Henry Barrow, had already arrived from England to ensure the precision and upkeep of survey instruments. He later became so troublesome and defiant, though, that Everest was forced to discharge him. Fortunately, Barrow's assistant, a native Indian named Mohsin Husain, would soon prove more than his equal and become invaluable to the GTS.* Everest

---

* Amongst his accomplishments, Husain designed a plane table that essentially remained the standard Indian pattern for 100 years.

lobbied hard for Husain's appointment, securing him a monthly salary of 250 rupees. Although only one-half of what Barrow was paid, this was nevertheless a princely sum for someone who had risen from humble beginnings as a jeweller's assistant in Madras.

Everest, too, had a good working knowledge of instrumentation, as demonstrated by his improvements to the common theodolite. The Everest pattern would be popular for many years, especially within the Revenue Survey. Another example was his design for a pump to fill mercury barometers in a vacuum, thereby avoiding the frequent problem of breakage of their long glass tubes, which had frustrated many a surveyor.* In yet another instance, after conducting a route survey, he redesigned the perambulator to halve the number of khalasis required to push it along—from two men down to one.

A Calcutta office was set up headed by de Penning, who was enticed back from retirement and given the task of processing the mass of calculations generated by the multiple surveys. During this period, the science underpinning geodesy was rapidly improving, as was the art of trigonometrical surveying, as better instrumentation became available. As a result, there were now five special effects which needed to be corrected for: the earth's curvature; its non-spherical curvature (spherical excess); the refraction of sight lines; heights above sea level, especially for mountains; and the gravitational influence of mountains or nearby mass on plumb lines.

De Penning had a team of eight 'computers' who worked on processing of the mass of data generated and the complex calculations required. Although they possessed the requisite skills, Everest was initially scandalized on seeing them wear the traditional dhoti in the office. He insisted they sufficiently 'cover the nakedness' displayed and 'wear a pair of clean stockings . . . well blackened shoes . . . and trousers' or work in a separate room.

---

* Barometers were used to measure altitude. The invention of the aneroid type in 1844, which worked on a different principle and did not need a column of mercury, would remedy this problem.

One of these human calculators was a young Bengali named Radhanath Sikdar, who quickly proved his mathematical mastery and would go on to become Chief Computer for the GTS. Everest would say of him: 'There are few in India, whether European or native that can at all compete with him. Even in Europe these mathematical attainments would rank very high.'*

Two young lieutenants joined Everest's growing team in 1832, one of whom was Andrew Waugh. They were given the task of triangulating the vertical arcs running off the Calcutta Arc. Both proved themselves capable and were soon promoted as his assistants; years later, following Everest's glowing endorsement, Waugh would go on to become his successor.

Around this time, despite objections from his superiors, Everest moved his headquarters from Calcutta to a property he had purchased in Mussoorie. This was a picturesque hill resort just north of the large town of Dehra Dun, set high in the Himalayan foothills with commanding views of the mightiest mountain range in the world. (Later, it would be moved again into the town itself, where it remains today as the Survey of India's headquarters.)

In the period following his return to India, Everest transformed the GTS from Lambton's under-resourced and family-like little department to a professional institution with superior capability and an expanded staff. The scene was set for a final push to complete the Great Arc, during the years from 1833 to 1843. Survey of India historians label this period 'the Everest decade', and his commemorative bust, which stands outside the organization's headquarters today, bears testimony to his lasting influence.

Difficulties on the Doab

Everest travelled down from Mussoorie to take charge of the Great Arc, and restart it from the Sironj base where it had come to a halt

---

* In 2004, the Government of India released a set of three commemorative postage stamps of the GTS, with Sikdar featuring on one of them (the Great Arc and Pundit Nain Singh were shown on the other two).

some years earlier. He was once again returning to fieldwork after an eight-year absence, including the five spent in England and the remaining ones worked in Calcutta. He would now spend large amounts of time in the survey camps—much to the consternation of his superiors, who had considerable difficulty contacting their surveyor general when they needed to consult with him. In typical Everest fashion, he would fire back curt letters reminding them he was a surveyor, not a clerk, and was working where he was most needed.

To counter his inaccessibility, a survey committee was formed by the government but, not surprisingly, there was much friction between the two parties. Everest regularly clashed with the Company's hierarchy at home as well, although Phillimore defends him in this:

> The Directors in England expected far too much of their Surveyor General. He was to bring the expensive work of the Trigonometrical Survey to speedy completion—he was to expedite the submission of material for the Indian Atlas, all accurately tied to the triangulation—and, whilst he was devoting his whole energies to the primary triangulation, they withdrew his Deputies at Madras and Bombay. They expected miracles.

Everest's base camp in Sironj was a large one, dwarfing previous numbers. Other than his key survey staff, it included some 700 khalasis and camp workers, plus elephants, camels and horses needed for transportation; their measurement apparatus alone, on one occasion, took thirty-four camels and three elephants to move. As the Great Arc progressed north along the 78-degree meridian, their challenge was to survey some of the most difficult terrain ever attempted in India: the smoke-laden and densely populated area known as the doab lying between the Ganges and Jumna (now Yamuna) rivers. The Jumna Valley, being practically dead flat except for a few low mounds, made it hard to establish a sight line over 5 miles. New surveying techniques and innovations would be required to overcome these obstacles.

Everest decided to take a fundamentally different approach in this region. He planned to undertake all the triangulation work simultaneously across this 400-mile sector, rather than build the arc sequentially, one triangle at a time. Standard practice required an advance party to first pick out the next tall landmark to be used as a trig point, which a surveyor would then sight from the previous station. Everest realized this method of 'hill-hopping' would not work in flat countryside; instead, he planned for all trig stations to be selected beforehand. Only then should the sight lines through these heavily populated areas be established, which would invariably require some degree of house demolitions, tree felling and ground levelling. Any work of this nature needed to be kept to an absolute minimum, to reduce disruptions to the populace and control costs, including compensation payments which would invariably be required.

Before any of the permanent masonry towers were custom-built for the final triangulation work, it was vital that their positions be precisely determined, as mistakes would prove costly. This was achieved by undertaking an approximate series of triangulations first, usually with a smaller 12-inch theodolite seated on top of a temporary 30-foot tower made from bamboo scaffolding. The surveyor would observe luminous signals burnt during the night at set intervals. These were lit and hoisted 90 feet high on another portable mast, many miles away.

One variant of these flares, known as a 'blue light', was the brightest available, and could be observed up to 60 miles away. It had to be carefully concocted using several chemicals, before being wrapped in cloth and contained in a sheep's bladder. Expensive to make, it would only burn for up to six minutes at a time, and its effectiveness was frequently interrupted by stormy or hazy weather. Another difficulty arose from not knowing whether an undetected flare was due to faulty signalling, or the presence of some obstruction. On other occasions the flares were barely observable with the naked eye, making it near impossible to point the theodolite in the right direction. Everest's frustration with all this messing about was evident as he wrote to Olliver:

> . . . I dare not put a blue light into the hands of any of you. You seem . . . to think they grow like grass, and all you have to do is to put them at the top of a pole and set fire to them, just as you would a wisp of straw.

At one point he fired off an angry note to one of his other sub-assistants:

> I have seen two of your blue lights, but only got an angle with one because your time was so irregular . . . You are the cause of the detention of my camp by this neglect of my orders. The other day when I ordered you to commence at 4 you did not commence till past 5, and now when I ordered you to commence at 5 you begin half an hour before.

When the poor man replied that his difficulty arose from not owning a watch, Everest was astounded and retorted:

> No decent person is ever without a watch, and a man who has no watch can never pretend to be respectable. You ought to be ashamed to acknowledge that you have no watch. You might just as well say that you have no coat or no shoes or no hat.

Finally, after trialling several different methods, Everest overcame the problems associated with night flares by inventing a reliable technique called 'ray tracing'. It allowed his team to work rapidly during the day using a perambulator and compass, or a small theodolite instead, to determine the true bearing of where the next signal mast should be erected. Then the 'ray' to this mast could be cleared of any obstructions, before the telescope was pointed in the exact direction to observe the brief blue flare at night, typically some 30 miles away.

For observations made during daylight hours, Everest introduced another instrument he had brought back from England. Known as a heliotrope, it could generate a powerful signal by using a mirror to reflect flashes of sunlight to a surveyor standing up to 100 miles away.

The whole process of ray tracing—preparing blue flares, handling the tricky heliotropes, and sighting from bamboo platforms susceptible to vibration—was an inherently troublesome one. For this reason, the survey teams were always on a sharp lookout for suitable buildings on which to place their trig stations, saving them all this extra effort. Near Agra, they were able to take advantage of the ancient city of Fatehpur Sikri by hoisting a signal there, and another on the rooftop of the tomb of its founder, the Mughal emperor Akbar. Still, many fruitless nights were spent attempting to burn flares and locate signals in the hazy, polluted atmosphere of the doab. These were trying times for all concerned, and Everest was a difficult taskmaster at the best of times. Phillimore describes it well:

> Continuing to storm and rage at each and all of his assistants in turn whenever anything went wrong—standing to his instrument for many hours through the evenings, and again an hour or two before dawn till 10 o'clock or so—spending the day at correspondence or computations—insisting on his assistants sending in their raw observations so he might compute them himself—praising—scolding—jeering—mocking—and sometimes patiently explaining—Everest steadily brought his team and his triangles within view of the Siwaliks [foothills of the Himalayas].

His bad temper and frequent outbursts may be better understood, although not excused, in light of his various painful and debilitating ailments. Everest was ordered to return to England on account of his failing health, but he saw this as impossible as there was simply too much left to accomplish. When his recovery was thought to be beyond all hope, his superiors appointed a successor, but without consulting him. This so enraged Everest that they backed off, and the officer concerned, witnessing his determination to see the Great Arc completed, accepted the inevitable and left India.

Sometimes the surveyor general could be his own worst enemy, as Phillimore comments after one of his episodes: 'Everest himself was constantly embroiled through impatience and insistence of his own importance. Delays and difficulties . . . were greatly magnified by his own intolerance and obstinacy.'

Years later, though, his niece, writer Mary Everest Boole, would shed light on a more tolerant side of his nature. It seems he had once been initiated into ancient philosophy by a learned Brahman, which changed his outlook: 'The whole idea of any particular religion being . . . truer or better than any other, became utterly abhorrent to him. That anyone . . . should speak of his own doctrines as essential to salvation, was enough to rouse his contempt and anger to the last years of his life.'

What was never in doubt was Everest's dedication and work ethic, which went well beyond the call of duty and earned him the nickname Neverrest from his contemporaries. If the 'cantankerous old sahib' did not spare his men, he did not spare himself either. Through sheer hard work and at a huge cost to his own health, he earned their respect and, finally it seems, a good deal of their devotion too.

The Final Push

By mid-1834, the positions of all the masonry towers had been mapped out and their construction could begin, but this work would prove to be slow and expensive. In all, fourteen towers were needed at a cost of almost 3000 pounds, and would take two years to build. They were between 40 and 60 feet high, with walls 5 feet thick at the base tapering to 2 feet at the terrace. The instrument table within each tower was set on a pillar isolated from the observation platform, to prevent any interference. A later surveyor general remarked: 'his towers always seem to me to be an amazing monument to Everest's enterprise and conception'. A few of these structures have survived, and can be seen on the doab to this day.

While they were being built, the survey teams worked on laying out a new base-line and completing astronomical observations. The site selected for the northern-most base-line was in the beautiful valley of Dehra Dun, between the Siwaliks and the Himalayas. Much of this work continued in the face of enormous obstacles, especially in the deadly terai, those marshy tracts of jungle near the foothills where the malarial mosquito and fever were rampant.

By late 1835, the new masonry towers had been erected, and Everest was ready to complete the last stage of the Great Arc, triangulating between the two base-lines at Sironj and Dehra Dun. All the meticulous work invested in locating the towers would prove its worth now. Fittingly, the Great Theodolite had been refurbished and would be called on to make some of the final measurements, after it had been hoisted on to the instrument table with a crane. Working from tower to tower, the triangulations progressed relatively smoothly, although a few problems of varying degree were encountered.

A major predicament arose when the sight line from a tower was blocked by some trees, a village and then more houses in another town further along. The trees were felled easily enough, but persuading the inhabitants to cut a 30-foot-wide gap through their settlement, demolishing 100 houses in the process, required a good deal of compensation and tact. Everest gave due credit to his sub-assistant who had to persuade these villagers, known for their hot temper, to leave their homes while hoar frosts were forming on most nights: 'How Mr. Rossenrode contrived to effect this severe operation, and reconcile all parties . . . surprises me . . . he ventured unarmed . . . without a single weapon of defence or any show of force . . .' For his part, Everest sincerely regretted this miscalculation, reporting: 'The list of dwellings destroyed, however, is disastrous, and I hope it will never again fall to my lot to have so disagreeable a task to discharge.'

More understandable were the problems stemming from arousing local superstitions, as a result of their night work and blue flares.

Olliver related how one local raja 'caused it to be proclaimed by beat of drum that his people should be cautious of falling into the hands of the surveyors lest they should have their children taken to burn in the signal fires'. There were also the expected sensitivities voiced by locals about the intrusion into their privacy, which the towers and spyglass were bound to generate.

A more worrying issue was the occasions when trig station markers were damaged or dug up by angry villagers. Everest described this state of affairs, which could undo weeks of work:

> The natives of India have a habit of attributing supernatural and miraculous powers to our instruments and the sites which have been occupied by them. In cases of death or any other natural visitations they often offer up prayers to those sites; and if the object of their prayers be not conceded, they proceed to all sorts of acts of destruction and indignity towards them.

In the end, though, the problem that hurt them most, delaying the completion of the Great Arc by many months, came from an unexpected source. Initially, the 7-mile length of the base-line at Sironj had been measured using Lambton's steel chain. Unfortunately, when it was compared with the triangulation brought down from Dehra Dun, a discrepancy of over 3 feet was discovered. Although the two base-lines were nearly 450 miles apart, for Everest this was far too large an error to concede. He strongly suspected it had arisen from small inaccuracies in the steel chain itself, and immediately resolved to re-measure the base-line with his new compensation bars. When this was accomplished some months later, it proved him right. The entire discrepancy across the eighty-six primary triangles between Sironj and Dehra Dun was subsequently reduced to an acceptable 6 inches.

If one might suggest, as Everest promptly did, that the detection of this small error should necessitate a re-measuring of all the other base-lines and the full length of the arc across India, then the government was certainly not about to countenance this argument, or the extra cost involved for that matter. Other than allowing for a small amount of re-measurement, his superiors firmly pointed out that, for all practical purposes, the Great Arc was more than accurate, and Everest had no option but to accept their stance.

Soon after the last triangulations were completed, Rossenrode and Olliver retired, and de Penning left two years later, although their sons would continue with the GTS for many years to come.

For Everest, one final piece of work remained, and that was to revisit the old geodetic question about the earth's shape. He and Waugh spent countless nights making over 3000 astronomical observations to determine the precise latitudes of the three separate bases: in the north near Dehra Dun; in the middle at Sironj; and a third further south at Bidar near Hyderabad. Once these measurements were in hand, the length of the arc connecting these bases, covering over 11 degrees of latitude, could be compared with the ground distance determined through triangulation. This work resulted in the most accurate measurement of the earth's shape in the tropics, and it was a major advancement on Lambton's initial effort based on 1½ degrees of latitude.

By this stage, Everest too was a colonel. With him at its helm, the GTS had surveyed 57,000 square miles of territory, at a final cost of nearly 90,000 pounds. Although this area was only a third of the total achieved under Lambton's stewardship, Everest's survey is considered unsurpassed because of its superior quality. For example, to ensure the highest levels of accuracy, Everest made his triangles as symmetrical as possible. He achieved this by instituting a strict rule that internal angles be kept between 30 and 90 degrees, and preferably closer to 60 degrees. Furthermore, as much as Everest appreciated the size of Lambton's large triangles, as a general rule, again in pursuit of accuracy, he favoured limiting each side to between 20 and 30 miles, even though this restriction would slow down the rate of advance of his survey.

Towards the end of 1841, the actual triangulation across the length of India—some 1600 miles spanning 22 degrees of latitude—

was completed.* When all the various computations were resolved in the following two years, after four decades of painstaking labour the Great Arc was finally finished; Everest pronounced it 'as perfect a performance as mankind has yet seen'.

Everest's health was failing by this stage. Other than ongoing battles with dysentery and fever, rheumatic pains wracked him. An inflamed hip joint in 1835 had cost him the use of his upper leg and rendered him a cripple. Failing eyesight and memory loss were also taking their toll. After twenty-five years with the GTS, it was clearly past the time to retire.

Everest sailed back to England in 1844, where he seems to have made a remarkable and happy recovery: he married at age fifty-five and raised a family of six children. He also set aside time to write his second book, which was published in 1847 in two volumes, titled *An Account of the Measurement of Two Sections of the Meridional Arc of India*. In 1861, he was honoured with a knighthood; Sir George lived on for another five years before passing away in London, aged seventy-six.

His other lasting contribution to Indian cartography, the gridiron system he had anchored to the Great Arc, was left to his successors to complete. It would take the GTS another forty years of continuous surveying to finally finish the principal triangulation of the subcontinent in 1883. A decade before this, the Survey of India had begun employing the electric telegraph, which would revolutionize surveying and cartography by simplifying the process for measuring longitude; remarkably, Everest had foreshadowed its use over twenty-five years earlier.

When the highest mountain in the world was surveyed by the GTS around this time, and after its computation staff confirmed this peak as the only one standing over 29,000 feet above sea level, the task of naming it fell to the incumbent surveyor general,

---

* This achievement remains embodied today in the motto of the Survey of India: *A Setu Himachalam* (From Kanyakumari to the Himalayas).

Andrew Waugh. He knew of no local name for the peak and, although it would generate much controversy, in honouring his predecessor he chose 'to perpetuate the memory of that illustrious master of accurate geographical research'. Curiously, Everest was never a recipient of a gold medal from the RGS, unlike Waugh and a number of others from the GTS. However, by this act, he arguably received the 'highest', most recognized, and lasting accolade—although the mountain's name remains mispronounced *Ever–est* rather than *Eve–rest*. Yet, despite the fact that most people today are readily able to identify this peak, few know of the man it was named after, or the accomplishments that earned him this singular honour.

Everest and Lambton's Legacy

The president of the Royal Astronomical Society, during his annual address in 1848, put the decades of work invested by these two pioneers into perspective:

> The two individuals, Col. Lambton and Col. Everest, who began and completed this important measurement, have earned for themselves a distinguished place amongst the benefactors of science . . . The Great Meridional Arc of India is a trophy of which any nation, or any government, of the world would have reason to be proud, and will be one of the most enduring monuments of their power and enlightened regard for the progress of human knowledge.

William Lambton and George Everest had made a lifetime commitment to science and, equally, to mapping India. In personality, these two men could not have been more different, but in purpose they were united. Their work would form the backbone of future maps of the subcontinent, and would benefit millions of ordinary people for generations to come. They had also answered the complex question about the earth's shape, which possibly only the geodesists of this world would fully appreciate. Ultimately, establishing the GTS of India and completing the Great Arc will forever stand as their lasting achievements.

PART THREE

THE PUNDITS

*'We of the Great Game are beyond protection. If we die, we die.
Our names are blotted from the book. That is all.'*

—Rudyard Kipling, *Kim*

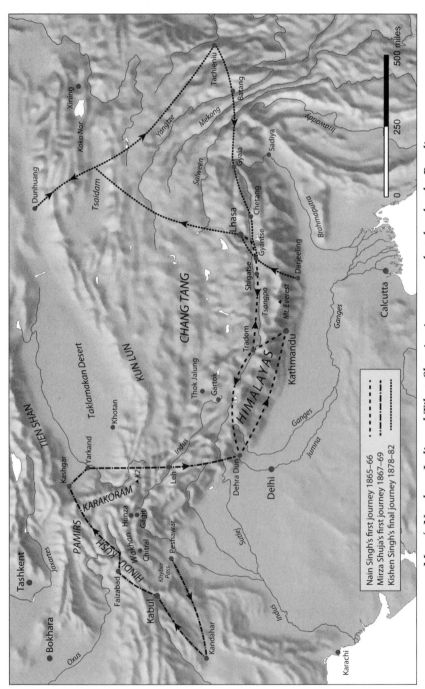

Map 4. Northern India and Tibet: Showing journeys undertaken by the Pundits

Nain Singh's first journey 1865–66
Mirza Shuja's first journey 1867–69
Kishen Singh's final journey 1878–82

0   250   500 miles

5

Montgomerie's Native Explorers

When Captain Thomas George Montgomerie of the GTS was surveying high up in the mountains of Kashmir, he noticed a curious thing. While the border crossings from India into China were supposedly closed to all foreigners, some Indians were able to cross the frontier freely. His observation, coupled with the insatiable desire of the British to explore and map new territories, would spawn an extraordinary group of native explorers. One of the first of these men would be Nain Singh, who was by profession a pundit—a title which in his case denoted a schoolteacher. He would prove to be so remarkable an explorer that his code name, the Pundit, would soon be used to refer to Montgomerie's entire group of native explorers. They would cross the formidable mountain ranges encircling northern India to explore and spy for their employer, the GTS, enabling it to map these forbidden regions.

Montgomerie arrived in India in 1852, aged twenty-one. The son of an English colonel, he had recently graduated as the year's top cadet from Addiscombe, the Company's military academy for its officers. Already showing a healthy interest in surveying and astronomy, his application to join the GTS was promptly accepted by the surveyor general, Andrew Waugh.

The Vale of Kashmir

By this stage, the GTS had mapped a large portion of northern India as it continued to extend Everest's gridiron system, and Waugh wanted to push into Kashmir before mapping the Himalayas. After Montgomerie had proved his abilities, following his first few years of fieldwork, Waugh entrusted him with the important survey of this region at the early age of twenty-five.

By all accounts, the beauty of this vale is worthy of the rhyming epithets *'Kashmir bi nuzir, Kashmir junta puzir'* (Kashmir without equal, Kashmir equal to paradise). For the next decade, mapping this state would consume most of Montgomerie's time and energy. It had been under Sikh control until 1846, when it was handed over to the maharaja of the neighbouring state of Jammu by Britain, following its victory in the First Anglo-Sikh War. Much of the terrain here is situated high in the western Himalayas and Karakorams, requiring survey work to be carried out in cold and trying conditions.

Lambton and Everest had triangulated on a horizontal plane to measure ground distances. The same techniques could be applied vertically to measure heights: the instruments used and the mathematics involved were identical.* Under Waugh, the GTS was determining the heights and locations of the highest and most inaccessible mountains in the world, many miles north of the Indian frontier, by triangulating from a distance while remaining within its own borders.

Montgomerie was fortunate to have as his second-in-command William Johnson, a civilian surveyor who had joined the GTS as a sub-assistant at age sixteen. He would go on to become something of a legend for his ability to work at high altitudes, his readiness to rescue others in strife, and his daring exploration across the border. Their survey teams were frequently required to set up stations at heights between 15,000 and 20,000 feet (it was here that a khalasi gained the world's altitude

---

*   Although when only the height of a peak was sought and it could be climbed, it was often easier to measure it with reasonable accuracy using a simple boiling-point thermometer.

record mentioned earlier). And for sixty years, four of Johnson's peaks would support the highest trig stations anywhere in the world.

The surveyors and their men had no access to mountaineering gear, nor did they receive any training in climbing. Yet the khalasis hauled up Montgomerie's equipment, including his 14-inch theodolite slung on a pole between two men, on to multiple peaks *averaging* 17,000 feet—more than 1000 feet higher than Europe's tallest, Mont Blanc. Amongst the dangers faced by teams working at these heights was the obvious one, highlighted when a khalasi fell down a precipice, as later reported: 'The scalp was dreadfully split and one eye completely gone. His back also and other portions of his body were seriously injured.' Although he managed to survive, he was left 'a sadly mutilated cripple' and was granted a pension.

The khalasis regularly suffered from snow blindness, since they owned no dark glasses, and had to resort to using fir tree twigs or horsehair to shade their eyes. Sometimes they had to first dig through many feet of snow and ice, to locate the actual mountaintop (as opposed to the top of the snow), before anchoring their trig point on solid rock. They also had to dig building materials out from under the icy covering, to construct an observation platform for the theodolite. The water for slaking the lime used during construction, and for drinking, had to be melted first, requiring large quantities of wood to be carried up as well. Often they ran low on food, and on a few occasions were starved out and forced to retreat from the summit.

On days when cloud cover—the bane of all mountain surveyors—prevented the use of heliotropes, observations had to be made using lamps after dark, in freezing temperatures. Cloud on the peak being surveyed from, or to, could undo all the exertions of a strenuous climb. The men built rudimentary stone shelters on the peaks, where they dwelt for many days and nights waiting patiently for the weather to clear. Years later, when another GTS officer was visiting one of these high stations, he found a human skeleton lying in the corner of one of these shelters—probably a khalasi whose companions were unable to carry his body back down for a proper funeral.

If the survey team was lucky, especially with the weather, all its observations from a peak could be completed within a few days and they could hurry back down, but this wasn't typical. At one station they were held up for twenty-two days, when snowstorms and fog made sighting impossible. At another, a senior khalasi named Daffadar Mulli camped on the summit for over two months under severe conditions to ensure his signals were seen and recorded. His was such a heroic effort, including once having his hair set alight from an electrical storm, that the 15,000-foot peak was dubbed Mulli Hill Station on all the maps.

Montgomerie would later write elegantly about the thrill of spotting 'the bright point of light shining from the apex of a noble snowy cone'. He describes working high up in the mountains:

> Stations over 15,000 feet . . . are unmistakably unpleasant, though there is some slight compensation . . . when the upper level of the clouds falls . . . leaving the camp on an island surrounded with a level sea of clouds from which the peaks . . . stood out like other islands, and the waves of clouds surged backwards and forwards across the lower ridges.

In addition to conducting the primary triangulation of Kashmir, Montgomerie was responsible for its topographical survey which followed closely, filling in geographic details using plane tables. He steadily worked his way across the Pir Panjal Range into the Kashmir Valley, where he surveyed the city and its lake, before moving on to a preliminary reconnaissance of the sparsely populated region of Ladakh (Land of High Passes). It had acquired a predominantly Buddhist Tibetan population during the ninth century, and is sometimes referred to as Second Tibet.* It was from here that

---

* Its northwestern neighbour Baltistan is known as Little Tibet, as its people are also of Tibetan descent, although they converted to Islam in the fourteenth century.

Montgomerie first set eyes on the majestic Karakoram Range and, later, after observing its towering peaks with his theodolite, simply numbered them from K1 to K32. His designation for the second peak, K2, standing at 28,250 feet, remains the name of the world's second highest mountain.

The years during the Indian Mutiny, and the death of the maharaja in 1857, were difficult and dangerous times for the GTS. Montgomerie soon lost his survey assistants, as these officers were urgently recalled to arms. He was ordered to stay behind, however, and continue his survey, thereby demonstrating to the maharaja Britain's belief that the outcome of the rebellion was not in doubt. The surveyor general would later applaud him 'as an officer of no ordinary stamp' who was able to retain, with 'tact, delicacy and ability', the confidence of the new maharaja's court, and ensure the work of the GTS was not halted during the turmoil.

Montgomerie's survey was also notable for achieving a remarkable level of accuracy. In early 1859, he produced a detailed and beautiful map of *Jammu, Kashmir and Adjacent Countries*, covering over 8000 square miles and some 4600 villages. The governor-general of India and the RGS in London greatly praised this map.

By 1864, the Kashmir Survey was complete and, after ten uninterrupted years dedicated to this work, Montgomerie returned home to England for two years. He was suffering from jungle fever, and hoped to recover his strength after prolonged exposure to an extreme climate. The next year, he was awarded a gold medal by the RGS for 'his great trigonometrical journey from the plains of the Panjab to the Karakoram Range'. This recognition also demonstrated the very high regard the GTS was held in around the world for its cartographical work. Important as this honour was for both employer and employee, it would be overshadowed by Montgomerie's work during the next decade, as he established the Trans-Himalayan Exploration (as it would soon be termed).

The Forerunners

The GTS had become adept at working in the challenging regions and climes of India. Whether its men surveyed down in the teeming jungles or high up in the freezing mountains, they had learnt to accept the dangers and discomforts from fever, dysentery, tigers, heat and frostbite. Yet there was one seemingly insurmountable problem the GTS faced, and that was being denied access to carry on its survey beyond India's borders. This was largely because of the dangers involved in venturing into these regions, whether it was going beyond the Northwest Frontier,* or into Chinese Turkestan or Tibet.

The authorities in British India had actively discouraged its people from crossing these northern borders, making it perfectly clear to the GTS that it was not to 'risk the safety of the party nor to entangle Government in political complications'. This edict applied even more stringently to army officers, for reasons that the fate of Stoddart and Conolly in Bokhara had already demonstrated. Such killings caused Britain much grief and, because often they could not be avenged, loss of face as well. But the Great Game was in full swing now, and the military desperately needed maps and information, if it was to defend India effectively.

Quite apart from this, the sheer thirst for exploration on all sides would not be denied—not when large tracts of Asia remained uncharted, and while institutions such as the RGS eagerly sought to publish the accounts of explorers and the new geographies they 'discovered'. Montgomerie was keen to play a part in this exploration effort. He estimated the Chinese territory alone that was accessible from British India, which the GTS was entirely ignorant of, to be approximately 1,000,000 square miles. His other hope was to

---

* These were the frontier districts of the Punjab, lying between the Indus River and Afghanistan, which were later established as a separate province of India in 1901.

survey north, and map the unexplored land between the British and Russian frontiers.

By the 1860s, the major cities and roads of Afghanistan had been mapped to a large extent, following the British missions to Kabul and during the First Afghan War, but travel through most of this area was still far from safe for Europeans. More than a decade later, the viceroy of India, Lord Lytton, was describing how 'the country within a day's ride of its most important garrison is an absolute terra incognita, and that there is absolutely no security for British life a mile or two beyond our border'. The Afghans had a saying that illustrated their deep mistrust of these interlopers, and the way to deal with them: 'First comes one Englishman for *shikar* (hunting), then come two to draw a map, and then comes an army to take your land. So, it is best to kill the first Englishman.'

On the other side of Afghanistan lay the khanates of Western Turkestan, which were still relatively unexplored. Individual officers such as Arthur Conolly and Alexander Burnes had made daring journeys into the heart of this hostile region a few decades earlier. These, however, were mainly for intelligence-gathering purposes and, apart from Burnes, without the specific objective or resources to conduct any serious mapping.

Tibet, in particular, remained a mysterious land that foreign geographers found frustratingly difficult to penetrate. Even the exact position of its capital, Lhasa (Abode of Gods), was not known, and the question of whether the Great River of Tibet, the Tsangpo, flowed into the Brahmaputra or Irrawaddy had yet to be settled. The best maps available of this isolated land had been drawn a century and a half earlier, by two Tibetans lamas who had been trained in rudimentary surveying by Jesuit priests residing in Peking. Decades earlier, the country had closed its borders to all foreigners. Although Britain did ratify a treaty with China in 1860, which theoretically gave its subjects the right to travel there, in practice this was foiled by the hosts; besides, China had only nominal suzerainty over Tibet during this period.

Chinese Turkestan was equally unwelcoming and dangerous. The last European to enter this region, a German geologist named Adolf Schlagintweit, was beheaded after blundering into a civil war there. His killing, in the city of Kashgar in 1857, had precipitated the designation by British authorities of the regions beyond India's northern frontiers as 'out of bounds' for its subjects.

A few years later, William Johnson would disobey these orders. He crossed the Kunlun Mountains in 1865 to visit the rebel ruler of the southern city of Khotan, mapping the terrain as he went. This feat made him the first European visitor there since Marco Polo and the Jesuit missionary Benedict de Goes; but the surveyor was taken hostage, and only released after a ransom was paid by the GTS. On his return, following the publication of his exploration notes, the RGS roundly applauded Johnson and elected him a Fellow. Lord Strangford, president of the Asiatic Society of Bengal, described it as 'one of the most important papers that had ever been read before the Society'. But, to Johnson's intense disappointment, the government rebuked him for disobedience, which soured his remaining time with his employer.

If the GTS was to map across India's borders, the problem of accessibility had to be overcome first. When Montgomerie was surveying in Ladakh, he had witnessed local Indians crossing into the city of Yarkand, located in southern Chinese Turkestan, without any difficulty. What if a few of these natives could be trained and sent across the frontier to explore for the GTS? This was the idea he conceived way back in 1861, even before completing his Kashmir Survey and returning home to recuperate.

Montgomerie outlined his thoughts in a memorandum to his superior, Major James Walker, then superintendent of the GTS, and gained his full support. Next, they overcame opposition from the government, who were not in favour of using natives for exploration work. Another hurdle was the stereotypical view held by the British that Indians were simply not capable of such work. As Andrew Waugh had once remarked: 'They have not, it is believed, the same *coup d'oeil** and power of drawing from nature that Europeans have.' In this, Montgomerie's native explorers would soon prove the old surveyor general quite wrong.

In fact, native explorers *had* been used in the past, although only in a limited and ad hoc way. Moorcroft and Hearsey had recruited Harkh Dev to pace out a route survey during their journey into Tibet in 1812, which was the first recorded instance of an Indian being deployed in this manner. Moorcroft had also used Mir Izzat-Allah to complete a year-long reconnaissance trip to Bokhara starting out that same year. Soon afterwards, however, the surveyor general reported: 'the government have now notified me that they wish to throw cold water on all natives being taught, or employed in making geographical discoveries'. In time this edict would be withdrawn, and three decades later 'Bokhara Burnes' would take a native surveyor with him on his celebrated visit to that city.

The other prominent forerunner to the Pundits was a mullah named Abdul Mejid, who was sent on a mission from Peshawar to Khokand in 1860 on the orders of the governor-general. His mission was to convey a letter and presents to the khan, and gauge the presence of Russian activity there. Mejid was successful in both objectives, and his report was well-received by the government on his return the following year, when he was rewarded accordingly. As an explorer, he completed the first recorded traverse of the Pamirs, and the RGS acknowledged this achievement by presenting him with a gold watch. When he accepted the award on Mejid's behalf in London, Strangford made a prophetic remark: 'to us as geographers it is a great advantage to have the means of exploring countries inaccessible to Europeans, in the cooperation of these meritorious native travellers'.

Mejid's success heartened Montgomerie and, at a meeting of the Asiatic Society of Bengal, he discussed how such missions could

---

* A French term, often used in a military context, referring to the ability to discern at one glance the tactical advantages offered by a terrain.

be extended to gather further geographical knowledge. He believed this could be achieved by training native explorers and equipping them with basic instrumentation, to carry out route surveys and take observations such as latitudinal positions. Both he and Walker discussed their idea again, and in some detail, with other members of the society at future meetings. This tendency to publicly discuss plans concerning their native explorers, and afterwards publish the results of their explorations, would continue to be a rather inexplicable move on the part of Montgomerie, Walker and other senior members of the GTS. It would soon become a highly contentious issue with their government as well.

Montgomerie and Walker finally convinced their superiors of the viability of their plan. It is likely the government saw this as a less risky undertaking compared to British officers venturing beyond India's borders, since native explorers could be simply disowned and given up as lost if they were caught. Montgomerie's initial proposal, with a request for 1000 rupees to allow him to begin recruiting and training, was approved in 1863. He and Walker were ready to launch the GTS on its big geographic adventure, which would come to include a good deal of espionage as well.

Abdul Hamid and Spy Craft

Montgomerie's first explorer was a munshi (translator or educated man) named Abdul Hamid, who had been recommended by the lieutenant governor of Punjab. Initially, Montgomerie planned to use Pathans* to reconnoitre both halves of Turkestan since these were Islamic regions, while using Bhotias and other races to enter Tibet: 'I have always endeavoured to secure the services of men who are actually natives of the countries to be explored, or who had been in the habit of travelling or trading in the said countries.'

---

* Pathans are Afghans living in India; the term is a corrupted form of their actual name, Pashtun.

Montgomerie wanted to use his first recruit to route-survey from Leh, the capital of Ladakh, all the way north into Yarkand. Primarily a trial run, it would test the feasibility of sending out more native explorers in the future. This objective of itself made Hamid's journey a crucial one for the GTS. In addition to this, Montgomerie wanted to use him for another purpose: to determine the geographical position of Yarkand, which previous explorers had fixed only approximately. It sat on the southern arm of the so-called Silk Road, between two other cities, Kashgar and Khotan, around which the population of Chinese Turkestan was clustered.

Hamid was now ready to learn the art of route surveying, and how to utilize the instruments he would need, just as the succession of others after him would be trained. Of course, none dared use a perambulator to measure out distances, as a normal route surveyor might, as this would certainly lead to being caught red-handed. Discovery of their clandestine activities would be the gravest risk the Pundits faced (as do all spies everywhere, and in all ages). At least in Hamid's case, because the people of Chinese Turkestan were mainly Muslim, his journey was somewhat less dangerous.

To estimate the distances Hamid would cover during the months ahead, Montgomerie measured the rate at which he normally walked, and gave him a watch to time the stages of his march. He was also equipped with both pocket and prismatic compasses,* to keep track of his bearings, and was required to jot down his times, number of paces, and route bearings in a small notebook.

* * *

In later years, Montgomerie would come up with many ingenious aids for his charges. To keep better track of the distances they

---

* A pocket compass is for common use, while a prismatic compass, with its extra attachments, can be used for taking bearings of distant objects such as mountains.

covered, he drilled each one, over many months, to walk constantly at their own standard pace whenever possible, regardless of the terrain. Where it became too rugged, they were taught to adjust the route survey accordingly using their timepiece. The faces of the compasses they were issued had either Persian or Hindi letters and numerals, depending on the country being explored; and the field books they were provided were made to look 'un-English', to avoid arousing suspicion.

For the Pundits who would explore Tibet a few years later, Montgomerie devised an ingenious way to keep a careful count of their paces, by giving them a modified string of Tibetan prayer beads. While the normal Buddhist rosary has 108 small beads (recalling the 108 Blessings of Buddha), these had eight removed, and every tenth bead was made slightly larger. As the Pundits marched, they moved a bead after every 100 paces, and a larger one after 1000 strides. Each completed circuit of the full rosary was marked with an additional big bead, representing 10,000 standard paces. Later, the distance of each stage could be determined simply by multiplying the total number counted with the length of their standard pace.

The Pundits recorded this data and other measurements religiously. They also noted any important features such as the topography of the region, plus any special military or political information they could glean. Montgomerie ensured there could be no falsification of the data his explorers gathered, by not showing them how to reduce their observations or map out a route survey. Nor were they taught how to determine latitude or longitude from the measurements they took, or supplied with astronomical tables. This precaution had its own advantages, since it shortened the time it took to train them, and meant those candidates not mathematically minded weren't necessarily excluded from selection. Their data would be processed by GTS staff only after the Pundits returned to headquarters.

The Pundits who explored Tibet after Abdul Hamid didn't write their daily records in a notebook as he had done. Instead, they kept their records hidden in a prayer wheel that Montgomerie gave them. Normally these have a revolving barrel filled with Buddhist prayers, which pilgrims twirl to send their prayers to heaven, bestowing merit on the one who spins the wheel. Although this was sacrilegious, the Pundits used the barrel to store their notes, out of sight from prying eyes.

One can imagine them disguised as pilgrims on the road to Lhasa, twirling their prayer wheels as they marched along the narrow tracks high up in the mountains. They would have repeatedly chanted the sacred Buddhist mantra '*Om mani padmi hom*' (Praise to the jewel in the lotus) to keep fellow travellers from interrupting them, while they quietly counted their paces with a 100-bead rosary in hand. The enormity of this task can be appreciated by considering one of the journeys undertaken by Nain Singh, which covered some 1600 miles. Since the length of his standard stride equated to almost 2000 paces per mile, this required him to diligently count out around 3,200,000 paces during this mission.

In addition to compasses, Montgomerie equipped his Pundits with other survey instrumentation: a clinometer to gauge the slope of roads, a boiling-point thermometer to determine altitude, a sextant for measuring latitude, and a chronometer for approximating longitude. The sextant could be used either during the day to observe the sun, or at night to 'shoot the stars', as the Pundits were trained to recognize the larger stars.

On later expeditions, they would carry even more sophisticated instruments: larger and more accurate sextants, better chronometers and aneroid barometers for measuring altitudes. These instruments had to be concealed carefully, especially from frontier officials who would thoroughly check the baggage of travellers. The smaller items could be hidden in the clothing worn, the compasses secreted in prayer wheels, and thermometers placed in hollowed-out walking sticks. Larger instruments were stashed in secret compartments built into their baggage, which staff at the GTS workshop would construct. As author Jules Stewart summed up: 'Montgomerie devised a bold scheme that must stand as one of history's cleverest pieces of spy craft.'

Each Pundit was given intensive training in the use of these instruments and the techniques of route surveying, which could take up to two years to complete. This was mostly carried out in Dehra Dun, usually by a British officer, and included some medical instruction to go with the small supply of medicines they carried. If necessary, they were even taught a trade, to provide them with a plausible cover story.

In the early years, however, there were many disappointments, and only two or three of the Pundits—from the six to eight men put through training—became first-class observers. The GTS tested their overall proficiency by sending them along routes previously surveyed. As the scheme developed, the best and most experienced amongst them would be used to train new recruits.

The Pundits were typically paid a monthly salary of between 15 and 50 rupees. This was given to them years in advance, as it included travel and living costs, and to provide for their families while they were away. As a precaution against robbers, some Pundits would convert the bulk of their funds into gold, for concealment in hollowed-out walking sticks. Others would take pearls and coral as well, to trade or sell along the way. On their return, they were often rewarded further, depending on the value of their work and for any political or military intelligence they brought back. A few were awarded handsome retirement payments, and the most successful went on to receive high honours from their government and the geographical societies in Europe.

* * *

Returning to Hamid's mission, in May 1863, he arrived at base camp in Kashmir ready to be trained, but his preparation was rushed as Montgomerie was pressed for time. This meant he received only about a month of training, although he was given books on route surveying and how to make astronomical observations, which he carried with him. Luckily he was a quick learner, already familiar with the basics of route surveying and parts of the road he was about to take.

Disguised as a trader, complete with merchandise, Hamid and his two servants joined a caravan of merchants bound for Yarkand, which left Leh in August 1863. He carried a number of basic instruments (and a spare of most items), including a watch, compass, thermometer, notebook and pocket sextant. The journey was a difficult one, and the party suffered from altitude sickness as they crossed the Karakoram and Kunlun ranges; at one stage the trail took them over 15,000 feet for nearly a month. Still, Hamid carefully timed his marches, and took his compass bearings hourly, and his astronomical observations daily.

When the caravan reached Yarkand, he spent the winter there and made observations secretly at night, to determine the city's position and its height above sea level. He noted the extent of Russian activity in Chinese Turkestan, and sketched a general map of the region. After residing in Yarkand for some months, in March the following year Hamid learnt that his activities had aroused the suspicions of the Chinese authorities. He wasted no time in joining a caravan returning to Leh, which followed the same route back.

His whole party successfully traversed the high mountains once again, but after reaching British territory Hamid died suddenly, most probably from eating poisonous rhubarb, which grew wild in the area. As this incident occurred close to a GTS camp where Johnson was stationed, he investigated the death; but although the surveyor suspected foul play, he could not prove anything. He did manage to recover the explorer's notebooks and instruments, though, and passed these on to Montgomerie.

Using Hamid's raw data, Montgomerie produced a route survey of his journey and determined the geographical position of Yarkand. He located the city some 100 miles from the position shown on earlier maps, and this correction has proven to be close to its present-day coordinates, both in terms of latitude and longitude. Although

Montgomerie had not given his explorer a chronometer, which would have allowed the GTS to determine longitude, back in Dehra Dun they were able to estimate this coordinate since Hamid had travelled almost entirely in a north–south direction to Yarkand.

Montgomerie presented the results of Hamid's expedition to the RGS in London soon afterwards, in a paper titled 'On the Geographical Position of Yarkand and Other Places in Central Asia'. The president stated this work was 'of the very highest importance to geographers', which *in some small way* made up for the death of Montgomerie's first native explorer.

Maintaining Secrecy

Even before Hamid completed his journey, Montgomerie had obtained approval to send out more native explorers. Unfortunately, the next attempt again ended in the death of his explorer. This time he was a Pathan of the Native Sappers and Miners whose name is not known. He had been travelling from Peshawar towards Chitral, a region located in India's far north. Just six weeks into his mission, he was murdered after a family blood feud, which the GTS had been unaware of, was settled against him. This was a setback, as another life and another year of training had been wasted, not to mention the trouble Montgomerie had gone through to find this capable and intelligent recruit in the first place. As Montgomerie discovered, the difficulty wasn't due to a shortage of volunteers or their lack of courage, but because of widespread illiteracy amongst the Pathans.

After each Pundit returned from his mission, the GTS was eager to publish any new information emanating from their journeys, including the all-important maps. There can be little doubt that, in doing this, they were primarily driven by a desire to share findings with geographical societies around the world—especially the Royal Geographic Society, which was the world's foremost at the time. An invitation to address this esteemed body, or to publish a paper in its illustrious journal, was highly prized by every explorer and geographer. On the other hand, much of the work undertaken by the Pundits was clearly of a secretive nature, especially within the machinations of the Great Game. Even though just code names were revealed in these publications, and only after they had completed the expeditions, their superiors still risked 'blowing their cover' for future missions, both of the individual Pundit concerned and for the group as a whole.

What is particularly mystifying is why the GTS revealed so many operational details as well: the routes their explorers took; the disguises they used and how they fooled the border guards; the survey instrumentation they carried and how they were concealed; and information about their other aids, such as the 100-bead rosary and the prayer wheel containing their notes. Granted, it was unlikely these publications would find their way into official hands in faraway places like Tibet and Turkestan, but they clearly had the potential of compromising the safety of their charges once they had ventured beyond India's borders.

The British and Indian governments were concerned about the Russians extracting sensitive military and political information from these publications, including descriptions of the terrain and mountain passes along the frontiers, as well as the detailed maps which usually accompanied the text. Members of the Imperial Russian Geographical Society were certainly reading these journals; and Walker readily swapped information with it and other like-minded societies, regardless of nationality. The Russians, too, were surprisingly forthcoming in sharing their material; but the RGS was still frustrated and annoyed by what it considered undue secretiveness by governments. Yet Calcutta went even further, finally imposing a degree of censorship on submissions by the GTS, although only in later years. This was an imposition which the likes of Walker thoroughly detested, and he tried to circumvent it on a few occasions; but it led to the government censuring him, and nearly cost him his career.

Understandably, officers of the GTS wished to receive accolades for their pioneering work, which they rightly deserved.

For his survey of Kashmir, Montgomerie had already won the highest geographical award, as would his replacement Henry Trotter, and so would one of his Pundits. Perhaps Walker, being their commanding officer, coveted a gold medal too, which may go some way towards explaining his actions in being so eager to publish. Nevertheless, the Survey of India was a part of the Military Department, whose prime focus was the defence of the nation, not the dissemination of geographical discoveries—and at times the GTS needed to be reminded of this.

With regard to its less-than-discreet handling of the identity and methods of the Pundits, it mattered little that the GTS saw its charges mainly as *explorers*. By secretly gathering information about foreign lands, in the eyes of these neighbouring governments they were *spies*, and would be treated as such if caught. The Russians, for example, had long suspected the GTS of being a cover organization for conducting espionage. It was clearly the direct responsibility of the GTS to ensure that the safety of its Pundits was not compromised, but through its eagerness to publish it fell short in fulfilling this duty.

Too much should not be made of the Pundits' label of 'spies', however, at least from British India's perspective. Neither were they Great Game players as such, despite Kipling's characterization of the Survey of India's secret agents in *Kim* (although he does capture the mood of this period rather well). This becomes evident when the Pundits' activities are compared with the British officers who crossed India's frontier as part of the Great Game, whose prime objective was the clandestine gathering of intelligence. The raison d'être of the Survey of India was just that, *surveying*; and the GTS sent out native explorers primarily to assist its mapping efforts. In the process they often did collect useful military and political information, which the GTS no doubt passed on to the relevant government departments.

The Indian government recognized this opportunity presented by the Pundits, as is evident from correspondence by the governor-general in council. The written approval Montgomerie received in 1867, following his request for another 5000 rupees to extend the

Trans-Himalayan Exploration, goes on to state: '[Let] it be intimated to each explorer who may be sent out by the Trigonometrical Survey that any important political intelligence he may bring back will receive a separate pecuniary acknowledgement, according to its value, from the Foreign Secretary.' It is probable, too, that the military and foreign departments exerted some degree of influence in deciding when and where the GTS sent its explorers—for example, the sensitive Afghan border region when it was later being delineated.

Montgomerie's Legacy

Montgomerie departed for England in early 1865, suffering from jungle fever, well before Nain Singh had completed his first mission. His indefatigable deputy, William Johnson, resigned from the GTS soon afterwards. Johnson left feeling disappointed at not having received more recognition from the government for his daring journey to Khotan. He also felt hard done by after being passed over as Montgomerie's successor in Kashmir, in favour of a recently arrived junior officer, despite his obvious merit. But Company rules were clear on this point, stating no civilian, however senior, could have charge over military officers. Johnson's background had also been a distinct handicap: to begin with, although his parents were English, he was native-born. He wasn't considered 'a proper gentleman', having been educated in India rather than back in England, probably due to the poor financial situation of his parents.

A long-running and acrimonious disagreement with Walker, after his foray into Chinese Turkestan, may have ended Johnson's prospects within the GTS; Walker had patronizingly written that he 'had neither the benefit of a liberal education, nor the ability to rise above the disadvantage of his position'. On the latter point at least, Johnson would prove him wrong. He later took up a lucrative offer, that paid three times his GTS salary, from the maharaja of Kashmir to become the governor of Ladakh, where he was well loved and served the people for many years. Unfortunately, he would ultimately fall foul to the intrigues of the maharaja's court, where he was thought to have been deliberately poisoned and died, at age fifty-five.

Montgomerie had often praised the work of his second-in-command, and on his recommendation the RGS had presented him with a gold watch. He wrote of Johnson: 'A surveyor and explorer from boyhood. As a mountaineer . . . always conspicuous. No height, no amount of snow or ice was sufficient to deter him if an ascent was necessary.'

James Walker wouldn't leave the GTS until 1883, after twenty-two years at its helm and having risen to the rank of general. He would be justly praised for his role in the GTS and the success of its Pundits. However, it was only after his departure, when he was no longer in a position to flout its censorship rules, that the government relaxed its restrictions around the publication of the Pundits' exploration efforts.

Like Johnson, Montgomerie's career with the GTS was cut short. After spending four years in England, he returned in 1869, now holding the rank of major. He was appointed deputy of the GTS under Walker, and officially put in charge of the native explorers. During his remaining years in India, he nurtured his Pundits, improved their training, and equipped them with better and smaller survey instrumentation that could be concealed even more cleverly. Unfortunately, his health did not improve sufficiently, and in 1873 Montgomerie returned home for good. Sadly, he failed to recover, and died five years later at the relatively young age of forty-seven, leaving behind a widow and three children. He had achieved international renown as a cartographer and recipient of the RGS's highest award, even before conceiving the idea of using native explorers. His work in launching the Pundits, though, will remain Colonel Montgomerie's most lasting contribution to exploration and mapping in Asia.

A Tally of the Pundits

There were many brave Indians who served as native explorers, taking the field for the GTS between 1863, when Hamid first travelled to

Yarkand, and their last exploration effort in 1899.* Records give the names of twenty-one Pundits, although this may exclude some that were lesser known and others who went unrecorded. Over this period, they undertook more than fifty explorations, mostly working individually, or with fellow Pundits on occasions.

Other than one notable exception, these men were not well educated or well-to-do; the exception was Sarat Chandra Das (code-named S.C.D.). He was a Bengali scholar of Tibetan language and culture who published widely (and is thought to be Kipling's inspiration for the character Hurree Babu in *Kim*).

The Pundits crossed India's northern frontiers many times to explore large portions of Central Asia and Tibet, almost entirely on foot. They helped the GTS solve many riddles surrounding the region's physical geography and map its topography, while spying for the British Raj at the same time. By any measure, their journeys were remarkable and taken at considerable personal risk, as discovery meant almost certain death.

In the next three chapters, the stories of some of the more notable Pundits will be told. For the sake of clarity, this will be related by region, rather than chronologically, first across the Northwest Frontier of India and in Chinese Turkestan, followed by Tibet and finally the land cradling the Tsangpo and Brahmaputra rivers, as we traverse vast stretches of the Asian continent.

---

* An extensive list of the Pundits and their forerunners has been detailed chronologically by Michael Ward in the *Alpine Journal* (vol. 103, 1998). Note: his entry for 1858 is incorrect; Bir and Deb Singh were with Moorcroft in 1812.

6

Northwest Frontier and Chinese Turkestan

The Pundits who explored beyond the Northwest Frontier of India and in Chinese Turkestan did so within the context of the Great Game, which had reached a decisive stage by the late 1860s. A few years earlier, Russia had taken the prized city of Tashkent and was set to advance across Western Turkestan; while Afghanistan continued to be a thorn in the side of Britain. Following the First Afghan War, many issues still festered, and a second war would be fought between the neighbours within a decade. Diplomatic negotiations between London and St Petersburg regarding Afghanistan's uncertain northern border would soon commence, eventually leading to the Oxus River being set as the Russo-Afghan boundary. Further east, the first Englishmen had recently penetrated the domain of the rebel ruler Yakub Beg in Chinese Turkestan, alerting Britain to the possibility of Russian influence there, and India's vulnerability from this little-understood flank.

Once Montgomerie had returned to India and taken charge of the Pundits, his intention was 'to extend the exploration northward into that great blank between the Himalayas, Russia and China proper', as he explained in a letter to the RGS. Soon, the GTS would send a number of Muslim native explorers into this blank, including two with the code names of the Mirza and the Havildar. Their journeys (plus the work of the future Forsyth Mission) will be followed here, to give a sense of the challenges faced by these Pundits and their accomplishments in these faraway Islamic regions.

Mirza Shuja (The Mirza)

Born around 1822 in his mother's country, Persia, Mirza Shuja's father was a Turkish trader from Afghanistan. He had come to be noticed by the British while serving as a lad under Lieutenant Eldred Pottinger in 1837, during the siege of Herat. When that was over, Pottinger took him to Kabul where the Mirza was of service to the British, who taught him English, adding to his Persian and Pushtu (the language of Pathans).

A decade later, Walker employed the Mirza as a munshi, and then as a stand-in surveyor when he couldn't find qualified men while conducting a military survey around Peshawar. The Mirza worked with his survey in a limited capacity for three years and 'rendered valuable assistance' according to Walker, who kept him on for a further two years until the Indian Mutiny. Speaking about the local tribesmen, Walker pointed out: 'To go into their country excepting by force is never possible for a European, and is at all times dangerous for a native.' He asked the Mirza to explore the valleys with a compass and locate the main villages in the region, while the survey team mapped the surrounding peaks. The other task entrusted to him was persuading the belligerent hill tribes around Peshawar to allow their territory to be surveyed, and Walker again had reason to praise the Mirza's efforts. During this time, he received further basic training in surveying, which would stand him in good stead years later with the GTS.

The Mirza wouldn't join the Pundits until 1867, as he first took up a post teaching English to Dost Mohammed's sons in Kabul. When the emir died in 1863, after regaining his throne following the First Afghan War, the Mirza continued this service for the third son and successor Sher Ali. This work was interrupted when the new ruler was temporarily forced from the capital, following a bitter rivalry for the throne with his brother. While the Mirza was there, he used the opportunity to secretly provide a stream of intelligence back to the British in Peshawar; but Sher Ali's departure from Kabul put the Mirza out of work, forcing him to return to India. At this point the GTS promptly rehired him, since Montgomerie had identified him as a first-class candidate some years earlier. At Dehra Dun, the Mirza underwent refresher training, before he was sent out on his first mission. He would be the first of the Pundits to explore extensively across the Northwest Frontier, before entering Chinese Turkestan.

The Mirza started out from Peshawar in the autumn of 1867, and headed for the Badakhshan region in northeastern Afghanistan. This area is renowned for its lapis lazuli, which has been mined since antiquity and used to make much-prized jewellery, or turned into the finest and most expensive of all blue pigments. His objective was to explore the upper Oxus and Pamirs, and then the route to Kashgar, before returning home.

Just as he made ready to start out, the Mirza became involved in a political wrangle that erupted between the GTS and the Foreign Department. This incident is insightful as it shows not only the lack of coordination between the two departments, but also how the Pundits generated interest at the highest levels of the Indian government. When the lieutenant governor of Punjab, who oversaw territory the Mirza would pass through, belatedly learnt of the proposed journey he complained to the Foreign Department, pointing out the dangers the Mirza faced if he was discovered. The viceroy, Lord Lawrence, was finally dragged into the dispute and threatened to call a halt to the mission. As a strong proponent of masterly inactivity, he opposed British officers exploring beyond India's border, for reasons he had outlined two years earlier: 'In the first place, we send them to certain destruction . . . If they lose their lives we cannot avenge their deaths, and so lose credit.' Now, he questioned the use of a native explorer crossing into foreign lands. When Walker pointed out that the Mirza had already departed and was 'beyond recall', the lieutenant governor reluctantly agreed to his proceeding, but suggested a good cover story be established for future explorers. At this point the viceroy made it clear this suggestion be 'rigidly attended to', and no native explorers were to be sent out in future without 'special sanction'.

The Mirza had his own problems to contend with, the crucial one being that winter was already settling in. This meant the passes through the Hindu Kush, which allowed for the most direct route north to Badakhshan by way of Chitral, were closed due to heavy snow. Making four separate attempts to cross into Afghanistan, he was forced to turn back each time. Either the country was in too unsettled a state due to the civil war raging there, or the people in the area were too hostile to enter it safely. To make matters worse, he found the other passes closed as well, even as far south as the Bolan. In desperation, he continued his march still further down the Indus, before using the Mala Pass to enter the town of Kalat in Baluchistan. Here he bought two donkeys, and hired a guide to take him back north into the city of Kandahar. The journey wasn't without its dangers, especially when he was denounced as a spy at one point, after some of his baggage and documents were captured, but he managed to talk his way out.

From Kandahar, the Mirza was able to join Sher Ali's army marching north to retake Kabul. He used the opportunity to supply the British with valuable information about this army and, later, when they arrived there, about the overall political situation in Afghanistan. He entered the capital in June 1868, having spent the best part of a year getting there because of his long detour south. Here, he was welcomed back by Sher Ali, once his old student, who had now regained the throne. He found the city still bearing the scars of the First Afghan War and the reprisals the British Army had wrought afterwards.

The Mirza left Kabul in October, which meant he once again had to face the hazards of winter travel through the mountains. He crossed the Hindu Kush and trekked northwest to Bamiyan where, like Moorcroft, he marvelled at the magnificent Buddha statues carved into the rock face. Nearing the city of Kulm-Tashkurgan, close to the Afghan border just south of the Oxus, bandits ambushed and robbed his caravan, wounding two of his party and making off with most of their goods. Further on, the Mirza experienced another unsettling incident when a stranger joined their caravan claiming to be a European. The man's perfectly spoken Persian made the Mirza suspect he was being interrogated to determine the true nature of his mission. When he stuck to his story, that he was a merchant travelling to Kashgar to trade, the stranger left and did not return.

From Kulm-Tashkurgan, the Mirza travelled eastwards through heavy snowfalls to arrive in Faizabad, the main town of Badakhshan, where he found the caravanserais full of pitiful Chitrali slave girls destined to be traded for horses. By this stage his servants were so worn out that they were becoming mutinous; one even denounced him as a British spy, and the Mirza had to bribe him to remain silent. They were reluctant to go on after hearing frightful stories of what awaited them in the Pamirs, but the Mirza managed to hold his group together. After hiring new guides, they set off again, and by early January his small party reached the Oxus, at the entrance to Wakhan Valley.

A few days later, they arrived at the main divide of this long and strategic river. Since Montgomerie hadn't specified which branch of the Oxus he was to take, the Mirza decided to pursue the southern one as it looked the bigger of the two. This turned out to be fortuitous, as a British officer, Lieutenant John Wood, had already explored the upper tributary in 1838 (for which he was awarded the RGS's gold medal).* Wood had been misled by his guides into thinking this branch, emanating higher up in the Pamirs from Lake Zorkul, was the source of the Oxus he so eagerly sought, and which he then erroneously laid claim to discovering. The Mirza's findings, upon taking the lower branch, would later allow Montgomerie to

---

* He had worked with Burnes on the Indus River survey, then accompanied him to Kabul in 1836, before exploring up the Oxus on a separate mission.

map the drainage of the headwaters of the Oxus. He could verify the Mirza's survey as far as the main divide by comparing this journey with Wood's and, because their routes were nearly identical to this point, he would find his native explorer's observations agreeing closely with the lieutenant's.

The Mirza now moved up the Wakhan for the most arduous part of his journey towards Chinese Turkestan, but only after he was forced to bribe the ruler and his officials to let his caravan pass. This section of the march would take twelve days, of which eight were beyond the last settlement. The river was frozen solid, allowing it to be crossed and recrossed easily, making winter the best time for caravans to take this torturous route through Badakhshan. Winter also forced the Kirghiz bandits, who were a constant threat, to leave the area as they moved their herds further afield to find pasture. Another advantage was that the meat carried by the Mirza's caravan remained frozen, ensuring they didn't run short of food. But both man and beast alike were severely tested, having to endure sub-zero temperatures and piercing winds.

Once they had left the last village behind, the men tried to keep warm at night huddled around small fires, but often these would be extinguished by heavy snowfall when they were forced to camp out in the open. The Mirza would later describe how, on some mornings, 'the men literally rose out of a bed of snow'. They constantly battled altitude sickness; and when their horses became sluggish from shortness of breath, they were relieved in the usual way practised here, with the use of a long dagger to bleed the animals by the nose. Even in the face of these hardships, the Mirza faithfully continued his route survey, although at times he had to ask his men to assist him in counting out the paces.

They finally reached the watershed of the Pamirs, where a drop of rain or snowflake falling on the western side eventually drains into Western Turkestan and the Aral Sea; whereas if it falls on the eastern slopes, it flows down into Chinese Turkestan, and would one day probably dry up somewhere in the Taklamakan Desert. The Mirza paid off the men from Wakhan here as they turned back for home, while the rest of his party entered the important frontier town of Tashkurgan (not to be confused with Kulm-Tashkurgan). Standing close to 11,000 feet above sea level, it commanded the whole area and the caravan trails which crossed it.

A Tajik from Khokand named Yakub Beg, who claimed to be a descendant of Tamerlane, ruled this town at the time, as well as most of Eastern Turkestan. This half of Turkestan is boxed in on three sides by mountain ranges with peaks exceeding 20,000 feet, and on the fourth side by the Gobi Desert to the east. In the early 1860s, following a general revolt against their Chinese rulers, this Muslim strongman had seized the province and made Kashgar the capital of his new domain which he named Kashgaria. During the rebellion, Yakub Beg besieged the Chinese garrison for over a year, but rather than give themselves up, its leaders chose to take their own lives by blowing up the fort and all in it. Although, reportedly, they did so only after spitting in Peking's direction, from where the help they desperately sought never arrived.

The new governor of Tashkurgan, Yakub Beg's brother, was immediately suspicious of the Mirza and interrogated him closely, before sending him under armed escort to Kashgar. The Mirza was able to prevent his baggage being searched by offering the governor gifts, and mentioning he was an associate of the chief of Yakub Beg's artillery. Fortunately for the Mirza, the Kirghiz chief and men who guarded him rode on ahead, allowing him to continue his survey unhindered. He did have one anxious moment, though, when a Kirghiz spotted him taking bearings with a prismatic compass, and reported him. When the chief challenged the Mirza, he switched it with a cheap *Kibla nama*—a compass which points in the direction Muslims face during prayer, Mecca. The workings of this simple instrument so astounded the chief that he begged to keep it as a present.

The ground they covered between the Pamirs and Yarkand was practically unknown to Europeans, which meant the Mirza's route survey would later help the GTS fill in the map of this desolate area.

One mountain pass along the way was so difficult to cross that the Mirza described it as 'fit only for goats', and its steepness compelled them to descend crawling on all fours through the snow. Thankfully, they found the fertile valley on the other side so lush and beautiful it buoyed the Mirza's party, putting an end to their grumbling as they finally left the cold mountains behind them.

In a few days, they arrived in the ancient city of Kashgar, strategically located on the old Silk Road as the furthest western entry and exit point of Eastern Turkestan. Caravans had passed through this famed oasis for centuries as they plied their way between 'Cathay' and Europe, until ships eventually replaced most of the overland trade. Marco Polo was one of the few Europeans to have visited this city and, more recently, Adolf Schlagintweit had lost his head here.

The Mirza now met his old acquaintance, an Indian jemadar (lieutenant) who had risen through the ranks to command Yakub Beg's artillery. At first, he did not want to acknowledge the Mirza, for fear of others finding out about his ordinary beginnings as a gunner with the Sikh Army. The jemadar was wary of the Mirza and examined his baggage carefully, taking whatever he fancied, before consigning him to miserable quarters while awaiting a meeting with the ruler of Kashgaria.

The Mirza had good reason to be nervous as he was brought before Yakub Beg the next day. Although the latter was religious and bore the title Atalik Ghazi (Champion Father), he was known to have a violent temper and dispense quick, rough justice. A distrustful ruler with a large secret police, he was detested by his people who lived under crippling oppression. The Mirza was relieved when Yakub Beg received him courteously, although he had many questions for him. He was quizzed again during their other meetings, but each time the Mirza was able to avoid being found out. Once, he felt a trap was being set, when he was shown a sextant and compass before being asked to explain how they worked, but he pretended to have no knowledge of these instruments.

There were heightened concerns in the Atalik Ghazi's court just then, due to the unexpected arrival of two other foreigners. They had reached the capital separately, a month on either side of the Mirza's entry in early February 1869, and were the first Englishmen to visit Chinese Turkestan.

The first to arrive was Robert Shaw, a tea planter from the Himalayan foothills in India, who had come looking for trade opportunities, especially for his crop. Following the revolt and expulsion of the Chinese from the region, tea supplies from China had been cut off, making this staple drink of Asia scarce. Shaw was equally driven by a desire for exploration and, on his return, would be rewarded with political appointments in the region. This would allow him to feed his pioneering spirit, even as he quickly compiled a book of the local language.

The second man was an ex-army officer and adventurer, George Hayward, whom the RGS had sponsored to explore the area. Both he and Shaw had entered Eastern Turkestan against their government's wishes, although there was a suspicion that Hayward's unstated objective was to spy out the passes and gather intelligence. As it turned out, his next adventure would cost him his life. While exploring the region the following year, he was waylaid and killed across the border in the district of Yasin. His violent end was later romanticized by Sir Henry Newbolt's epic poem *He Fell among Thieves*.

Yakub Beg effectively imprisoned all three men for a time, within the confines of the new part of the city. He didn't believe their protestations that they were travelling independently of each other, instead suspecting all were spies; and each one now had good reason to fear for his life. Without revealing he was working for the GTS, the Mirza approached Shaw by way of a note written in English, which he had his servant deliver. He requested the loan of a watch and wanted to know the exact date by the European calendar—as this information would be essential for the GTS later, to determine the city's geographical position from his sextant readings (after consulting a nautical almanac for that year). But Shaw was in a precarious position himself and, wary the Atalik Ghazi may be using the Mirza to entrap him, would not render any assistance. Disappointed, the Mirza didn't trouble him further, or Hayward for that matter.

During his stay in Kashgar, which lasted over four months, the Mirza succeeded in gathering information about all manner of things, more so than either Shaw or Hayward were able to. He found Yakub Beg and his court officials to be mostly uneducated. Their illiteracy meant that the government was unable to keep financial records, so they collected taxes in a haphazard manner, sowing much dissent amongst their people. The Mirza made notes about the city, its population, and the various ethnicities and their customs. By bribing his guards, he even visited the old part of city, which was off limits to all three travellers, but this made the jemadar angry when he learnt about it.

The Mirza estimated the size of Yakub Beg's army, which he put at 20,000-strong plus a similar number of reservists from the nearby Kirghiz hordes; they were supported by seventy artillery pieces. He made notes about the army's composition, training and readiness. By sending a friend to reconnoitre on his behalf, the Mirza even managed to gather intelligence about the closest Russian frontier posts and military forts, including the number of men and guns stationed at each.

When both Shaw and Hayward were eventually allowed to leave Kashgar in April, the Mirza, who was running low on funds by now, borrowed money and made ready to return too. He began fearing the worst, though, when the jemadar continually frustrated his departure, and only relented when he threatened to take his case to Yakub Beg directly. The Atalik Ghazi was gracious in bidding the Mirza farewell, giving him a dress of honour and gold dust worth 60 rupees to buy a horse for his return journey. The Mirza finally left Kashgar, passed through Yarkand, and headed directly south, returning to Leh in August 1869. His survey had taken him nearly two years, during which time he had diligently paced out around 2200 miles across some of the most challenging terrain in Central Asia.

Back in Dehra Dun, Montgomerie evaluated the Mirza's observations and found them to be remarkably accurate, especially given the difficult conditions he had encountered; other European explorers would later confirm his work. He had route-surveyed 18,000 square miles of unexplored territory and confirmed the position of Yarkand, which Montgomerie had previously fixed based on Abdul Hamid's journey. In addition to this, the Mirza's observations helped the GTS reset the position of Kashgar made by earlier European travellers.

His survey from Kabul to Kashgar and then on to Yarkand, covering just over 1000 miles, was particularly important. Before this time, little had been known of the last 350 miles between these key cities of Chinese Turkestan. Their relative positions on the map were altered as a result of the information the Mirza brought back, and helped explain why Marco Polo had visited Kashgar *before* Yarkand on his travels. By demonstrating that Faizabad was almost twice the distance from Kashgar than previously thought, the Mirza's journey also explained why the Venetian traveller, as well as Benedict de Goes and others, had taken so long to cross the Pamirs from Western to Eastern Turkestan.

From the Mirza's observations, the GTS could demonstrate that this range was a continuation of the Himalayan chain. This fact would have comforted the military chiefs in Calcutta, as it implied there was no easy invasion route through these mountains into India. His description of the Pamir watershed contained hydrographical information sought after by geographers. He managed to fix the height of over two dozen places through boiling-point readings, as well as taking twice as many latitudinal readings with his sextant, at more than a dozen locations.

Montgomerie would spell out these findings in his 'Report of the Mirza's Exploration from Caubul to Kashgar', which was published in the annual *Journal of the Royal Geographic Society*. It was readily available to the general public, less than two years after the Mirza's return. Surprisingly, the report included details of the military intelligence garnered, even while the GTS was sending other Pundits into this sensitive region.

In an indirect way, Shaw and Hayward finally did render the Mirza some assistance: being British, their observations added credibility to the native explorer's efforts. This is evident from the statement by the famous orientalist and pioneer scholar of Marco Polo's travels, Colonel Henry Yule:

> Had we not been prepared for his results by the labour of Mahomed Hamid [Abdul Hamid], corroborated by Messrs. Shaw and Hayward, which showed how erroneous were the longitudes heretofore assigned to the great cities of Eastern Turkestan, there can be little doubt that the accuracy of the Mirza's work would have been subject to general misgiving.

Shaw and Hayward would each go on to win a gold medal from the RGS for their exploration efforts in Chinese Turkestan. The Mirza, whose journey had covered far more territory and was at least as valuable to geographers, received no such reward, other than the GTS and RGS praising him for his 'pluck and endurance'.

A few years after his return to India, the Mirza was slain in his sleep by his guides, somewhere on the road to Bokhara while undertaking a second mission for the GTS. Montgomerie had recently returned to England, and wrote to Walker on hearing about it: 'I shall be very sorry if the old fellow has been murdered, and you must see if you can get something done for his family if true.'

Hyder Shah (The Havildar)

Unlike the Mizra, the Havildar's code name originated from his rank: he was a havildar (sergeant) in the Bengal Sappers and Miners. His real name was Hyder Shah, and he was a Pathan from Peshawar who had been recommended to the GTS by his commander. Montgomerie wanted him to explore north from his hometown into Swat, Dir, Chitral, and then across the Hindu Kush into Badakhshan. This direct route through the mountains was a possible invasion route into India, and the path that the Mirza had originally planned to take before he had been foiled by winter. This time Montgomerie made sure his explorer was trained and ready to start in August, while the passes were still open.

The Havildar took as his assistant another Pathan named Ata Mahomed, who would soon join the ranks of the Pundits and be assigned the code name of the Mullah. In 1870, accompanied by a few servants, they crossed the Malakand Pass into the stunning Swat Valley. However, the natural beauty of this region was not matched by the welcome outsiders received from its many lawless tribes. Walker had been forced to give up his trigonometrical survey of the area twenty years earlier, after his camp was continually shot at by snipers.

The party marched as ordinary travellers as far as the town of Dir, with the Havildar using a cover story of wishing to buy hunting falcons from Chitral, which were highly prized in the Punjab. They felt particularly vulnerable from Dir to Chitral, as Kafir bandits were known to infest this road. The Kafirs were an unusual people, in that they stood out as non-Muslims in a devoutly Islamic country. Legend had it, incorrectly, that they were descendants from the remnants of Alexander the Great's army after his failed invasion of India. Their corner, Kafiristan (Land of the Heathens), lay just to the west of Chitral; and the surrounding Muslim tribes, who hated these 'non-believers', took them for slaves whenever they could.* The Kafirs, for their part, raided their neighbours and regularly attacked

---

*   In 1896, the emir of Afghanistan would subjugate the region and force the Kafirs to convert to Islam, renaming the province Nuristan (Land of the Enlightened).

passing caravans; the road to Chitral was littered with hundreds of flags marking the graves of unfortunate travellers.

Only large caravans braved this route, but when the Havildar arrived in Dir he learnt the last one had already left. By presenting the local chief with a gold-laced scarf and begging for his assistance, the Havildar secured an armed escort of twenty-five men to accompany them but, even then, Kafir bandits persistently troubled them at night. This whole region was far from wealthy, and Chitral was a particularly poor and impoverished province. Years later, a British officer would describe the situation: 'Food is so scarce that a fat man has never yet been seen in the country . . . and the most effective form of bribes is a full meal.'

When he heard of the Havildar's arrival in Chitral, the provincial chief, Aman-i-Mulk, summoned him to a durbar together with Mir Walli, the local chief of neighbouring Yasin. The Havildar had heard rumours of the Mir ordering his men to rob and kill George Hayward (also leading to the death of seven of his eight servants). When he asked the Mir about this, the latter readily admitted to it, claiming Hayward had abused and insulted him. Although Aman-i-Mulk had denounced the killings, he was known to be a deceitful man, and it was strongly rumoured that it was he, in fact, who had ordered the ambush in Yasin, as his renewed friendship with Mir Walli seemed to imply.

Fearing he would not leave the durbar alive, the Havildar carried a loaded revolver hidden in his pocket, ready to kill the two chiefs if it came to that. As it turned out, they accepted his explanation of travelling north into Bokhara to recover money owed to him. They warned him, though, that he would not be able to cross the Oxus into that khanate, as the road had been closed on Sher Ali's orders.

The Havildar's party left Chitral in early September and arrived in Faizabad twenty days later, following an arduous crossing of the 17,000-foot Nuksan Pass, all the more difficult as this was his first experience marching in mountain snow. The road on the crest was cut through solid ice up to a depth of 12 feet, and they encountered large crevices which had to be avoided with extreme care. Although the Havildar did not realize the significance of these fissures in the ice at the time, his would be the first report of a glacier existing in the Hindu Kush.

When he arrived in Faizabad, the Havildar found the road across the Oxus to Bokhara closed, just as he had been advised. After staying in the town for a month, he had no option but to turn for home. Fortunately, he was able to join Mir Walli's caravan, which was also returning to Chitral, and provided his party much-needed protection from the bandits. As snow had already closed the Nuksan, they returned via the Dorah Pass a little further west; but without two of the Havildar's servants, who deserted him rather than face another crossing of the Hindu Kush. Although this pass was lower in comparison, he found the going even tougher, and would later relate that he had 'never in his life experienced such hardship'.

Back in Chitral, Aman-i-Mulk confronted the Havildar about rumours circulating that he was in the pay of the British, but he refuted this. Montgomerie later explained: 'his undaunted bearing on his return journey, when the chief had guessed his secret, was the means of preventing himself and party from being sold into slavery, or possibly from a worse fate . . .'

The Havildar returned safely to Peshawar in mid-December, after four months on the road. Back in Dehra Dun, Montgomerie was able to connect his route survey with the Mirza's, because at one point they had passed through the same town. This meant that for the first time, the GTS had a continuous route survey from Peshawar to the Hindu Kush, a distance of almost 300 miles. The Havildar had explored 13,000 square miles of new territory, and helped fix the height and position of Chitral and other important places. He also returned with information about the passes across the Hindu Kush, which the Military Department would find particularly valuable. Montgomerie's full report, 'A Havildar's Journey through Chitral to Faizabad in 1870', was published in the *Journal of the Royal Geographic Society* two years later.

After his first successful mission, the Havildar would complete two more for the GTS in the next five years. There is no account of the second, which took him from Kabul to Bokhara, as Walker believed he had begun falsifying some of his observations. Montgomerie, too, later admitted having some doubts about this trip, commenting: 'It is the Pathan blood coming out. It is very annoying, for otherwise the man is very satisfactory.' The issue must have been resolved satisfactorily, since Montgomerie sent him on a third and final mission in 1873.

The Havildar set out from Peshawar in September, with the aim of surveying the unexplored sections of the Oxus. There were six in his party including a corporal of the Sappers and Miners, and the Mullah; the latter broke off once they crossed into Afghanistan, to undertake a separate mission for the GTS (the first of three, spanning five years). They travelled disguised as cloth merchants, but this time the Havildar donned the disguise of a servant attending to the corporal. First, they made their way to Kabul, crossing the main range of the Hindu Kush using the Sarolang Pass, before reaching Faizabad two months later. After a delay of some six months here, waiting for the road north to become passable, they crossed the Oxus on a raft of inflated skins.

The Havildar explored along the deep river valley travelling south towards Ishkashim, where the Oxus turns abruptly to make its big swing north. The trail became precarious here as it wound its way through narrow defiles. There were times when his party had to make their way along ropes suspended from iron pegs driven into the cliff face with the river thundering below, when a lost foothold would have surely meant death.

Despite several attempts, the Havildar could not reach Ishkashim, which is unfortunate as it would have connected his survey with the Mirza's and completed the route map of the upper Oxus. Even so, before returning home, the Havildar worked west along the river to Kulm-Tashkurgan, extending the total distance of his route survey to nearly 800 miles. In doing so, he solved a puzzle that had previously confounded geographers: identifying that the Surkhob and Vahksh rivers were, in fact, one and the same; and showing that this major tributary joined the Oxus 80 miles further downstream than was believed at the time.

The Havildar's findings were beneficial not only to geographers, but also had a bearing on the Great Game, as Anglo-Russian efforts were already underway to mark out Afghanistan's northern border. He, together with a few other Pundits, would help shed more light on the geography and people of this little-known region, at a time when much was at stake. Russia had its surveyors working in this area along the northern bank of the Oxus, and the positions they fixed for two towns, using sophisticated instrumentation, were found to match closely with the Havildar's observations.

Little is known about the Havildar following his return to India, except that he died of cholera in the Afghan city of Jalalabad in 1879. His short obituary in the *Proceedings of the Royal Geographic Society* observed: 'Hyder Shah's services to geography are most conspicuous . . . They undoubtedly call for some public recognition of their value.' Although no such acknowledgement followed, at least today there is increasing recognition of his accomplishments as an explorer, as well as the efforts of some of the less well-known Pundits.

The Forsyth Mission

The second Forsyth Mission to Chinese Turkestan in 1873 was the one occasion when a group of Pundits was attached to a British diplomatic mission; it was also notable for allowing Hindu Pundits to explore in predominantly Islamic regions. Douglas Forsyth, a commissioner with the Punjab government, headed the mission, which included six European military officers and scientists, plus 350 other men and 550 baggage animals. The geographer for his large party was Captain Henry Trotter, who had succeeded Montgomerie as the GTS officer in charge of native explorers.

Trotter took with him four Pundits from the Singh family, as well as two assistants and a trained sub-surveyor. The last member was Abdul Subhan from the Topographical Survey, who effectively took on the role of a Pundit, and was code-named the Munshi. From the Singh family came Nain Singh (code-named the Pundit), his brother Kalian Singh (G.K.), his first cousin Kishen Singh (A.K.), and Jusmal Singh. For the sake of clarity, of the Hindu Pundits, only Nain Singh will be referred to by his code name, as those of the others were generally made up by just letters. These were usually derived by reversing the first and last sounds from their names: thus Kalian SinGh became G.K.; while Kishen Singh, who was also known as KrishnA, became A.K.*

Forsyth's first mission to Chinese Turkestan, undertaken three years earlier, had been a smaller one, but had soon fizzled out, with his party getting only as far as Yarkand. It came about following a request from Yakub Beg, after he had sent an envoy to India to establish diplomatic ties. The envoy requested a reciprocal visit by a British officer, who was expected to return with him to meet the Atalik Ghazi. Forsyth was chosen, and Robert Shaw volunteered to accompany his mission. On this occasion, no Pundit joined them, as Yakub Beg's envoy was reluctant to let Nain Singh into Chinese Turkestan when it became known he was a 'surveyor'.

As it turned out, after they crossed the border into Yarkand, Forsyth was told the Atalik Ghazi was not available for talks as he was campaigning 600 miles to the east, putting down a rebellion. At this point the mission hurriedly returned, rather than risk being trapped on the wrong side of the mountains for the duration of winter, since the passes would soon be closed by snow.

The whole political situation in Chinese Turkestan had altered with Yakub Beg's rise to power, and this had a bearing on India's defence—although, realistically, the Karakorams formed a formidable barrier to any serious invasion attempt. Nevertheless, Britain still feared the possibility of Russia annexing this region,

---

* Jusmal Singh's code name is not known, and his name does not appear in Michael Ward's list of the Pundits.

with some justification, as it had already gobbled up large tracts of Western Turkestan.

Earlier, the Atalik Ghazi had received a commercial mission from Russia and signed a treaty with them, which made Britain decidedly nervous about Tsar Alexander II extending his influence into this half of Turkestan as well. As a minimum, India needed Kashgaria to remain a friendly buffer state, although it was eager to develop stronger commercial ties with its northern neighbour if possible. Shaw's recent visit there had highlighted the opportunity for increased trade, even though the physical barrier posed by the Karakorams limited the extent to which this would be possible. The viceroy's expectation was that Forsyth's second attempt would result in British India gaining further political influence with Yakub Beg, and lead to the signing of a commercial agreement.

This mission presented the GTS with a golden opportunity to explore and map the topography between Afghanistan and the two halves of Turkestan, high up in the Pamirs. It could also open the way to discovering more about the lesser-known parts of Chinese Turkestan, especially those areas east of Kashgar. The oasis settlements here stretch for some 700 miles, dotted along the rim of the Taklamakan, a desert almost the size of Germany. They are often hidden by a haze of *loess*—dust particles so fine they remain suspended in the air for long periods, until the wind or rain finally disperses them. This gives rise to mirages, which for centuries have enticed passing caravans into the depths of the desert, requiring travellers to remain close together at all times and tie bells around the necks of their animals. The shifting sands of the Taklamakan are known to have swallowed up hundreds of towns in the past; a few have been recently rediscovered, but many others lie waiting to be uncovered. It is one of the harshest places in the world, as one translation of its name attests: None who enter, return.

This region hadn't been explored by Europeans since Benedict de Goes in 1604—when the Jesuit had travelled overland from India into China, and identified the latter as the country known to the

Middle Ages as Cathay. Trotter was optimistic of carrying out a trigonometrical survey as far north as possible, and to this end his team packed small theodolites amongst the equipment they carried.

Forsyth's mission started out from Leh late in the summer of 1873, and was away for more than a year. They travelled across the Karakorams towards the town of Shahidula, located close to the Indian border. A summer start had its disadvantages, though, as the riverbeds, which had little water in winter, now became raging torrents making them difficult to ford, and the risk from avalanches increased in warmer weather.

The surveyors soon encountered bleak weather that made triangulation work near impossible. A frustrated Trotter would later describe in his report how, nine times out of ten, they would struggle up a high mountain only to find that snow and cloud had entirely obscured their vision of other peaks. Another challenge was to keep up with the main party, who set their own rate of advance. These problems meant Trotter's team could only carry out a limited amount of mapping with theodolites; in the end they abandoned these efforts in favour of topographical surveying using plane tables. Moreover, the extreme temperatures made their pocket chronometers unreliable, compelling Trotter to rely on the pacing of his Pundits to estimate longitude. He had them working in pairs, relieving each other where possible. As the days got shorter, it meant having to deal with one other imperative: the Pundits had to complete each stage before darkness overtook them, or face having their days' work nullified.

The mission proceeded in two main groups along separate routes, with Trotter's surveyors and the Pundits periodically splitting off to explore other trails. In this way, they were able to map the routes across the mountains 'with an amount of accuracy not hitherto attained', as Trotter would later submit. Still, he was frustrated and disappointed in not achieving a good deal more, which was largely due to the inherent difficulty of surveying at such high altitudes. At one point, Trotter travelled for twenty-three days continuously above 15,000 feet, and on four consecutive nights their camp had to be pitched over 17,000 feet. The temperature seldom rose above freezing point during the day, and fell as low as –26 degrees Fahrenheit (–32 degrees Celsius) after dark. Taking astronomical observations during the night was testing to say the least, as the blood would stop circulating in their hands, while the ink in pens and the oil in lamps would freeze. The exertions from this high-altitude work would ultimately cost one of Forsyth's officers his life: Dr Stoliczka, the geologist in the team, died after he had recrossed the mountains, just before making it back to India.

Once past Shahidula, upon entering Yakub Beg's domain, Forsyth placed restrictions on Trotter's team to ensure their survey work would not compromise the overall mission. He did not wish to arouse the suspicions of the Atalik Ghazi's envoy, who was travelling with them. To avoid being accused of spying, Forsyth had carefully explained the work of the GTS and shown the envoy the instruments they carried, including the cameras he had brought. Now, only one of the Pundits was allowed to secretly continue the route survey to Yarkand, aided by a small pocket compass. Trotter split the Pundits up after Yarkand: the Munshi travelled with the main group, while Kishen Singh followed a few days later, but Nain Singh and his brother Kalian had to remain behind.

The mission arrived in Kashgar at the start of December, where Yakub Beg and his court warmly welcomed them. He approved the use of all scientific and surveying instruments, and even permitted them to visit the old quarter of the city, normally off limits to foreigners. Since they were also allowed to venture outside Kashgar on hunting expeditions, Trotter's team used the opportunity to route-survey all the way to the Russian frontier passes, located at the start of the Pamirs. Although they did not manage to shoot any of the famed Marco Polo sheep on this occasion, Trotter bagged one on his return, probably making him the first European to have done so.

Within two months of their arrival, Forsyth secured the desired commercial treaty with the Atalik Ghazi, but his mission had to stay on some weeks longer, waiting for the passes to reopen. This gave the officers a chance to survey eastwards and complete two more expeditions. They managed to travel some 200 miles along the northern rim of the Taklamakan, but still well short of the other townships they had hoped to visit.

By mid-March, the whole mission had retraced its steps back to Yarkand, and made ready to recross the mountains. Trotter, together with three other officers and the Munshi, took a separate route to Wakhan via Tashkurgan, planning to explore new territory. Kishen Singh accompanied them, and shared the pacing with the Munshi as far as Tashkurgan; but at that point he had to turn back, as they were leaving the protection of Yakub Beg's domain and entering other Muslim lands. The British officers, too, had to return once they reached Wakhan, as they could not gain Sher Ali's permission to travel in Afghanistan, due to continuing political tension between their countries.

Only the Munshi pushed on and secretly surveyed the missing section of the Oxus, which neither the Mirza nor Lieutenant Wood had been able to complete. This was the portion going north from Ishkashim, after the big bend in the Oxus, into the barely known districts of Shighnan and Roshan, where the river flows through many narrow gorges. For centuries, this region was famous for its ruby mines, but the Munshi found them practically exhausted, although a ruby the size of a pigeon's egg had been unearthed the previous year.

Unbeknown to Trotter and the Munshi, the Havildar, who was on his final mission for the GTS, was exploring the upper Oxus at the same time. Even though both Pundits marched towards each other, unfortunately they did not ever meet up. This meant one portion of the river, stretching for 25 miles, remained the only gap left in the route survey of the upper reaches of the river.*

The work of these Pundits would lead to a redrawing of the map of the Oxus, and hence the delineation of the Afghan border with

---

*   Another Pundit, Mukhtar Shah, finally closed it seven years later.

Russian Turkestan. The Munshi's other discovery, that the emir of Badakhshan controlled some land *north* of the Oxus, was also politically significant. Since the emir owed his allegiance to Sher Ali, albeit reluctantly, this effectively meant this area was Afghan territory rather than Russian—a revelation that would be factored into the boundary negotiations and the final agreement.

* * *

Meanwhile, Kishen Singh had returned to Yarkand, and was sent out on a separate expedition—while the rest of the Forsyth Mission returned home (except for Nain Singh and Kalian who stayed on in Yarkand to undertake further explorations). Kishen Singh headed for the centuries-old city of Khotan, which William Johnson had contentiously visited some years earlier. Sitting on the southern branch of the ancient Silk Road, it represents a haven wedged between the Taklamakan Desert and the Kunlun Mountains. Lying south of the confluence of the Karakash (Black Jade) and Yurungkash (White Jade) rivers, even today it remains a rich source of this exquisite gemstone that washes down the mountains.

Kishen Singh sketched a plan of the city, and the superior accuracy of his observations in fixing its position led Trotter to move it more than 30 miles from Johnson's placement. In fact, Trotter was so confident of the coordinates determined for Yarkand from Kishen Singh's measurements that he used the Pundit's data in favour of his own. Geographer Kenneth Mason later pointed out: 'Had still more reliance been placed upon the evidence collected by him [Kishen Singh], the map of the headwaters of the Yurungkash would not have remained incorrect for nearly fifty years.'

Kishen Singh continued east as far as the town of Keria, and from there visited the goldfields Yakub Beg monopolized as a source of his wealth. He then crossed the Kunlun Range and climbed on to the western end of the Chang Tang (Northern Plain), which sits within the Tibetan Plateau, the world's largest and highest plateau.

Like the Pamirs, it too is sometimes referred to as the Roof of the World, but otherwise the regions have little in common. The land here is undulating, with gentle slopes and few precipices. It represents an enormous closed basin with brackish lakes, stagnant marshes, and without external drainage other than on its far eastern and western rims, which become the source of the mighty rivers of Asia.

The Chang Tang stands at over 15,000 feet above sea level and covers an area close to 500,000 square miles, including almost half of Tibet. Being in the lee of the Himalayas, the plateau is treeless and arid, rarely receiving more than an inch of rainfall annually. It freezes most days of the year, yet the ground is free of snow. A clear sky can cloud over within minutes, and give rise to deadly hailstorms which the locals fear greatly. Sometimes the hailstones are larger than chicken's eggs, capable of killing whole herds of yaks. The wild variety that inhabit this barren land are enormous—some stand over 7 feet at the shoulder—and hunting them was historically considered the sport of kings. They are capable of feeding on moss and lichen, enabling them to survive the long winters, and have evolved a substance that prevents freezing of their hooves and legs. The severe climate of the plateau reduces it to being sparsely populated—mainly by nomads, the Changpa (people of Chang), who are amongst the highest-living inhabitants on the planet.

Advancing on the Chang Tang, Kishen Singh didn't meet another traveller for 250 miles, but this allowed him to take observations without risk of discovery. He finally returned to India using a long-forgotten route, which headed towards Lake Pangong and then skirted just north of it. This road from Chinese Turkestan could be traversed in summer without once crossing through snow. Better still, by circumventing Kashmir, one could avoid the crippling taxes this state imposed on passing merchants—a valuable piece of commercial information if Tibet was to open its western border again.

At the lake straddling the border between Tibet and Kashmir, Kishen Singh had the presence of mind to hide his survey instruments and notes before the border guards carefully searched him, only retrieving his cache afterwards and then crossing safely into Leh. In his report, Trotter gave due credit to Kishen Singh, stating his journey to be 'one of the more important geographical results secured by the Mission'.

After Forsyth returned to India, it soon became evident the commercial treaty he had negotiated could not be implemented, mainly because of political complications that had developed on Yakub Beg's side. This meant Robert Shaw could not take up his appointment as the permanent British representative in Kashgar, and India's trade with Chinese Turkestan did not increase significantly, as Forsyth and others had hoped. Nevertheless, the mission was highly successful from a geographical standpoint, having collected valuable information and created better maps of this little-known region.

On his return, Forsyth was made a Knight Commander of the Star of India, and Trotter's survey efforts would later win him the RGS's gold medal. For the native explorers involved, this had been a unique opportunity to work in the field shoulder-to-shoulder with British officers and demonstrate their true worth. By the end of the mission, it was clear the Pundits had given a good account of themselves.

7

Tibet and Lhasa at Last

By the mid-1870s, the GTS was winding down its work beyond the Northwest Frontier. Large tracts accessible from this border into Afghanistan had been mapped by British surveyors, often during their military expeditions. The Second Afghan War would break out in 1878, and a boundary commission would endeavour to settle Afghanistan's northern borders with Russia. The Forsyth Mission had mapped the main routes and oases of Chinese Turkestan along its western edge—the area most relevant to British India.

Now, the focus of the GTS shifted east to Tibet, which lay between the moisture-laden Himalayas and the deserts of Eastern Turkestan. It had to find a way into this closed kingdom and the geographical prize of its holy capital, Lhasa—which, like Mecca, Europeans were expressly forbidden from entering. The GTS was also anxious to determine the true course of its principal river, and resolve the question surrounding the unity of the Tsangpo and Brahmaputra.

The Bhotias

Sitting on a plateau surrounded by mountains, which makes it fortress-like, Tibet has been aptly described as a last redoubt of the unknown. Much of the difficulty in understanding its geography during the nineteenth century lay in the ban on foreigners instigated by the emperor of China. His standing order was: 'No Moghul, Hindustani, Pathan or *Feringhi* (European) shall be admitted into Tibet on pain of death.' This edict was similar to one already enforced in China except that, while trade with foreigners was limited to the port of Canton, in Tibet no Europeans whatsoever were permitted entry. Almost a century earlier, the emperor's troops had entered Tibet after coming to its neighbour's aid to drive out the Nepalese, who had first invaded Tibet in 1788 and again three years later. But after defeating the Gurkha Army the Chinese chose not to leave.

From the East India Company's perspective, as early as 1768, its Court of Directors had sent messages to staff on the subcontinent stating its 'earnest wish' to begin trade with Tibet. It followed up on this directive a few years later, remarking, 'we are surprised you have not already made an attempt to carry so desirable an object into execution'. The Tibetans, however, favoured the emperor's exclusionary policy, especially towards the British who had not come to their assistance against the Nepalese, and were becoming more powerful along their frontier with India. The Chinese insinuated that Britain had had a hand in the Gurkha invasion, and played on Tibetan fears of their religion being replaced by Christianity should they allow Europeans in.

Tibetan border officials proved most efficient at guarding the mountain passes, and stopping all intruders. The GTS was determined to work around this ban, by deploying some of its most daring Hindu Pundits to secretly enter, explore and map Tibet, and attempt to solve the mystery of 'the River'.*

Many of these Pundits would be Bhotias: a people of Tibetan origin who speak the language, share their customs, and are a hardy race used to living and working at high altitudes.† Their valley lies

---

* The Pundits would learn that the Tsangpo was referred to by various names and, often, simply as 'the River'.
† In 1953, Edmund Hillary and a Bhotia named Tenzing Norgay would be the first men to summit Mount Everest. (Tenzing would later refer to himself as a Sherpa, when this branch of Bhotias became the preferred high-altitude porters for climbing expeditions in the Himalayas.)

in Kumaon, a large province bordering Tibet, which Britain had annexed after defeating the Gurkhas in 1816. The region is one of raw beauty, as this old Bhotia song describes:

High are the mountains; Shiva lives in them.
This is my homeland; it is more beautiful than heaven.

Historically, the Tibetans had allowed Bhotias to monopolize the regular trade with its western region during the summer months. They were one of the few people permitted to travel freely across the border, becoming the go-betweens of the central Himalayas. The Bhotias brought items such as grain, cotton cloth and manufactured goods from India, and returned with wool, borax,* salt, gold dust and ponies. Interestingly, each Bhotia would initially pair up with a merchant from across the border, with each side holding on to one half of a split stone to mark this partnership. From then on, they would only trade with a Tibetan holding the matching half of their stone. For their part, the people of the plateau love to buy and sell, and it is said every Tibetan is a trader at heart.

When Montgomerie was looking for new recruits to penetrate into Tibet, he approached Major Edmund Smyth, who was the inspector of education in the area and an enthusiastic mountain climber-cum-explorer. Smyth was part of an effort to provide an all-English, Western-style education to native Indians, in the belief this would help integrate them with their British masters. He described the Bhotias to Montgomerie, noting how their flexibility in religious matters helped their cause:

These Bhotias are just the people for your purpose, as they are allowed by the Tibet authorities to go to certain parts of Tibet for purpose of trade and having this advantage, would not find much difficulty in going beyond these limits . . . The origin

---

* Borax was used to spice meat and tea, and to wash clothes and bathe with.

of these people is uncertain; they have Hindu names, and call
themselves Hindus, but they are not recognised as such by the
orthodox Hindus of the plains or the hills. While in Tibet they
seem glad enough to shake off their Hinduism and become
Buddhists, or anything you like.

Smyth went on to recommend Nain Singh and his cousin Mani
Singh as candidates, although in his opinion Nain Singh was the
more capable of the two: 'He is one of the best natives I know, and
thoroughly honest and trustworthy.'

Nain Singh was born in 1830 into the Rawat family, who
have lived in the Johar Valley for many generations. He was one
of Smyth's English-speaking Pundits (schoolmasters), eager to
improve his poor financial situation, and attracted by the extra pay
the GTS offered. Mani Singh was a *patwar* (chief native official),
and superior to his cousin in position, wealth and intellect. But this
seems to have made him less-suited for the rough life of exploration,
although he, too, was keen to find better-paying employment with
the government.

The cousins came from Milam, whose market was frequented by
Tibetan traders during summer. This small village, situated high in
the mountains, is dominated by India's second-highest peak, Nanda
Devi (25,643 feet). It could only be occupied during the warmer
months, forcing inhabitants on to the plains for the remainder of
the year. Both men already had some exploration experience, having
accompanied two British officers into Tibet a few years earlier.
Later, starting in 1855, they had accompanied the three German
Schlagintweit brothers (one of whom, Adolf, met his end in Kashgar).
The pair acquitted themselves well, just as their fathers had over fifty
years earlier, when they befriended Moorcroft and rendered him
valuable assistance.

The Singhs arrived in Dehra Dun in February 1863, ready to
start their training; they would go on to graduate as the first of the

Hindu Pundits. Mani Singh was given the code name of the Patwar or G.M., while Nain Singh was referred to variously as 'the first Pundit', Chief Pundit, or simply 'the Pundit'.

Walker and Montgomerie devised a demanding training regime for their recruits, who were quick learners and soon proved adept at using basic survey instruments, and even the more sophisticated sextant. They were drilled on the parade ground to walk to a constant pace of 31½ inches, the equivalent of almost 2000 steps per mile. Finally, after a year of training, the GTS tested them along routes already mapped; and once they demonstrated competency, the cousins were ready to take the field. Each would be paid 50 rupees per month, and given two years' salary in advance—in gold, allowing them to easily conceal these large sums. Montgomerie realized that once they set out, their whereabouts and length of absence would be virtually impossible to determine; nor would they be contactable until their return.

Nain Singh's First Expedition

Nain Singh started out in March 1864, first travelling with Mani to Bareilly, a town whose location was precisely known to the GTS. Here they took their initial latitude observation, calibrated the instruments, and commenced their route survey.* Then, after returning home to Milam, which bordered Tibet, they tried to cross into Gartok. This was the major trading town of western Tibet, but they found the route not practical to use. Perhaps this delay was fortuitous, as an opportunity now arose that would provide them with a cover story for wishing to enter Lhasa. Earlier, the property of some Bhotias trading in Tibet had been mistakenly confiscated by local authorities and forwarded to the capital. Once the traders had

---

*   The thermometers they carried had been boiled near Bareilly, where the altitude was known. All heights measured by boiling point during their journey would be referenced against this as the zero point.

returned home, they appealed to their own government prompting the British Commissioner of Kumaon to enlist the cousins to travel to Lhasa in an attempt to recover the goods.

Montgomerie directed the pair to go by way of Kathmandu, where a well-used border crossing intersected the so-called Great Road between Gartok and Lhasa. As this road was thought to run the length of the Tsangpo Valley, traversing it would allow them to survey the river as well. Additionally, they were given the important task of determining Lhasa's true position, which had yet to be accurately located on maps.

The Singhs set off for a second time in January 1865, while Montgomerie sailed home on leave (and would only return four years later). After walking 450 miles, they reached the Nepalese capital in two months, silently counting their paces with the aid of rosary beads, and secretly taking observations with their otherwise concealed survey instruments. The prayer wheel they carried openly, finding that it doubled as an ideal place to conceal their notes and compass—being a religious object, it wasn't examined by border officials. They also carried a 6-inch sextant and used mercury to provide its artificial horizon, rather than the dark glass Abdul Hamid had utilized.* The mercury was kept hidden inside a coconut, with reserves concealed in cowrie shells sealed with wax; when needed, it was poured into a wooden bowl, which Bhotias typically carry for their food. The sextant was used under the cover of darkness, and read using a bullseye lantern. This procedure became more difficult later, when the Pundit was forced to sell the lantern in Tibet to admiring officials rather than arouse their suspicions, after which he had to resort to using a common oil-wick.

In Kathmandu, they learnt that snow still closed the pass they had intended to use, forcing the cousins and their four servants to detour through the small town of Kirong. They travelled disguised as

---

* On land (unlike at sea), the horizon is often not visible, so an artificial one must be created before sextant readings can be taken.

Bashahris, another people of the region traditionally allowed to cross into Tibet without question. To their surprise, border officials *did* stop and search them. Luckily, their well-hidden survey instruments were not detected. The guards, however, would not believe their story—that they wished to buy horses and go on a pilgrimage to Lhasa—as this route via Nepal was an unusual one for Bashahris to take. They refused to let the party cross, leaving the disappointed cousins no option but to return to Kathmandu.

At this point, they decided to split up and try to reach Lhasa separately, particularly when they learnt Mani Singh was well known to the governor of Kirong, who would probably see through his disguise. Mani then tried a more circuitous route, but eventually returned to Dehra Dun after this attempt failed. According to him, this was due to ill health and the unsafe state of the roads, but Montgomerie felt his failure was 'in a great measure due to his own want of determination'.

Nain Singh switched his disguise to one of a Ladakhi, complete with a pigtail hairstyle, to fool the border guards who might otherwise recognize him after his last attempt. He took along a servant named Chumbel, who would prove to be a faithful companion not only to him, but also to another Pundit in times to come.

The Pundit made an agreement with a merchant who was going with others to Lhasa: in exchange for a loan of 100 rupees, he was permitted to join their caravan. Unfortunately, after waiting many days to get started, the merchant failed to appear. Nain Singh then approached the man's family and persuaded his brother to act as his guarantor; this allowed him to cross the frontier at Kirong on the pretext of visiting relatives. At the border, he had to sign a declaration agreeing, on pain of death, to not proceed to Lhasa within the year, even though he had every intention of doing so.

Once he crossed into Tibet, the Pundit reverted to his old disguise after he met other Bashahri merchants, who were travelling in a caravan with 200 domestic yaks. These are the famous pack animals of Tibet—about half the size of wild yaks, from whom they are descended.* Able to bear extreme cold and altitudes, yaks struggle to survive much below 10,000 feet. They are slow, lumbering creatures which groan at every step, and the domesticated variety is well-deserving of its Latin name *Bos grunniens*. Although hardy and surprisingly surefooted on steep mountains, they have also been characterized as stupid and stubborn animals.

The Bashahris were headed west for Lake Manasarowar, by way of the Tradom monastery sitting on the main road. The Pundit was invited to join them after he declared his desire to worship at the monastery; he added that he intended to travel to the lake as well, despite this being in the opposite direction to Lhasa.

They crossed the towering Himalayas using the No La (*la* means mountain pass) at 16,600 feet, and made their way down the other side. Here, the Pundit finally encountered the Tsangpo River, the highest major waterway in the world. Any thoughts of crossing it using a coracle were quickly dismissed when, to their horror, they witnessed three men drown while using these flimsy wooden-framed craft. This prompted the party to march further upstream and use a ferry instead, before arriving at the revered monastery in the first week of September. The Pundit's initial enquiries with locals, as to what became of the Tsangpo after it left Tibet, revealed that they unanimously believed the river turned south into India to become the Brahmaputra (Son of Brahma, the Hindu god of creation).

At Tradom, the Pundit feigned illness to give the Bashahris the slip, and remained there after they turned west towards the lake. He now learnt that another party of traders with some 300 horses and yaks was due in a month's time, bound for the capital. The maharaja of Kashmir sent this large caravan once every two years to trade in Lhasa, and the Tibetans would reciprocate with a mission of their own. A high-ranking Ladakhi official, with the honorary title of

---

*   In Tibetan, the word *yak* refers only to the male species, the female being called a *dri*; the cross between a cow and a yak is a sterile male *dzo*, or a fertile female *dzomo*.

Lopchak, always led the caravan. Great attention and respect was paid to him as he passed by, and the Tibetans would provide free food and shelter for his entire party. As well as being accompanied by merchants, the Lopchak was given 15,000 rupees worth of goods to trade by the maharaja, and he was expected to contribute twice that amount to the treasury on his return. The merchants took a variety of goods with them, including silks, saffron and their prized cashmere shawls woven from the soft wool of the Tibetan goat.

The Pundit rented a house while awaiting the caravan, then quickly befriended the Lopchak's headman after its arrival and secured his onward passage. He seems to have made friends easily, and quickly became a favourite with almost everyone he encountered.

The Ladakhi caravan headed east for the capital along the Gartok to Lhasa road, which was something of a mystery itself. Europeans had not travelled this Great Road since two Jesuit priests had used it to visit Lhasa in 1716, and none would traverse it again until the twentieth century. On his return, the Pundit would report that this vital 800-mile 'road' was, in fact, an unpaved although well-maintained track. It never fell below 10,000 feet, while at other times climbing to over 16,000 feet; yet a man travelling on horseback between the two cities need never dismount, except to cross rivers.

The Great Road was interspersed with twenty-two *tarjums* (staging posts) along the way, each between 20 and 70 miles apart, with the larger of these able to accommodate up to 200 travellers at a time. These distances required ordinary folk with baggage animals to make up to five marches between tarjums. This meant having to sleep in simple tents or even out in the open at times, exposed to the cold and buffeted by strong winds, huddled around dried dung fires at night. Each tarjum had a resident in charge, who was required to keep horses, yaks and porters ready for whenever he received notice of an official approaching from Lhasa. Every three years, a high-ranking official would make his way from the capital to inspect the entire length of the road and its tarjums, travelling in a large caravan comprising up to 1000 yaks. The nomadic tribes along the way were required to provide these animals as a form of tax, and were held strictly responsible for the safe transit of the caravan.

Official couriers on horseback also traversed the Great Road, usually completing the full journey between Lhasa and Gartok in just over a month, but in as little as twenty days when carrying urgent dispatches. The Pundit saw how these couriers would stop only for food and to change horses, arriving at their destination looking haggard: 'Their faces were cracked, their eyes blood-shot and sunken, and their bodies eaten by lice into large raws, the latter they attributed to not being allowed to take off their clothes.' This directive applied during the entire journey, and officials sealed their overcoats to ensure compliance. The Pundit's description of the Great Road and how, through an iron rule, Lhasa maintained a rapid communication system along the length of the country, would prove to be valuable information for British India.*

Every morning the caravan started out at dawn, and stopped for the day around mid-afternoon. The Pundit found it safer to march separately; his pretence at religious devotion—twirling his prayer wheel and chanting the Buddhist mantra—kept others from interrupting him, as convention demanded.

In places the road became ill defined, as it opened out on to the barren plateau. To avoid going astray, travellers erected piles of stones with a flag on top at frequent intervals to mark the way. It was usual for others who followed to add another stone to these piles; or they would tie another flag, believing merit is obtained for the initiator as the mantras printed on the fluttering flags are recited by the wind. These cairns soon grew to a considerable size, making them ideal markers for the Pundit to take compass bearings to. Further down the river, five days from the town of Shigatse, when most travellers continued by boat, he could indulge in no such luxury as it would

---

* This was similar, although on a smaller scale, to the *orto* system used by Genghis Khan and his Mongol hordes in the thirteenth century to govern their empire, which stretched all the way to the gates of Europe.

interrupt his pacing. In the few instances when he was not able to complete a route survey during a particular stage of his march, the Pundit would pace these out during his return journey.

After reaching Shigatse in just under four weeks, the caravan stopped here for close to two months. This was a large town with some 9000 inhabitants, including a garrison of Chinese and Tibetan troops. The massive Tashilhunpo monastery stood nearby, where the Panchen Lama resided with a further 3300 monks. Although he was reluctant to join the Ladakhis when they paid their respects to Tibet's second-highest priest, the Pundit went along anyway, rather than be seen as being impolite. He feared this holy man would see into his heart and penetrate his disguise. To his relief, he turned out to be an eleven-year-old boy, who asked him three innocent questions: 'Is your King well? Is your country prospering? Are you in good health?'

The long stay in Shigatse meant that the Pundit was starting to run low on funds. To earn a few rupees, he resorted to teaching Nepalese shopkeepers the Hindu method of accounting. The caravan's last major stop, three days from the capital, was the large trading town of Gyantse; this was the centre for the manufacture of small bells, an item in much demand in Tibet.

Afterwards, they continued around the sacred Yamdok Tso (*tso* means lake), whose stunning turquoise surface is almost entirely taken up by a seemingly large island sitting within it—a curious topographical feature unknown anywhere else in the world.* On its shores, a band of brigands ambushed the caravan; in his diary the Pundit describes what happened next:

> One of them took hold of my horse's bridle and told me to dismount. Through fear, I was on the point of resigning my horse to him, when a Mahommedan who accompanied me

---

* Montgomerie would claim: 'The evidence as to the lake encircling a very large island is unanimous.' However, later explorers would disprove this; the 'island' is, in fact, joined to the surrounding land.

raised his whip; whereupon the robber drew a long sabre and rushed on the Mahommedan. Taking advantage of this favourable moment I whipped my own horse forward, and as the robbers could not catch us they fired on us, but without effect . . .

Finally, on 10 January 1866, after marching nearly 500 miles from Tradom, on the banks of the Kyi Chu (River of Happiness), the Pundit set eyes on the holy capital of Tibet.

Lhasa

Nain Singh rented a room in a caravanserai, before proceeding to explore the city and its environs. Lhasa was built on a circular plan, 2½ miles in circumference, encircled by a well-made road. It had a population of 15,000 and retained a military garrison of 1500 Tibetan and Chinese soldiers. The city's demography was quite imbalanced, though, with women outnumbering men three to two, because many men became priests and took vows of celibacy. This situation was further exacerbated by the custom of polyandry regularly practised in these parts. It took the form of several brothers in a family sharing the same wife—thus keeping sons at home to work the fields, and avoiding the unsustainable division of inherited land, as cultivable plots were already scarce.

The Pundit found the city centre dominated by the holiest shrine in Tibet and its spiritual heart, the Jokhang. This large golden temple, containing idols richly inlaid with gold and precious stones, had thousands of flickering butter lamps and a giant statue of Buddha, in front of which pilgrims prostrated. For many of them, entry into the temple represented the culmination of an act of piety which may have started months ago, after walking from their homes possibly hundreds of miles away, making obeisance along the way. And for the exceptionally devoted who, after every three paces, chose to prostrate fully and touch their foreheads to the ground, this would be a particularly sweet day.

Bazaars surrounded the Jokhang, and the Pundit saw many merchants from other neighbouring states in India, China and Nepal. The traders came to the city at the onset of winter in December and left in March, before the rains came and made the rivers impassable. There was brisk trade in all manner of exotic goods: silk, saffron, carpets, tea, tobacco, rice, musk perfume, cloth, saddles and various other manufactured goods. He also witnessed large quantities of fossil bones for sale, including a 2½ foot-long skull, and learnt that these bones were valued for their healing properties: after being powdered, they were applied to wounds.

The Pundit visited the magnificent Potala Palace, built on a rocky outcrop on the outskirts of the city. At thirteen stories high, it ranked as one of the world's tallest buildings during the eighteenth and nineteenth centuries. It was home to 7700 priests, whom the ordinary people revered, but no women were permitted to live there. The Pundit accompanied the Lopchak to pay homage to the Great Lama, known to the outside world as the Dalai Lama, regarded by his people as the thirteenth incarnation of the historical Buddha. Tibet's highest priest left the affairs of state to his raja and four ministers, but these officials also came under the power of the Chinese Amban (high official), who could have them removed from office if necessary.[*]

Inside the palace, sitting on a throne 6 feet high, the Pundit found this god-king to be another boy, this time aged thirteen. During his brief audience, Nain Singh was asked the same three innocuous questions the Panchen Lama had put to him. Again, he was relieved not to have been unmasked; nor was the prayer wheel he carried, stashed with his survey notes, discovered. After his audience, on his way out, the Pundit even managed to pace out the dimensions of the palace.

At night, from his rooftop in the caravanserai, he took observations with the sextant, allowing the GTS to later fix the

---

[*]   This is disputed by some Tibetan historians today, who claim the Amban's power was largely ceremonial.

position of the Tibetan capital for the first time ever. Using his boiling-point thermometer, he measured the city's altitude as 11,700 feet above sea level (closely matching today's accepted figure of 12,000 feet). Despite this elevation and the freezing temperatures, he rarely encountered snowfall in Lhasa or anywhere else in Tibet, and learnt that locals regard anything other than a light fall as a sign of displeasure from their gods.

On his return, the Pundit's report of Lhasa would be the first since the account by the two Lazarist priests, Huc and Gabet, who had arrived twenty years prior (to hear rumours of William Moorcroft's supposed visit there, a year *after* his reported demise). Due to the limitations of his disguise and the need to move principally among the lower orders of society, Nain Singh, like all the Pundits penetrating Tibet, would be restricted in the information he could reliably gather about the country's overall economic and political conditions. Still, he carefully observed life in the capital, and the vivid descriptions he noted in his diary would shed further light on this mysterious kingdom and its people, including their customs and the food they consumed.

Throughout the day, Tibetans drank copious quantities of salted tea. Tea is not only a stimulant, but also reduces the oxidative stress of living at high altitude. Tibetans turned their salted tea into a nutritional drink by mixing it with butter made from yak's milk. When roasted barley flour was added, it became a full meal called *tsampa*, an ideal dietary supplement in a land that does not readily support fruit or vegetables; it remains a Tibetan staple today. They also ate various meats, but within the limits of the holy city no blood was permitted to be shed, which meant any slaughterhouses were placed outside its boundaries. Wheat and other kitchen produce were cheap; but rice was not eaten because of its high price, and as it was considered a source of disease. A type of beer known as *chhang* was commonly brewed from barley, by fermenting it with a spice. It was kept in closed earthen vessels for some days before being consumed, or further distilled into a type of spirit.

The households in the city received water from nearby wells, for which they had to pay a fortnightly tax of one *anna* (one-sixteenth of a rupee). In winter, the water kept in even the warmest parts of houses regularly froze, bursting the vessels holding it. The Pundit noted how the houses were mostly made from mud bricks due to the lack of wood, as the hills were barren except for a thorny bush that grew wild. He saw people wearing elaborate ornaments made of coral, regarded as one of the Seven Treasures of Buddhism and much sought-after by Tibetans, who considered it to be worth more than gold. They displayed other gemstones as well; and sometimes the women wore gold and silver on their heads.

The poorer classes of Lhasa would dispose of their dead in an unusual way: after first binding the corpses tightly with ropes, they placed them erect against the inner walls of their houses for two or three days, to prevent them becoming demons. Afterwards, the priests would advise them what to do with the body: sometimes to cut it into pieces and scatter the fragments to birds and animals, while at other times to bury it.

During his stay, the Pundit witnessed the unusual customs surrounding the city's New Year celebrations which began around the middle of February, marking the official end of winter. At its commencement, the priest who bid the highest sum of money was appointed judge of the court for twenty-three days. Thereafter, he was referred to as the Jalno, and carried a silver stick to signify his new position. Over this period, he and his henchmen were allowed to tax every house in the capital, and levy heavy fines for the slightest faults—to such an extent that it sometimes drove the working classes out of the city for the duration.

Another curious custom was played out on the second day of festivities, to commemorate the legendary descent of their first kings from heaven. All the people of Lhasa, including the Dalai Lama, would gather in front of the soaring Potala to witness a dangerous sport. One end of a rope was fastened high up on the palace walls, while the other stretched down to rivets secured 100 yards from its base, before two men were required to slide down its length. In the process, they often fell to their deaths, but if they were successful, they were rewarded by the court.

Twenty-four days after the Jalno's first period of authority, he was permitted to resume issuing arbitrary fines for another ten days, finally profiteering by around ten times the initial purchase price of his temporary appointment as judge. At the end of it all, the Jalno played dice with a sacrificial peasant whose face was painted half black and half white, and who was first pelted with grain before receiving small donations from everyone assembled. If the Jalno lost, it was considered a great evil; whereas if the victim lost, it was seen as a sign from the gods that he bore the sins of the whole city. He was then hooted and shouted at by the people as they drove him outside the capital to a monastery nearby. If he died there shortly afterwards, it was considered an auspicious sign; but if he didn't, he was kept prisoner for a year before being released. The day after his banishment, all the state jewels together with the treasury's gold and silver were paraded through the streets, followed by thousands of spectators. The next day huge images of their gods, made from colourful paper and set on wooden frames, were dragged through the streets. Finally, the coming of New Year ended with a big celebration held on the plains of the city, which everyone attended.

The Pundit made ready to leave Lhasa after residing there for over three months. During his long stay, he had again run low on funds, and once more had to resort to teaching accounting. He also borrowed money from two Kashmiris, after leaving his survey watch with them as surety. This last incident demonstrated the Pundit's ability to turn a bad situation to his advantage. It came about after the pair saw through his Bashahri disguise, but he convinced them not to denounce him to the authorities and gained their assistance instead.

Another dangerous moment arose one day when Nain Singh spotted in the street the governor of Kirong—the same official to whom he had staked his life, on the promise of not entering the capital. To avoid any chance encounter (Lhasa being a city of only 15,000 inhabitants), the Pundit hurriedly changed his accommodation and laid low until departure. The Ladakhi caravan was fortunately returning to Gartok soon, and his friendship with its leader meant he could again secure a passage with them.

The return journey west initially took him back to Tradom, and then along the northern bank of the Tsangpo, at an even higher altitude averaging 15,000 feet. From Tradom, his route survey of the Great Road would cover new territory all the way to the area around Lake Manasarowar, which mirrors the holiest of peaks, Mount Kailas. This mountainous region is also the ultimate source of the four major rivers of the Indian subcontinent: the Indus, Sutlej, Ganges and Brahmaputra. The Pundit found this part of the main road to be desolate, inhabited only by nomads and their flocks of yaks, sheep and goats. At the lake, he was fortunate to meet a friend from Kumaon, who helped pay off all his debts except for the watch pawned to the Kashmiris. Soon afterwards, the Pundit parted from the caravan and headed for home, but was forced to leave without Chumbel who had become ill, and as a surety for repaying his friend from Kumaon.

Since the road was now unsafe due to heavy snowfall, the Pundit had to make a large detour before he could cross the Himalayas in late June. Once he was back in British territory, he dispatched two men to Kumaon to pay off his loan and collect Chumbel, who returned in good health. At this point the Pundit met up with Mani Singh, and learnt of his unsuccessful attempt to enter Tibet. He asked Mani to proceed to Gartok and redeem his watch from the Kashmiri merchants, and at the same time complete their route survey to that city. Once Mani achieved this, the cousins returned to Dehra Dun in late October 1866, after an absence of almost two years.

Montgomerie's commentary on Nain Singh's first journey, titled 'Report of a Route-Survey made by Pundit ___, from Nepal to Lhasa . . .', was read out to the RGS in March 1868. He did not name his native explorer to maintain secrecy, but the RGS was instructed not to censor or suppress any part of the document. Its contents detailed the four major findings from Nain Singh's explorations. The first was his thirty-one observations for latitude at Lhasa and other important places; until then only the town of Shigatse had been fixed, way back in 1783. The second was his route survey over 1200 miles, including the whole of the Great Road from Lhasa to Gartok. It helped the GTS map much of the Tsangpo River, from its source near Lake Manasarowar to the Kyi Chu tributary joining it at the capital. Third, he determined the altitude of some thirty-three places through boiling-point measurements, measured air temperatures and noted climatic conditions. Finally, the Pundit had gathered valuable information about many aspects of Tibet, its people and their customs. Further to his report, in a letter to the RGS, Montgomerie added: 'The Pundit, I think, deserves all praise; his work has stood every test capitally.'*

The RGS and its members were greatly impressed by the efforts of both Nain Singh and Montgomerie, and the way in which the GTS had conducted the expedition. They awarded the Pundit an inscribed gold chronometer valued at over 30 pounds, although, to his lasting disappointment, it was later stolen by a Pathan whom he was training up as a Pundit. For Montgomerie and Walker, Nain Singh's success did much to prove the viability of deploying native explorers, and it would soon lead to many more exploits by other Pundits.

The Pundit's Later Expeditions

Nain Singh would undertake four assignments in all for the GTS (including his work with the Forsyth Mission), spanning a decade of active service. After resting for a few months, he was sent back out on his second expedition. He was accompanied again by Mani Singh, and this time he took his brother Kalian as well.

---

*   In extracts published from the Pundit's diary, he acknowledged Mani Singh's assistance (referring to him as his brother, although Smyth, Phillimore and others believed them to be first cousins).

They started out from Dehra Dun in May 1867, travelling north-east through the foothills of the Himalayas into Badrinath, regarded by Hindus as the sacred source of the Ganges. At the 18,000-foot Mana Pass, they were required to wait for Chinese officials to open the border, which was regulated to prevent the outbreak of disease, after the scourge of smallpox had been spread from India in prior years. This border control was a bone of contention with the British, as Montgomerie's later comment reveals: '[B]efore this is done, the Jongpon [fort master] . . . makes inquiry every year as to the political and sanatory condition of Hindustan . . . Looking down from their elevated plateaux, they decide as to whether Hindustan is a fit county to have intercourse with.'

Once they were allowed entry, the trio crossed into western Tibet with a party of eleven men, including guides and servants, all well-armed against the threat of bandits. Their disguise was that of Bashahri traders, ostensibly to sell the coral they carried in exchange for shawl wool. They crossed the Sutlej using a remarkable iron bridge which was 76 feet long, 7 feet wide, and suspended high above the rushing water. Locals believed Alexander the Great built this structure more than 2000 years ago; and it had lasted through the ages due to their efforts, which involved lubricating its thick chain links annually with clarified yak butter.

The Pundits skirted Gartok to avoid arousing suspicion but, further on, the Tibetan headman in the town of Giachuraf penetrated their cover. Unbeknown to them, the previous year Bashahri traders had introduced smallpox into the area, leading to the death of many inhabitants. Consequently, they were barred from trading this season, which the Singhs would have known had they been genuine Bashahris. Moreover, they had ventured well past Gartok, the centre for the shawl wool trade, making their cover story even less convincing. After repeated requests, the headman agreed to let some of the party through, provided others remained as hostages. This condition of entry forced the Singhs to split up, with Mani being left behind in Giachuraf as surety, and because he seemed to have lost his nerve for fear of discovery.

Nain Singh travelled alone to reach their initial objective: the fabled gold field at Thok Jalung, which has been written about since antiquity. In what was probably Europe's first reference to Tibet, the Greek historian Herodotus had sparked one of the longest treasure hunts in history, starting with Alexander the Great and his troops. Describing a land to the north of India, Herodotus mentions 'ant-like creatures bigger than foxes yet not so big as a dog, which bring up great quantities of gold-bearing sand as they dig their burrows'.* Tibet was thought to be rich in this precious metal. The British had long been interested in confirming the existence of this mine, and any others in the country. Locals were reluctant to exploit their mineral wealth for religious reasons, believing the nuggets contained life, but lamas did permit digging if the activity was undertaken well away from any monasteries or the holy capital.

The Pundit gained access to the mine site after offering a gift to the headman, and selling some coral to his wife at a bargain price. He was granted permission for a stay of five days, although the exchange did cause him an uneasy moment. His coral had been stored in a handsomely crafted box which attracted the chief's attention but, despite carefully examining it, he failed to discover the Pundit's sextant hidden within the box in a secret compartment.

During his stay, Nain Singh took detailed notes of the mining techniques practised there, while keeping well clear of the fierce black mastiffs which Tibetans everywhere used to guard their encampments. The miners would only excavate near the surface, as they considered it a crime to dig deeper and deprive the earth of its fertility, fearing retribution would come in the form of hailstones and rain storms. The Pundit found the water around Thok Jalung so brackish that it could not be drunk, unless it was first frozen and then melted. He saw how the miners toiled in extreme conditions,

---

*   Explorer Michel Peissel believed these creatures to be marmots, as expounded in his book *The Ants' Gold*. In 1982, he visited tribesmen in the Himalayas who claimed to collect gold from the burrows of marmots.

16,000 feet up on the plateau, living in yak hair tents pitched in deep holes to find whatever protection they could from the bone-chilling winds. To keep warm as they slept at nights, they would curl up, balancing on their knees and elbows, piling every scrap of clothing they owned on their backs. Even faced with this intense cold, the miners preferred to work in winter, since the frozen ground reduced the danger of mine collapses.

At the height of the mining season, the site housed as many as 6000 tents of diggers, who were each required to pay a small annual tax in gold. There were rich pickings to be had, and the Pundit saw one recently recovered nugget that weighed nearly 2 pounds. Over the years, much of this gold would be used to thickly coat the enormous stupas of the Potala Palace, and lavishly decorate other monasteries all over the country. On his return, the Pundit's report would spark enormous interest within the Company, and in Europe generally, regarding Tibet's gold reserves and the prospect of exploiting them.

While Nain Singh was visiting Thok Jalung, Kalian had gone off to explore separately, and succeeded in reaching an upper eastern branch of the Indus River, the Gartang. Geographers had doubted its existence because no European had ever seen it, but he was able to confirm it was the main tributary of the Indus. Later, Kalian would route-survey parts of the headwaters of the Sutlej River—the first time this area was explored.

Once they were reunited with Mani, the Pundits continued their pacing through various other stretches of this region. But they left hurriedly after Nain Singh learnt of rumours circulating that some locals believed he was a British spy. All three managed to return home safely, after route-surveying 850 miles of new territory covering 18,000 square miles of western Tibet. During their six-month mission, they took 190 latitudinal observations and altitude readings at eighty locations. They also determined the position of several peaks from various points, including the previously unheard-of Aling Kangri (*kangri* stands for mountain) group, which they estimated to be around 24,000 feet high. Montgomerie was particularly pleased with this aspect of the Pundits' proficiency, and commented how they had 'succeeded in the difficult art of intersecting and fixing distant peaks'.

* * *

After Nain Singh's involvement with the Forsyth Mission, his fourth and final expedition was planned as his most ambitious. Starting out from Leh, he was to travel to Lhasa again, although taking a more northerly route this time, before walking all the way across China to Peking. Montgomerie had left India by this stage, and been replaced by Captain Henry Trotter. The captain enlisted the help of William Johnson, by then governor of Ladakh, to find a way of getting his Pundit safely across the border, as Tibetan officials now knew of Nain Singh and were on the lookout for him.

This time he went disguised as a trader going north into Chinese Turkestan, complete with a flock of twenty-six sheep to be used as baggage animals. Although sheep carry smaller loads, ranging in weight between 20 and 25 pounds, and are slower than pack animals, they are a good option in pastoral country as they are entirely self-sufficient in terms of their food. They can easily be replaced along the way, or eaten should the need arise—although a handful from the Pundit's original flock would make it all the way to Lhasa.

As a trade mission was about to leave Kashmir around this time, Johnson imposed on the Lopchak to carry the funds Nain Singh would need for his later journey from Lhasa to Peking, which could be handed over when the two met up in the capital. The Pundit concealed the balance of his money in a worn and ragged pad covering the back of an old donkey he took, which he dubbed 'the government treasurer'. Planning for his return trip from Peking to Calcutta, Trotter provided the Pundit with a letter of introduction to the British minister in the Chinese capital, who would arrange his passage home by sea.

His party of five set out from Leh in July 1874 claiming to head for Yarkand, but quickly turned east once they successfully crossed the border. They travelled roughly parallel to the main Gartok–Lhasa road, keeping about 150 miles north of it, along the virtually inaccessible Chang Tang. On the plateau, they encountered few living creatures other than the nomadic Changpa, and herds of wild asses, antelope and giant sheep. They came across marshes from which large quantities of salt were being extracted. The workers would sink to their loins in mud to remove the salt crust, before washing and drying this much-prized product in the sun.

The Pundit visited another gold mine, this time at Thok Daurakpa (*thok* means gold or goldfield), but found it to be less lucrative than was previously thought. Pushing on, he surveyed a chain of unknown lakes across central Tibet. He learnt that the locals considered one large lake named Dangra Yum (*yum* means mother) and its adjacent tall peak Targot Yap (*yap* means father) to be the progenitors of the world. These sites attracted pilgrims from as far away as Lhasa. It took the devotees a month to complete a full circuit of both the holy lake and mountain, in the belief this would absolve their ordinary sins. To cleanse the sin of murder, however, required two full circuits, and three were needed for the vilest crime of all: murdering a parent.

Almost a month later, just north of the capital, the Pundit reached the Tengri Nor (*nor* being the Mongolian word for lake), which wouldn't be explored by a European for many years. In fact, his whole northerly route across the high plateau of Tibet, from Leh to the Tengri Nor, was practically a blank on maps until then.

When he finally reached Lhasa, the Pundit's stay was unexpectedly cut short to just two days, giving him no time to recover from his arduous four-month crossing of the Chang Tang. This change of plan became imperative when he heard of a rumour that the Chinese were looking for a British agent from India. To make matters worse, he ran into a merchant from Leh who knew his real identity and could denounce him. This made the Pundit fearful, as he had actually seen people beheaded in Lhasa for lesser crimes than spying.

Originally, he had planned to stay until the Lopchak arrived, collect his money, and then join the caravan all the way to Peking. Now the risk was clearly too high to remain here any longer. Before leaving, worried that he may not make it back, the Pundit took the precaution of sending complete copies of his survey notes back to Trotter with two of his men, who returned via Leh. He then made for home using the quickest route possible, while initially pretending to head in the opposite direction on pilgrimage to a monastery.

The Pundit travelled south-east with his remaining two servants, and crossed the Tsangpo by boat on the last day of November. Ever the explorer, he approximated its flow by throwing a piece of wood into the water, before timing how long it took to be carried 50 yards by the current. He estimated the river's width to be 500 yards, and its maximum depth to be no more than 20 feet judging by the long poles used to punt the boat across. On the other side, he surveyed the lower course of the Tsangpo as far as the town of Chetang, including parts which hadn't been charted. He was even able to approximate its course for a further 100 miles downstream from where he stood, by taking bearings of distant peaks the river was said to pass beneath.

On his final leg, the Pundit marched south from Chetang, crossing the main Himalayan Range using the Karkang Pass which rose over 16,000 feet. Here was another route not previously mapped which he managed to survey. Just before the frontier, he was detained for six weeks at the large market town of Tawang, as the merchants there had monopolized the cross-border trade, and were preventing other traders from crossing into India. Only by leaving all his goods with them, and pretending to go on pilgrimage, was he finally able to cross into British India on the first day of March 1875.

The Pundit had walked almost 1500 miles since leaving Leh, without any time to recuperate in Lhasa. Most of this trek—1200 miles—had passed through unexplored territory. He would provide the GTS with a solid framework to map this region, making over 275 astronomical observations with his sextant for latitude, and nearly 500 measurements of altitude by boiling point. His frequent measurements of air temperature and wind direction would also help geographers better understand the Tibetan climate.

By this stage Nain Singh was a spent force. A decade of exploration in harsh country and at continuous personal risk had taken its toll. His eyesight, too, had been seriously impaired, after prolonged exposure and incessant observations made at high altitudes. There would be no more missions now, and at last the secrecy around his identity could be lifted. His name was made public the following year; and he was given a land grant by the Government of India with an annual revenue valued at 1000 rupees, while the Paris Geographical Society awarded him a gold watch. Yet although he expressly requested a replacement chronometer from the RGS for the one stolen from him, even offering to bear its cost, this was not forthcoming.

Interestingly, there was much disagreement in the RGS council when it came to deciding who was most deserving of its highest award for the following year. The two contenders were: Trotter, for planning this last expedition, processing its findings, and his work with the recent Forsyth Mission; and the Pundit, as the actual explorer undertaking this and previous missions. It seems the former president of the RGS had informally promised Trotter the gold medal, but senior members disagreed. Colonel Henry Yule, himself a gold medallist and someone who carried real weight in the council, argued: '*either* of his great journeys in Tibet would have brought this reward to any European explorer; to have made *two* such journeys . . . is what no European but the first rank of travelers like Livingstone or Grant have done'.

Nain Singh was awarded the Patron's Medal for 1877.[*] His citation reads: 'For his great journeys and surveys in Tibet and along the Upper Brahmaputra, during which he determined the position of Lhasa and added largely to our positive knowledge of the map of Asia.' The new president of the RGS, in advising the viceroy of India

---

[*] Trotter would receive a gold medal the next year, for connecting the Russian Survey with the GTS.

of its choice, wrote: 'No more could have been looked for from any British explorer, from any British officer.'

Lord Lytton presented the Pundit his gold medal on the first day of the following year, and appointed him a Companion of the Indian Empire. On some maps, at least for a period of time, there was even a chain of mountains on the Chang Tang named the Nain Singh Range (the Aling Kangri group noted by the Pundit during his second journey in 1867). He was honoured again more recently when he was featured on an Indian postage stamp in 2004.

The Pundit would spend his final years before retirement helping train new recruits to take the field for the GTS. He is credited with having written two books, which were published over a century later in India in the early 1990s: *Itihas Rawat Kaum* (History of the Rawat Community) and *Akshansh Darpan* (Mirror of Latitudes). In 2006, his three-volume biography by Uma Bhatt and Shekhar Pathak was released, titled *Asia Ki Peeth Per . . .* (On the Back of Asia: Life, Explorations and Writings of Pundit Nain Singh Rawat).*

There has been considerable confusion around when and how the Pundit died. The *Times* of London printed his obituary in 1882. His old school supervisor Edmund Smyth, who knew him better than most, wrote a longer obituary in the *Proceedings of the Royal Geographic Society* confirming this date, putting his death down to cholera. Smyth estimated his final age to be fifty-seven, but this does not tally with his year of birth being 1830. Other writers, including one who was a close relative,[†] claimed he lived on for another thirteen years, finally dying of a heart attack in 1895 while tending to the estate he had been granted.

---

*   The first two volumes are in Hindi. The third, which is in English, comprises the reports of the Pundit's explorations published by the GTS in the journals of the RGS.

†   Indra Singh Rawat was Kishen Singh's uncle. He spent forty-one years with the Survey of India, and wrote a book about the Pundits in 1973 titled *Indian Explorers of the 19th Century*.

Whatever the date or circumstances, one element remains indisputable: that Nain Singh has a place amongst history's premier explorers, despite remaining relatively unknown to this day. Yule, who had intervened decisively when the RGS council was wavering on awarding him its highest honour, best summed up the Pundit's achievements: 'His observations have added a larger amount of important knowledge to the map of Asia than those of any living man . . .'

8

The River

Another remarkable Pundit would now take centre stage—one whose accomplishments would rival those of his cousin Nain Singh. So much so that it would start a rather pointless debate in some quarters as to who was 'the greatest' amongst the native explorers employed by the GTS.

The question as to whether the Tsangpo and Brahmaputra rivers were, in fact, the one and same was now demanding an answer from geographers as never before, and this Pundit would bring back substantial proof.

Kishen Singh (A.K.)

Kishen Singh was born in the early 1840s, although some records put the year of his birth as late as 1850; either way, he was much younger than his cousin. Yet, the pair would work together on the Forsyth Mission, which would be the junior Singh's third journey. On his first mission, while only eighteen, he made a route survey of some 400 miles of countryside around Kumaon and into Tibet, although no account of this trip was ever published.

His second journey started in late 1871, when he marched via Shigatse, circumnavigating the Tengri Nor, to reach Lhasa three months later. Of the memorable sights his party encountered, one involved a series of hot springs—part of a geothermal belt in southern

Tibet. Here, they would witness an unusual geyser on the banks of the Lahu River, a tributary of the Tsangpo. The jet of water, which was close to boiling, shot 60 feet into the air before freezing into a pillar of ice about 30 feet in circumference. The river was so hot here that it remained unfrozen three miles downstream.

Along the way they were attacked and robbed, and left with only the bare essentials despite pleading with the bandits. The robbers did not take Kishen Singh's survey instruments, though, for fear of being caught by the authorities with no plausible explanation for possessing them. This incident forced the party to beg their way to Lhasa, and Kishen Singh became so weak that he had to shorten the length of his pacing. Only with considerable difficulty, and after pledging his survey instruments to a trader, was he able to borrow a little money in the capital. As this amount was insufficient to fund his mission going forward, he had no choice but to return to Dehra Dun, abandoning his final objective of reaching Xining, the capital of the Tsinghai province in western China. Despite this setback, he managed to route-survey over 300 miles of new territory, take latitudinal observations, and explore the upper reaches of the Tsangpo River.

* * *

Kishen Singh's fourth and final mission would be his crowning achievement. One prominent Himalayan explorer and RGS gold medallist, Michael Ward, has described it as 'the most substantial and important journey in the history of Central Asian exploration'. Walker, now a general and in the twilight of his career, organized this mission, as Trotter had already left the GTS for a career in diplomacy.

Kishen Singh set out from Darjeeling in April 1878, aiming to traverse the entire Tibetan Plateau from south to north all the way into Mongolia, exploring as much of the unknown regions of Tibet as possible. This time he took only two others with him: Chumbel, who had earlier travelled with Nain Singh, and a servant, Ganga

Ram. Other than his usual survey instruments, the GTS supplied him with a larger and more accurate 9-inch sextant.

His party arrived in Lhasa in the first week of September, after being delayed for three months when Ganga Ram fell ill on the way. Here, they found few caravans were travelling to Mongolia, and the caravan leader was evasive about a start date. Bitter experience had taught him not to divulge this information, for fear of spies in Lhasa alerting bands of robbers along the road, who would then lie in wait. In Tibet, outside of the main centres, many tribes adopted banditry as a profession; however, as an unwritten law, they would never plunder their own people.

The wait to join a caravan dragged on for twelve months; but Kishen Singh had no alternative than to wait, as it was simply too dangerous for the trio to travel on their own. He put this time to good use, though, learning Mongolian well enough not to require an interpreter, and studying the sacred books of the Tibetans; both skills would prove invaluable later. Working secretly and carefully, he also prepared a plan-to-scale of the city and its surrounds, which would prove of immense value to his masters in the coming years.*

From his daily interactions, he recorded details about the people of Lhasa and their customs, adding to Nain Singh's observations from a decade earlier. He, too, witnessed their intriguing new year celebrations, observing how religion dominated life here. Every morning he saw crowds making a circumambulation of the Dalai Lama's residence—the Potala Palace—which also housed the remains of former great lamas. Some devotees would complete the ritual again in the evening, although the wealthy could pay the less fortunate to carry out this extra act of worship on their behalf.

Eventually, in September 1879, Kishen Singh's party of six, including three new servants, joined a caravan of over 100 travellers

---

* In 1904, British surveyors attached to the Younghusband Expedition to Lhasa would praise his plan as 'very accurate and reliable', and it was the only such map available at the time.

returning to Mongolia. More than half were Mongolians, who could ride before they could walk, and remain mounted even when excessively drunk. The Tibetans, on the other hand, chose to walk; either way, everyone had to keep up with the caravan or face being left by the wayside, with little chance of survival. And everyone was armed, even the lamas, while mounted scouts were constantly on the lookout for any sign of the marauding bandits known to infest the area. When they set up camp each night, the Tibetans in their black tents made from yak hair could be distinguished from the Mongolians, whose shelters were of coarse white woollen felt. But everyone remained vigilant, as the brigands were notorious for mounting an attack when travellers were resting, cutting the ropes which held their tents up before murdering the trapped victims.

Some 60 miles north of Lhasa, the caravan started its traverse of the endless Chang Tang. They were soon in virtually uninhabited territory left to wild animals, while past the Tengri Nor lay uncharted land. Further on, they forded the headwaters of the Salween River, before crossing the Tanggula Shan (*shan* means mountain range) which separates the upper sources of the Salween, Mekong and Yangtze. All these rivers flow south here, before the Yangtze makes its big turn and eventually heads north on to the plains of China.

At times, it was wretchedly difficult for Kishen Singh and his men, and when Chumbel lost a toe, possibly to frostbite while crossing a freezing river, it further slowed the group's progress. Their baggage animals fared even worse: one perished from the extreme cold, another two had to be abandoned after they became stuck in a bog, and a further pair died from lack of food. Distressingly, this caused their party to become separated from the main caravan; but they pushed on and, by late October, managed to reach the Kunlun Range on the northern edge of the plateau. Here, they met passing nomads who sold them fresh horses, allowing them to rejoin the main group.

Soon afterwards, the caravan split up and the Mongolians left for home. Just when the Tibetans thought they had crossed the plateau safely, a band of 200 mounted robbers ambushed them. They stripped Kishen Singh of much of his goods and baggage animals, but he managed to hang on to some items of value, including his survey instruments. He resolved not to give up his mission, even after the rest of the caravan decided to return to Lhasa, but had to discharge the new servants. With Chumbel and Ganga Ram, he pushed on all the way up through the Tsinghai province of China, passing between the Koko Nor (Blue Lake) and the eastern edge of the immense Tsaidam (salt marsh) with its many brackish lakes—although the Tsaidam is labelled a 'depression', it actually sits at an altitude of 8500 feet.

By this stage they were running low on funds, and were thus fortunate to find work with a Tibetan lama for almost three months, looking after his camels during winter in return for food. Once spring arrived, they continued north, stopping for a further three months at a village in the hope of joining another caravan. Here, Kishen Singh bartered and sold the last of his goods for three horses and four guns, plus 200 rupees in silver; but a second theft now seriously upset his plans. Ganga Ram, fearful after hearing tales of unfriendly Muslims to the north, deserted, taking two of the horses, three guns and 150 rupees with him.

Even now, despite being desperately short of funds, Kishen Singh would not abandon his expedition; and the ever-faithful Chumbel had chosen to remain with him rather than abscond with Ganga Ram. The pair found employment as herdsmen, and after five months their generous employer gave them a horse, warm clothing and provisions, as they prepared to continue north. Joining a caravan, they crossed a ridge of mountains into the province of Gansu. Shortly afterwards, they arrived in Dunhuang, the northern-most point of their journey, in the first week of 1881.

This famed 'City of Sands' is an oasis located on the old Silk Road, which Marco Polo had visited centuries earlier, and where Benedict de Goes had finally succumbed in 1607. Close by are the Caves of the Thousand Buddhas, comprising many hundreds of temples and grottoes hewn out of the cliff face. They contain some of the finest examples of Buddhist art spanning 1000 years, including stunning wall paintings and clay sculptures. One special cave hid a library, into which archaeologists would later gain entry to find an enormous hoard of ancient manuscripts. Amongst these scrolls they would discover the *Diamond Sutra*—the world's earliest known printed book, published 600 years before the Gutenberg Bible.*

Unlike Lhasa, Dunhuang's population was almost exclusively Chinese. The governor of the city suspected Kishen Singh and Chumbel of being spies. He would not let them proceed further north, holding them prisoner within the city limits for seven months. Under constant surveillance, Kishen Singh kept his instruments carefully concealed, not daring to take astronomical observations even at night. During this time, to make ends meet, he was forced to sell the horse and work as a fruit seller. Later, Chumbel had to nurse him when he became ill with fever and found it hard to walk. Their luck finally turned when they met an influential Tibetan lama who had come to visit the Caves of the Thousand Buddhas, and he convinced the governor to release the pair to him as servants.

They left Dunhuang together in August, heading south and for home. On the way back, they learnt Ganga Ram had settled down with a group of nomads nearby. Kishen Singh, bearing his old servant no ill will, sent him an offer to rejoin them, but was refused. Fearful of bandits, the lama sometimes required them to ride, so they could make a run for it in case they were attacked. During such times, Kishen Singh cleverly managed to continue his route survey by counting his horse's paces instead of his own.

From the Tosun Nor, an opportunity arose to explore new territory, after the lama decided to return to Tibet by a different route, one which lay hundreds of miles further east from Kishen Singh's initial journey north. After recrossing the Kunlun Range and climbing back on to the Chang Tang, they crossed one of the main

* In 1907, the Hungarian-born Briton Aurel Stein would be the first of several foreign archaeologists to controversially remove most of the library to their own national museums.

tributaries of the Huang Ho (Yellow River) and arrived at the lama's monastery.

Here, the pair had to wait for two months before the lama paid them. However, he did give them a letter of introduction as well, addressed to an influential friend in the next town. His friend's recommendation, in turn, allowed them to join a trader's caravan as servants, on a 400-mile journey into the southeastern corner of Tibet. They travelled to the border town of Tachienlu—today the modern city of Kangding in China's Sichuan province—which sits high in the mountains at an altitude of over 8000 feet, arriving there in February the following year. It was the furthest point east Kishen Singh and Chumbel would reach; looking back, once they finally returned to Lhasa, their journey would trace out a rough triangle with the Tosun Nor at its northern apex.

Tachienlu was the centre of the tea trade, and a key stop on the old Tea Horse Road. Like the Silk Road, it too dated back many centuries, when China traded its tea for the sturdy Tibetan ponies needed to fight the fierce nomads to its north. Enormous loads, pressed into bricks for easier transportation, were brought to the town on the backs of 'coolies', who marched up from the tea-growing areas in China some twenty days to the east. Here the loads were transferred on to yaks and other pack animals for the long journey west to Lhasa, about 900 miles, or three and a half months, away. From the capital, traders and their caravans would distribute the tea bricks across the entire country over the following months.*

In Tachienlu, Kishen Singh used a letter of introduction Walker had given him to make contact with the Jesuit missionaries based there. When he left, they gave him a small gift of 6 rupees; but he was reticent to ask for a more substantial loan, which he desperately needed. The priests sent word back to the GTS that its native explorer

---

* Years earlier, China had enforced a complete embargo on the importation of Indian tea into Tibet; otherwise it would have required only a short haul across the mountains.

was safe. For Walker this was wonderful news, as he had not heard from Kishen Singh in nearly four years. His relief was considerable since he had heard wild rumours that Chumbel had been executed, and the authorities in Lhasa had chopped off Kishen Singh's legs to put an end to his exploring.

The pair crossed over from China back into Tibet, before walking to the major town of Batang, with its monastery of 1000 monks. It is situated on the banks of Asia's longest river, where the immense watershed belonging to the Yangtze, Mekong and Salween rivers run roughly parallel across a narrow 50-mile corridor separated by high ranges. Crossing the latter two rivers proved to be a hair-raising affair. They had no option but to use a dangerous-looking flying fox contraption to negotiate the Mekong, and were paddled across the Salween on a plank of wood guided by a long rope stretched across the river.

At this point, they tried to take a shortcut back to India, by heading directly south into the British territory of Assam. En route, they encountered the Mishmi people, who monopolized the trade between Tibet and their lands, and were known to kill all trespassers. They were a ferocious and primitive tribal people, whose trade in slaves included selling kidnapped children from Assam into Tibet. Maddeningly, just 30 miles from the British frontier, Kishen Singh realized they risked certain death if they attempted to cross Mishmi lands. So, they resigned themselves to backtracking and taking the long route home by way of Lhasa.

Unfortunate as this was for them, for the GTS this detour would prove to be a boon, as it would give Kishen Singh an opportunity to survey a further 600 miles of fresh territory. His new route would take him around the eastern basin of the Tsangpo, traversing the entire area between the rivers. Since he did not cross the Tsangpo at any time on his return trip, it indicated the river must flow into Assam further to the west. This finding would lend added weight to the majority view held by geographers at the time, that the Tsangpo flowed into India to become the Brahmaputra, and not into Burma (now Myanmar) as the Irrawaddy.

For Kishen Singh and Chumbel, this delay posed two further problems: because spring was late in coming, the mountain passes were still blocked with snow; and their money had almost run out now. To fund their six-month-long trip back, Kishen Singh went from village to village reciting the sacred books of the Tibetans, and in this way earned 20 rupees. But, as luck would have it, at one village he and Chumbel were placed in quarantine for twenty-two days, after they inadvertently crossed over from a district where there was an outbreak of smallpox.

They set off for Lhasa in early July, although in such a shabby state that they were mistaken for escaped convicts when passing through a penal settlement, and were promptly arrested. Fortunately, they were released a few days later when another traveller vouched for them. By October, they managed to reach Chetang and cross the Tsangpo here, before marching on to Gyantse and finally arriving in Darjeeling in November 1882. They had been gone four and a half years, and forced to beg their way for much of this time.

Walker, in his report of the mission, published by the RGS, noted: 'They arrived in a condition bordering on destitution, their funds exhausted, their clothes in rags, and their bodies emaciated with the hardships and deprivations they had undergone.' Kishen Singh returned to find that his only son, a two-year-old when he left, had died during his absence. His relatives had long given him up for dead, his wife had taken up with another man, and at one point it was feared he would not survive his ordeal.

It had been a mammoth journey, one that no other Pundit would surpass in terms of the distance covered or the time spent in the field. Kishen Singh had maintained an unbroken route survey throughout, totalling about 2800 miles (*not* including the distance back from Tibet, after he closed out his survey and retraced his outward march). Of this distance, around 1700 miles was through uncharted country. Even when he was forced to ride some 230 miles with the lama, he took careful latitudinal observations at certain points, to allow the average length of his horse's pace to be calculated afterwards. Otherwise, he had always insisted on walking, even though the Mongolians looked down on this practice, as even the poorest among them had horses and rode everywhere.

True to form, Kishen Singh brought back all his survey instruments, even the bulky 9-inch sextant. And, of course, all his tiny notebooks, hidden in the barrel of his prayer wheel and in his clothing. He had managed to take twenty-two latitudinal observations and seventy boiling-point determinations for height at various locations along the way. Latitude readings made by later European explorers would tally closely with his measurements; and a British explorer-cum-plant collector, Captain Kingdon-Ward, who travelled over the same ground, would endorse his work: 'AK's report and route survey . . . are excellent. It is hard to find a mistake.'

After Walker read out his paper describing this epic effort, the chairman commented on the valuable role the GTS and its Pundits had played over the years. They had uncovered substantial new geographical information about Central Asia and Tibet; of General Walker's contribution, he stated: 'his crowning success had been this marvellous journey of the Pundit A-K.'

Within a few years, Kishen Singh would receive gold medals from both the Paris Geographical Society and its Venice counterpart; but although the RGS was full of praise and gave him a grant of money, it chose not to award him its highest honour. The Government of India conferred on him the title of Rai Bahadur and, on his retirement in 1885, granted him a village generating an annual income of almost 2000 rupees. The government also did not overlook Chumbel's services, providing him a monthly pension of 15 rupees.

After his gruelling final journey, Kishen Singh did manage to recover his health; but, as the Tibetans had put a price of 500 pounds on his head, he did not cross their frontier again. He lived to enjoy his handsome pension for another twenty-six years until, in 1921 at the age of seventy-one, he passed away.

Kintup (K.P.)

The controversy surrounding the Great River of Tibet had looked all but settled after Kishen Singh's final report, based on his observations of the land between the rivers. As far back as 1765, James Rennell had explored up the Brahmaputra into Assam and concluded there was the 'strongest presumptive proof possible' that it was an extension of the Tsangpo. Other European geographers, though, continued to link the waters from Tibet to the Irrawaddy, Burma's main transport artery. Even if Rennell was right, it was still unclear which of the four major tributaries of the Brahmaputra connected it to the Tsangpo: was it through the Lohit, Dibong, Dihang or Subansiri?

India's 2000-mile northeastern frontier was virtually unmanned by the British. It ran from Ladakh all the way along southern Tibet to Assam, which was something of a forgotten province during this period. The Himalayan region was thickly vegetated here, making it impossible to survey any significant distance up the Brahmaputra, even with elephants. Furthermore, the British maintained a policy of appeasement, prohibiting any exploration or mapping in these sensitive areas, after a punitive force had taken to the field in 1862 against the local Abors. A fierce tribal people, they were divided into warring clans and weren't welcoming to outsiders. They went around almost naked and were labelled 'savage tribes' by the authorities, since a favourite pastime of these hill people was to raid the richer villages on the plains below them. The Survey of India had failed in its attempts to enlist natives of Assam as Pundits because, once they completed their training, recruits proved unwilling to travel through this dangerous region and explore upriver.

From the Tibetan side, Nain Singh had charted the river as far as Chetang in 1874. A second Pundit named Lala had tried to get further downstream two years later, but had returned after sixteen months, unable to continue due to the threat posed by bandits.

After Trotter left the GTS in 1875, Captain Henry Harman took charge of the Pundits together with another officer, both working under Walker. Harman carried the survey of the Brahmaputra upriver, close to the town of Sadiya, where three of its four main tributaries converge.

Walker had tasked Harman with determining which of the tributaries connected with the Tsangpo, the Dihang and the Subansiri being the two most likely contenders. The captain measured their flows, finding the Dihang discharged three times the volume of the Subansiri and was therefore the prime candidate. But whether it was indeed the connector could not be confirmed by direct observation, due to the difficulty in penetrating this area. And the earlier question of whether the Tsangpo flowed into the Irrawaddy had not been settled beyond doubt either, and refused to go away.

Harman planned to answer both these questions, and solve the mystery of the river, once and for all. He recruited and trained a lama called Nem Singh (code-named G.M.N.) to route-survey along the Tsangpo as far downriver from Chetang as possible. This new Pundit took as his assistant a man named Kintup, and the two travelled to the town via Lhasa in October 1878. They discovered that downstream from Chetang, rather than continue in a southeasterly direction, the Tsangpo bent back towards the north-east. This information was important, as it implied the river probably did not flow into the Subansiri.

From this point, they marched almost 300 miles downstream to a village called Gyala which, by their estimation, sat 8000 feet above sea level. As far as this village, the river had flowed placidly through a wide valley, but soon afterwards they encountered rugged mountainous terrain, and could proceed no further. They learnt from the locals that the river entered a deep gorge further on, as it turned southwards. At least by reaching Gyala, they left only about 100 miles of the river uncharted, but final proof that it was the connector had eluded them.

At this point, Harman decided to use Kintup (now code-named K.P.) to accompany a Chinese lama and complete the survey of the remaining section.* Kintup, a native of upper Sikkim, was thirty-one years old at the time and a tailor by trade, with a shop in Darjeeling. He had previously acted as a guide for travellers in this region, and possibly would have done more work for the GTS but for his being illiterate and unable to record survey observations. A British army doctor who often hired Kintup described him as:

> A thick-set, active man with a look of dogged determination on his rugged, weather-beaten features. His deep-chested voice I have often heard calling clearly from a hill-top some miles away, like a ship's captain in a storm. He has all the alertness of a mountaineer and with the strength of a lion he is a host in himself.

The GTS trained the lama in route surveying, and designated him the leader of this expedition, but its choice turned out to be a poor one. In the event the pair was unable to survey the missing section, Harman devised an ingenious backup plan. They were to throw a large number of specially prepared logs into the Tsangpo, each 1 foot in length and containing a tin tube with an identification paper. If they had to resort to this plan, they were to alert Harman beforehand. He would then arrange to have men stationed on the banks of the Dihang, at its junction with the Brahmaputra, to be on the lookout for the logs. The recovery of any one log would prove beyond doubt that the Tsangpo became the Brahmaputra, with the Dihang their connector as it flowed from the Abor Hills on to the plains of Assam.

The lama and Kintup left Darjeeling disguised as pilgrims, making their way via Lhasa to Chetang in August 1880. At times, when they ran out of provisions, they had to beg for food. They reached Gyala in March the following year, after being held up for four months at a village they stopped at along the way. This delay

---

* The lama is not named in the Survey of India's records, and another account mentions that he was Mongolian, not Chinese.

occurred after the lama began an affair with their host's wife, and would not leave. Once he was found out, it was only with considerable difficulty that Kintup managed to convince the man of the house to accept 25 rupees as compensation, before the pair could continue their journey.

Around this time the lama started treating him badly. Although Kintup bore this with patience, the situation would soon take a turn for the worse. After reaching the most northerly point of the Tsangpo, they continued further inland to stay in a *jong* (fort) by the road, which taxed passing travellers. At this point the lama disappeared and, when he did not return, Kintup learnt he had sold him as a slave to the *jongpon* (fort master).

He was forced to work as a servant now, and it was only after nine months that Kintup found an opportunity to escape. Rather than give up and return home, however, he decided to see his mission through. He had gone 35 miles downriver from Gyala before the jongpon's men, who had been in hot pursuit, caught up with him at a monastery. Kintup pleaded with the head lama there for refuge; the latter then paid the jongpon 50 rupees for his release. But Kintup soon realized that he had only succeeded in trading one master for another, although certainly a more compassionate one, as events would prove.

After serving the head lama for four and a half months, Kintup successfully pleaded for a month of leave, on the pretext of making a pilgrimage. Fortunately for him, a pilgrim can travel throughout Tibet relying solely on the generosity of its people, who would never let a devotee starve for fear of the retribution they would face in the next world. Despite this second chance to make a run for home, Kintup remained steadfast to his mission, even without the funds to continue downriver as originally planned. Instead, he decided to activate Harman's backup plan now, using marked logs, since he had retained the tin tubes they were given.

During his stay at a monastery across the river, Kintup carefully cut and prepared 500 logs, each 1 foot in length. Since he had lost the gouge Harman had supplied them with, to bore into the logs before inserting the tubes, he used bamboo strips to tie a tube to each log. He then hid his cache in a cave, and returned to serve the lama.

After a further two months, Kintup begged his master for more leave to make yet another pilgrimage. This time he walked all the way back to Lhasa, where he dictated a letter to the chief of the Survey of India, to be sent via Nem Singh in Darjeeling, stating:

> Sir, The Lama who was sent with me sold me to a Jongpon as a slave and himself fled away with the Government things that were in his charge. On account of which the journey proved a bad one; however, I, Kintup, have prepared the 500 logs . . . and am prepared to throw 50 logs per day into the Tsangpo . . . from the 5th to the 15th of the tenth Tibetan month of the year . . .

Although Nem Singh did receive this letter, it never reached Harman for reasons which aren't clear. Just before the letter's arrival, the captain had left for Europe due to ill health, suffering from severe complications caused by exposure and frostbite from his earlier survey days. He died a few months after arriving, never having heard from his two native explorers since the day they started out. Harman had, in fact, anticipated the possibility of his backup plan being used, stationing men by the Dihang to keep a lookout for any logs. But eventually, after two years, the watch was abandoned when he was forced to depart India on sick leave.

Kintup, meanwhile, returned to the monastery biding his time, unaware that no one knew of his plan or would be on the lookout for his logs. After another nine months of servitude, the head lama set him free, impressed by his work and piety. Kintup returned to the cave, retrieved his 500 marked logs, and diligently threw them into the Tsangpo over ten days, just as he had promised.

After finding some work in the area to fund his return trip, Kintup turned for home. He hoped to reach India by taking the shortest path possible, following the Tsangpo downriver. However, the track became impassable after a while, and the Abors would not let him cross their land. Like Kishen Singh before him, he came within miles of completing the shortcut to the Indian frontier, only to be disappointed. Forced to take the long way home via Lhasa, he had to break his journey several times to earn enough money to continue on.

Kintup finally returned to Darjeeling in November 1884, after a mission lasting more than four years. He received no hero's welcome, though, or even any immediate acknowledgement of his efforts; instead, he had to deal with the death of his mother during his absence.

It was only two years later that he was asked to dictate from memory to a fellow Pundit an account of his travels, which was then translated into English. Another three years would pass before a report of his exploits was published, although it wasn't given the credence it deserved, probably because he was not a trained Pundit. Being illiterate, he hadn't brought back any field notes for the GTS to process, nor had he completed a route survey. Yet he had traced the course of the Tsangpo nearly 100 miles further downriver than any previous explorer, to a point only 35 miles from the plains of India.

Regrettably, in the process of telling his story, Kintup was either misunderstood or mistranslated as witnessing a point where 'the Tsangpo . . . falls over a cliff . . . from a height of about 150 feet. There is a big lake at the foot of the falls where rainbows are always observable'. These few lines from his narrative proved controversial, and sent European geographers scrambling to discover another natural wonder akin to the Victoria Falls.

There had been speculation about the existence of such a waterfall, because the Tsangpo drops from a height of almost 10,000 feet at Chetang down to a mere 500 feet by the time it reaches Assam as the Brahmaputra. What wasn't clear was whether the river ran through a series of deep gorges, and dropped in a succession of cataracts; or did it, perhaps, contain a single massive waterfall?

Kintup *never* claimed he had seen a 150-foot fall on the Tsangpo. Colonel Frederick Bailey, the intrepid explorer and master spy, finally cleared up this misconception years later, when he and another British officer, Henry Morsehead, retraced Kintup's route in 1913. Bailey went on to prove irrefutably that the Tsangpo did become the Brahmaputra, and the rivers were indeed linked by the Dihang—for which he won the RGS's gold medal three years later.[*] He tracked Kintup down, almost thirty years after his remarkable mission, and they went over the details again. Bailey's view was 'that the whole story was remarkably accurate', given the time that had elapsed since Kintup's journey had been initially recorded, and considering he was fleeing captivity then.

When the colonel met Kintup, he had returned to working as a tailor in Darjeeling, and was living under poor circumstances. This, despite a note in the *Geographical Journal* of the RGS (vol. 4, 1894), titled 'Rewards to Tibetan Explorers', which mentions Kintup 'has since received a gratuity of Rs. 3000 from Government'. What he did with this large sum is unclear. Perhaps the report was inaccurate and meant to say 300 rupees; it goes on to incorrectly state that he was 'kept a prisoner for nearly six years'.[†] Nevertheless, through Bailey's efforts, and with the help of the surveyor general, a one-off payment of 1000 rupees from the government was secured for him. Soon afterwards, the viceroy received the tailor to present him what he was due, together with a parchment of honour. This recognition couldn't have come any sooner for Kintup, or his family, as he died a few months later.

---

[*]   Bailey also won the MacGregor Medal in 1914, for valuable military reconnaissance on India's behalf.

[†]   Further to this, the same note mentions a more senior, well-known Pundit, Ugyen Gyatso, receiving 1000 rupees with his medal and title of Rai Bahadur; hence 300 rupees for Kintup sounds more plausible.

Servants of the Map

One wonders what drove these native explorers—men such as Kintup, the Singhs, the Mirza, and the many other Pundits—and what lay behind their extreme dedication to the hazardous work they undertook. One explanation, offered by author Showell Styles, is the deep sense of service and devotion to duty that makes up part of the Indian psyche, even more so in times gone by. This is one reason why Indian pilgrims are considered holy and hold such a special place in the community, which so readily supports them with food and alms.

An extension of this concept is the idea of serving a higher cause with enduring loyalty. This is what the Pundits had demonstrated to their employer, the GTS, as 'servants of the map'. Cartographer Matthew Edney explains a wider role the Pundits had played, as 'the only Indians ever to be accredited by the British as autonomous field surveyors *in their own right*' [his emphasis]. He goes on to conclude that they 'are thus essential to the self-image of the modern, independent Survey of India'.

Today, however, when a roll call of the great explorers is taken, the Pundits are largely forgotten. Even Nain Singh, for example, despite winning its highest honour, doesn't rate a mention in the RGS' recent book *Explorers*, published in 2010. Neither does he feature as an individual entry in *The Oxford Companion to World Exploration*, but is listed generally under 'Pundit Mapmakers'. Nor are any of the Pundits listed in *any* capacity in many other books about eminent explorers.

Yet if success is measured not only by what one achieves, but also from where one starts in life *and* the resources at hand, then surely the achievements of the Pundits must be judged as extraordinary. During nearly four decades of exploration, up to the end of the century, they route-surveyed over 25,000 miles of territory north of India's frontiers, covering a staggering 1,000,000 square miles. Much of this region was previously uncharted, and where most European explorers had dared not venture. The American oriental scholar and traveller William Rockhill, writing close to this time, noted:

> If any British explorer had done one-third of what Nain Singh ... or Kishen Singh [he lists others Pundits] accomplished, medals and decorations, lucrative offices ... and every form of lionizing would have been his; as for those native explorers a small pecuniary reward and obscurity are all to which they can look forward to.

The Pundits remain unsung heroes of the British Raj. Although their achievements were diminished in the eyes of many Westerners at the time because they were natives, at least some of their number should rank equal amongst other renowned explorers. Native or otherwise, though, when considered as a whole, the Pundits were undoubtedly the greatest *group* of explorers the world has seen in recent history. *They deserve to be well remembered.*

PART FOUR

THE GREAT GAME ENDS

'When everyone is dead the Great Game is finished. Not before.'

—Rudyard Kipling, *Kim*

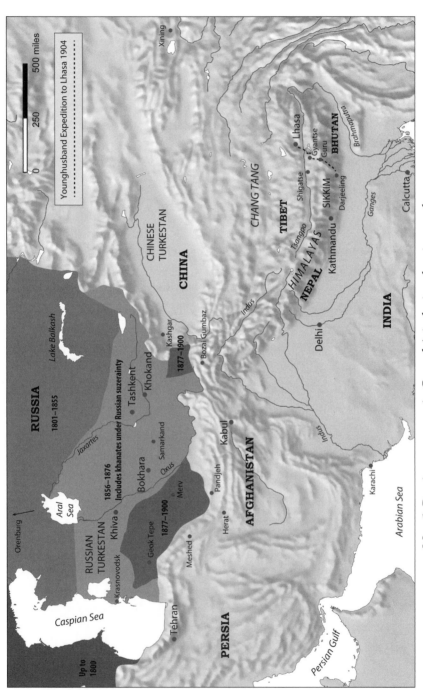

Map 5. Russian conquests in Central Asia during the nineteenth century

Caspian Sea

Aral Sea

Lake Balkash

Orenburg

Krasnovodsk

RUSSIAN TURKESTAN

Khiva

Geok Tepe

1877–1900

Merv

Meshed

Tehran

PERSIA

Herat

Pandjeh

Kabul

AFGHANISTAN

Karachi

Arabian Sea

Persian Gulf

RUSSIA

1801–1855

Jaxartes

Tashkent

1856–1876

Includes khanates under Russian suzerainty

Bokhara

Samarkand

Oxus

Khokand

Kashgar

1877–1900

CHINESE TURKESTAN

Bozal Gumbaz

Indus

CHINA

Delhi

Indus

Ganges

INDIA

Calcutta

CHANG TANG

TIBET

Tsangpo

Shigatse

Lhasa

Gyantse

Guru

BHUTAN

SIKKIM

Darjeeling

HIMALAYAS

NEPAL

Kathmandu

Brahmaputra

Xining

Up to 1860

0   250   500 miles

Younghusband Expedition to Lhasa 1904

9

Russia Advances into Central Asia

With Britain behaving so aggressively during the First Afghan War, justifying its moves as legitimate action taken in its own sphere of influence, Russia would be provoked into doing much the same, and more. The second half of the Great Game would be marked by the latter's inexorable advance into Central Asia during the second half of the nineteenth century, and a rapid expansion of its territory there.

Russia's first target was Khiva, the closest of the three Muslim khanates in Western Turkestan. In this case, the tsar believed his action was justified, in wanting to free his people from slavery and stopping this inhumane trade emanating from the city. Khiva was home to one of two infamous markets in Central Asia (the other being Bokhara), and well known for its brisk trade in Russian citizens

The Slaves

Many of these slaves were ex-soldiers, while others had been captured from caravans or frontier towns by Turcoman raiders. It was said of the Turcoman that they would not hesitate to sell the Prophet himself into slavery if he fell into their hands. So terrible was their raiding and banditry that many settlements in northern Persia and western Afghanistan had been abandoned during this time, and the whole region depopulated.

As far back as 1819, Captain Nikolai Muraviev, one of the early Great Game players, had travelled to Khiva and seen the wretched condition of the Russian slaves first-hand. They had even smuggled a message to him, secreted in the barrel of a gun he had given for repair, begging their tsar's help to end their bondage. But, try as he might, the tsar could not even *buy* the freedom of his own people, as the khan had threatened to execute anyone found selling slaves back. What particularly angered Russians was the forced conversion of their Christian fellowmen to Islam by their captors. Other than many hundreds of Russian slaves, there were some 30,000 Persians held in captivity as well. They were also regarded as kafirs by the locals, rather than as Muslim brethren, because they belonged to the minority Shiite sect and were therefore considered fair game. The markets in Khiva were said to be thriving, with the highest prices being paid for young Russian males as workers and Persian females for the harem. Muraviev had urged his superiors to annex this khanate, but nothing had come of his proposal back then.

Now, twenty years later, as the political timing became more opportune, Tsar Nicholas proclaimed his determination to free his people and put an end to this trade. In the process, Khiva would have to be subsumed, and the khan replaced with a ruler who would do Russia's bidding. Under General Perovsky's command, an expedition set out from Orenburg for the 900-mile march south in late 1839— timed to avoid the heat and lack of water, while expecting snow to protect the grazing underneath. The army comprised around 5000 troops, including artillery, and a baggage train of 10,000 camels. They began cursing their luck, though, as they encountered an early and acute winter with heavier snowfall than normal, and the freeze prevented access to grazing for their animals. As they battled incredible hardship, often trudging through waist-high snow, it must have brought back memories of Russia's failed invasion attempt of India in 1801. Soon, the hardy camels, which were critical to the expedition's advance, began dying off at an alarming rate: around 100 every day. The cold was so severe that many men could not take off their clothes during the entire march, and became covered with vermin and dirt. Sickness was rife, the men were steadily dying as the army trudged on, and packs of wolves stalked the column, ready to devour any stragglers.

Three months out and only halfway to Khiva, Perovsky had no option but to turn back. When his army finally limped back into Orenburg seven months later, they counted their losses: 1000 men and upwards of 8500 camels had perished. For the Khivans this was a welcome reprieve, at least for now. The Russian slaves, too, wouldn't remain in bondage much longer: help was on its way, although from a completely unexpected quarter.

On hearing of the Russian advance, the British dispatched Captain James Abbott from Herat some 500 miles away, with the intention of reaching the city first. His mission was to convince the khan of Khiva to release all Russians and, in doing so, take away any pretext for the tsar to annex his country. On the way there, Abbott overtook a group of slaves being marched to the markets by their Turcoman captors, including women and children, and he later described the plight of their menfolk: 'The men are chained together by the throats at night, so that rest is scarcely possible, whilst the contact of the frozen iron with their skin must be torture.' He went on to add: 'Alas! He who once enters Khiva abandons all hope, as surely as he who enters hell.'

A somewhat confused khan received the captain, since he had little knowledge of Britain, as no one from that distant island nation had ever visited Khiva. He and his court were astounded to learn its monarch was a woman, enquiring: 'Do you always choose women as your kings?' After hearing what the Englishman had come to propose, the khan remained unconvinced and suspected, somewhat ironically, that he was a Russian spy.

Abbott's effort to secure the slaves freedom was unsuccessful, but the khan imposed on him to undertake another mission instead on his behalf—one that might still achieve this aim. He was to travel to St Petersburg with a letter for the tsar, offering the freedom of his subjects in return for Russia dropping all designs on Khivan territory.

Unfortunately, on the way there, Abbott was betrayed by his guide, and suffered greatly after he was robbed and wounded by brigands in the desert. They only released him on learning of his mission, fearful of incurring the khan's wrath. Eventually, after recovering from his injuries in a Russian fort, Abbott did manage to reach St Petersburg and deliver the message from Khiva.

Meanwhile, Abbott's superiors, unaware he had left for the capital (since the khan had been intercepting his mail), or of the disaster befalling Perovsky's army, dispatched a second officer to try and complete the mission. This man was Lieutenant Richmond Shakespear—another young and ambitious political who, like Alexander Burnes, would seize his opportunity to make a name for himself.

By the time he arrived in Khiva in June 1840 with his party of twelve, the full extent of the General Perovsky's misfortunes were known to all. With this threat now neutralized, Shakespear had lost his prime argument but, to his lasting credit, he managed to convince the khan that Russia might try again in the near future. The slaves were handed over by their reluctant owners, and in the final tally 416 were released, including women and children, many of whom had been in bondage for over a decade.

Two months after arriving, Shakespear left Khiva accompanied by his jubilant group. The khan wisely gave them an armed escort, to prevent other slavers recapturing the party along the way. They headed for the nearest Russian post of Fort Alexandrovsk, over 500 miles away on the eastern shore of the Caspian Sea. Here, an incredulous camp commandant received them, while the liberated slaves showered Shakespear with gratitude. And when he arrived in St Petersburg, the tsar thanked him personally, although he was known to be privately furious that a lone, junior officer had thwarted his plan for Khiva.

On his return to London, not yet thirty years old, Shakespear was knighted by his queen. Abbott was initially not as fortunate, and he lamented on his return: 'All the sufferings fell to my lot, all the laurels to his.' In time, though, he too went on to great things. He later became a general, was knighted, and founded a garrison town that has grown into a city that still bears his name today.*

Many Russian historians, however, discount the role Abbott and Shakespear played in the liberation of these slaves, and regard the two officers as mere spies. Be that as it may, neither Russia nor Britain seemed as concerned about the fate of the remaining 30,000 Persian slaves, who remained captive in Khiva.

The Indian Mutiny

With the end of the First Afghan War in 1842, a period of relative calm and détente seemed to descend on Central Asia—but it wouldn't stop Britain or Russia continuing their territorial expansion towards their final 'natural' frontiers. During this decade, the aggressive forward policy of the hawks in both camps would find less favour, with the doctrine of masterly inactivity gaining ascendancy.

Britain used this time to make further territorial gains within India. First, they seized the large province of Sind in 1843 in an example of raw colonialism and, according to some historians, as a morale booster to offset its defeat in Afghanistan. Mountstuart Elphinstone, once governor of Bombay, who later wrote the *History of India*, went even further: 'It put me in mind of a bully who had been kicked in the streets and went home to beat his wife in revenge.' The commander of the expedition, General Napier, a man known not to mince his words, would say of this land grab: 'We have no right to seize Sind, yet we shall do so and a very advantageous, useful, and humane piece of rascality it will be.' The satirical magazine *Punch* would jokingly publish how, on conquering the province, Napier had sent back a one-word dispatch: *Peccavi* (Latin for 'I have Sin[ne]d').

This conquest was followed by two wars against the Sikhs, after the death of the old ruler Ranjit Singh. Without his strong hand, the

---

* The city of Abbottabad is located in northern Pakistan.

previously resilient alliance between the neighbours had crumbled—just as Alexander Burnes had predicted—and the kingdom disintegrated. Victories in these Anglo-Sikh wars in 1849 allowed Britain to claim the larger and more valuable prize of the Punjab, that fertile land of the five rivers. British India could move its border well beyond the Indus now, to become Afghanistan's immediate neighbour.

A few years earlier, in 1844, Tsar Nicholas I had visited Queen Victoria and impressed upon her Russia's desire for peace, assuring Britain he had no designs on India. His biggest worry was containing the fallout from the imminent collapse of the Ottoman Empire—'the sick man of Europe', as he termed it. He returned home convinced he had extracted a promise that the two nations would work together in the event of such a crisis. Britain, however, believed it had given no such undertaking—a misunderstanding soon to prove costly to both sides. The subsequent and senseless Crimean War, which claimed around 500,000 lives, highlighted yet again the immense divide between the two empires and their readiness to lock horns.

The Persians had remained neutral during this war—although only after a little persuasion from the British, who had a warship sitting in their gulf. Britain's policy towards them continued to vacillate, however, as one contemporary English writer observed: 'Persia is attracted to Britain by her hopes, driven towards Russia by her fears.'

In an effort to undermine its foe, St Petersburg persuaded Tehran to lay claim on Herat again, while the two powers were preoccupied fighting each other in Crimea. The shah's troops quickly captured the city in October 1856 after a brief siege—a move that greatly alarmed London, since Herat could be used as a forward base against India. Britain again resorted to the gunboat diplomacy that had worked so effectively during their last dispute, although this time it actually shelled the city of Bushire from its warships. This countermove quickly brought the shah back to his senses: he withdrew his forces from Herat, forever abandoning all claims to this once-coveted prize.

While this was occurring, some strategists and generals in Russia sought to launch an attack on India, in the hope this would divert British troops from Crimea, where Britain and its allies were winning the war. Their other hope was that this action might provide the spark for Indians to rise up against British rule. This plan was never executed, though, as the tsar desperately needed all his troops at home.

As it transpired, the Indians didn't need a spark from *outside* their borders: they were quite capable of lighting the fuse themselves, as the Indian Mutiny of 1857 would soon prove. Historian Brian Gardner, who wrote *The East India Company: A History*, described it as: 'The most bitterly contested and terrible war in which the British had ever been engaged in their long history of wars.' Author John Masters commented: 'Twelve centuries of English history show nothing remotely like it. This was at once the noon of courage and the midnight of barbarism.'

The causes and conduct of the Indian Mutiny have already been thoroughly documented by others and, like the Crimean War, it falls outside the scope of this book. The last of the rebels were defeated just over a year later, but the consequences for British rule in India would be dramatic, and Britons' relationship with their fellow Indians would be altered forever. It led Parliament to hurriedly pass the India Act in August 1858, transferring all powers to rule on the subcontinent from the East India Company to the Crown, firmly putting imperial interests ahead of the Company's profits. This event marked the start of the British Raj, otherwise known as Crown rule in India, and the governor-general was given the additional title of viceroy of India.

The years following the mutiny were a time of extreme caution for Britons in India, as they concentrated on internal problems and tried to repair the enormous damage done—although for many Indians 'the milk had already been spilt'.

In the immediate aftermath of the 1857 uprising, there was one other noteworthy loss to India's cultural heritage. Just as they had blown up Kabul's iconic bazaar in retribution for insurrection there, British troops destroyed large parts of the magnificent sixteenth-century Red Fort in Agra, sister monument of the nearby Taj Mahal.

Finally, it is worth mentioning the stance taken by Dost Mohammed while the bloody rebellion was underway. He had signed a treaty of friendship earlier that year after Herat was restored, and now maintained: 'I have made an alliance with the British Government and, come what may, I will keep it till death.' He was true to his word and kept Afghanistan strictly neutral—an act of inestimable value for Britain as it fought for its very survival in India.

Creating Russian Turkestan

The war in Crimea and Russia's subsequent defeat had spawned many Anglophobes, especially in the tsar's military ranks. Russian generals wanted to get their own back, favouring a big push into Asia, ready to force Britain back wherever they could. But the war had drained the empire's coffers, so, regardless of the ascendency of its hawks, any suggestion of forward moves was hotly debated in St Petersburg. Losing this war on the periphery of its empire made Russia even more determined to secure its frontiers in Central Asia. In the coming years, its generals would advance rapidly, on occasion annexing new territory first and seeking permission afterwards, although mostly with tacit support from St Petersburg. Meanwhile, Cossack freebooters had begun ranging further eastwards, with Russian settlers following in their wake. For Britain, the old question again loomed large: what was Russia's real intention in Asia, and how should Britain respond to this?

These events set the scene for another young and daring Great Game player to take the stage. Chosen by his tsar, Count Nikolai Ignatiev was to lead a secret mission deep into Central Asia, to understand the extent of Britain's penetration and influence in the region. Just as Lord Ellenborough had demanded first-hand information from his officer spies, the tsar, too, needed intelligence, and an understanding of the increasing presence of foreign traders in the bazaars here.

Ignatiev arrived in Khiva in 1858, at the head of an impressive mission of nearly 100 staff and soldiers, bearing royal gifts. Just as Burnes had used a ruse years earlier, with his coach and horses providing a cover to map the Indus, so too did the count. Only this time it was a large musical organ to be ferried up the Oxus, while charting as much of the river as possible. The khan was happy enough to receive him and accept the gifts offered, but wouldn't be duped into letting Russian vessels continue further upriver, or allow the party to complete its surveying. From Khiva, Ignatiev rode to Bokhara for an audience with Emir Nasrullah Khan—the one and same who had had Stoddart and Conolly beheaded. He, too, readily accepted a share of the gifts Ignatiev bore and, in return, promised trade. In a flush of eastern magnanimity, he even agreed to release any Russian slaves held in Bokhara—but thought the better of it once the count departed.

Ignatiev returned to St Petersburg a hero, having entered a little known and dangerous land, and brought back all kinds of valuable intelligence. In his report, he urged the tsar to quickly subjugate the khanates, eliminating any possibility of Britain seizing them first. The count would go on to even bigger and better things after this mission. Soon he was off to China, where he deftly negotiated the Treaty of Peking with its Manchu rulers. It resulted in Russia acquiring a staggering amount of territory on its Pacific seaboard, the size of France and Germany combined, at virtually no cost to themselves. This time he returned home to a tsar who was even better pleased, and who promptly awarded him the Order of St Vladimir.

It was the disruption to Russia's cotton supply caused by the American Civil War that finally convinced the tsar to act decisively. He was determined to grab the fertile cotton fields of Central Asia before anyone else. Ignatiev's report had argued that, given the backwardness and lack of trust in dealing with the khans, any treaties or commercial agreements should be discounted in favour of straight-out annexation. This view was finally accepted in St Petersburg, and Russia's double-headed eagle standard was made ready to be raised anew.

In 1864, Russia took its first step, taking a large tract of land in northern Khokand, including two key oasis towns. The khan sent an emissary to India begging for help but was refused, as Britain's policy had once again shifted towards masterly inactivity. This, despite the threat by Count Milyutin, then minister of war for Russia, who reasoned: 'We ought to particularly value the control of that region, it would bring us to the northern borders of India and our easy access to that country. By ruling in Khokand, we can constantly threaten England's East Indian possessions.'

Prince Gorchakov, Russia's foreign minister, issued his controversial 'Gorchakov Manifesto' soon afterwards, explaining his country's new stance. Its intention was to allay the fears of other European powers, while putting Russia's advances in context of Western expansion around the world. He went on to argue the merits of colonization, pointing out:

> The position of Russia in Central Asia is that of all civilised states which are brought into contact with half-savage nomad populations possessing no fixed social organisation . . . The civilised State is thus in the dilemma of abandoning attempts at civilisation or lunging deeper and deeper into barbarous countries. The United States in America, France in Algiers, Holland in her colonies, England in India—all have been inevitably drawn into a course where ambition plays a smaller part than imperious necessity, and where the greatest difficulty is in knowing when to stop.

The prince stressed to other European powers that, having consolidated its frontier with Khokand, Russia would encroach no further. The truth of this assurance, particularly for the tsar's 'half-savage' neighbours, would soon be laid bare.

Britain believed the Russian Army itself was the main problem, as its ambassador to St Petersburg explained:

> Where an enormous standing army is maintained, it is necessary to find employment for it . . . Fresh conquests of territory are laid at the Tsar's feet, gained by the prowess and blood of his troops. He cannot refuse them without offending his army; and troops so far distant are difficult to restrain.

Russian eyes now turned towards the richest prize in Western Turkestan: the prosperous city of Tashkent and its large population of 100,000 ruled by the khan of Khokand. This was a region the emir of Bokhara also coveted and, as the ruler of the holiest city in Central Asia, he had the support of the powerful Muslim clergy in Khokand. In 1865, the two khanates were once again at war but, before the emir could lay claim to the city, the Russians moved in.

The commander of their column was Major General Mikhail Cherniaev, who had led the conquest of northern Khokand the previous year. With a force of less than 2000 troops and a dozen artillery pieces, he arrived at Tashkent to face some 30,000 defenders fortified behind its walls. In the meantime, St Petersburg telegraphed the major general instructing him not to advance. They were worried about Britain's probable reaction; moreover, it was doubtful victory could be achieved with such a small force, which wasn't large enough to first lay siege to the city. Suspecting the envelope might contain such an instruction, Cherniaev chose not to open it; instead, he attacked. With clever tactics and resolve, his forces took the city after fierce fighting, earning Cherniaev the title of Lion of Tashkent, bestowed on him by the city elders. The tsar honoured him with the Cross of St Anne, choosing to ignore his disobedience, and commenting how the expedition had been 'a glorious affair'.

Britain protested, as expected, but to no avail. And despite assurances from St Petersburg that the occupation would be only transitory, there was, of course, no withdrawal. This would set the pattern for further Russian expansion into Central Asia over the next twenty years. It would take the form of a series of smaller annexations, never large enough to draw other European powers into a conflict, followed by early assurances that its presence was only temporary— but it would invariably prove to be permanent.

There were several reasons for Russia's steady and deliberate advance. Foremost was the fear of Britain penetrating the region first and monopolizing trade, which would lead to Ellenborough's 'commerce prepares the way for conquest' scenario. Whoever controlled these regions invariably taxed its own goods at a favourable rate, giving its merchants a healthy advantage. Second, there was the simple matter of imperial pride. After its loss in Crimea, and being thwarted in Constantinople and the Near East, Russia wanted its fair share of the spoils of colonization, which other major European powers were busily engaged in. Finally, this was an effective way of keeping Britain's power in check: by ultimately threatening India, Russia increased its bargaining power elsewhere in the world.

With Tashkent theirs, the new post of governor-general of Russian Turkestan was established there, together with a permanent administrative and military headquarters. The first to occupy this powerful position was General Konstantin Kaufman, who would hold it until his death. The city stood isolated, well away from the rest of the Russian Empire, separated by steppe lands which took two months to cross. The tsar gave Kaufman a free hand and, in time, he would become the uncrowned king of Central Asia, even having one of its highest mountains named after him.*

The khanates' days of independence looked to be numbered; and although the emirs would still reign, soon it would be the Russians who ruled. Count Milyutin argued in defence of his country's actions: 'It is unnecessary for us to beg the forgiveness of ministers of the English crown for each advance we make. They do not hasten to confer with

---

* Mount Kaufman (23,406 feet) was renamed Lenin Peak following the Russian Revolution.

us when they conquer whole kingdoms and occupy foreign cities and islands. Nor do we ask them to justify what they do.'

The next to fall was Samarkand, the fabled capital and final resting place of Tamerlane, who had conquered most of Central Asia and Persia five centuries earlier. In this case the emir of Bokhara himself provided the excuse needed. In April 1868, marshalling his troops in the city, he proclaimed his determination to drive the Russians out of Western Turkestan. On hearing this, Kaufman acted quickly and, with a force of just 3500 troops, he took the fight to them instead. After a brief skirmish the emir's troops fled, and Samarkand was taken with minimal Russian losses. The general then pursued the would-be aggressors back to Bokhara, defeating them a second time despite being again outnumbered. The emir had no option but to accept the harsh surrender terms that followed, which allowed him to retain his throne but only as a vassal of the tsar. After absorbing Bokhara, Kaufman wasted no time in shutting down the slave markets, and slashing tariffs on Russian goods sold in its bazaars.

The general next turned his eyes towards Khiva, well aware this was not Russia's first attempt to seize the khanate. It sat between the Kizilkum and Karakum deserts, naturally protected by the unforgiving terrain and suffocating dust storms which engulf the area. Vast distances would have to be traversed to get an army there, especially if it were to start out from Orenburg and travel south. Obtaining adequate water supplies for his men and baggage animals would be the critical challenge. Alternatively, they could proceed in winter, but then faced the murderous option of marching through heavy snow, as General Perovsky's army had attempted decades earlier. Thinking ahead this time, Kaufman landed his troops on the eastern Caspian shore at Krasnovodsk, where they built a permanent fort in 1869 and effectively opened a new route from the west. Now his men could be ferried down the Volga, then across the Caspian Sea, to disembark a lot closer to Khiva. This route would also get them within striking distance of Turcoman country around Merv, which was in Kaufman's sights as well.

The new fort at Krasnovodsk made Britain decidedly nervous, as it dramatically reduced the distance an invading army would have to march before reaching Herat, and force open the doorway into India. The viceroy at the time was Lord Lawrence, who explained why Russia would be wise to proceed with caution: 'an advance towards India, beyond a certain point, would entail on her a war, in all parts of the world, with England'.

To counter the potential for conflict, Britain put forward the idea of a permanent neutral zone. Russia agreed, suggesting this could be Afghanistan, as neither power had any real desire to acquire it, and both seemed to have expanded their respective empires to their natural frontiers. The precise borders of this soon-to-be buffer state were uncertain, however, and required further mapping, particularly along its unexplored northern frontier in the Pamirs and the upper reaches of the Oxus River. The sovereignty of these peripheral areas was still in dispute, and would bring the two empires close to conflict in the coming years. Yet early in 1873, much to Britain's surprise, the Russians unexpectedly conceded that these regions were a part of Afghan territory. The reason behind this backdown soon became evident: Russia had its eyes on bigger game, as it activated its plan for Khiva.

This time Kaufman was determined not to repeat the mistake Russia had made in 1839 and botch the operation. He advanced on the khanate with 13,000 troops in a three-pronged attack from Tashkent, Orenburg and Krasnovodsk. The khan of Khiva, knowing he had little hope of standing up to such a large and well-disciplined army, offered to surrender unconditionally if Kaufman held off the attack. The wily general knew how to push home his advantage, though, starting an artillery bombardment while advising the khan that negotiations could begin only when his army was *within* the walls of the city. Not wanting to risk capture, the khan fled his capital, allowing the Russians to enter Khiva unopposed.

Just prior to the final push, a young journalist named James MacGahan from the *New York Herald*, risking his life, had crossed the searing Kizilkum Desert on his own and begged Kaufman to be allowed to accompany the troops. Impressed by his boldness, the general had agreed and, in the closing stage of the campaign, MacGahan reported on the ragged-looking inhabitants who lined the streets: 'with hats off, bowing to us timidly as we passed . . . not yet sure whether they would all be massacred or not'. There was one group who had no such doubts: 'Then we came upon a crowd of Persian slaves, who received us with shouts, cries and tears of joy. They were wild with excitement. They had heard that wherever the Russians went slavery disappeared, and they did not doubt that it would be the case here.'

This latest acquisition meant Russia now dominated the eastern Caspian shore, and controlled the lower Oxus, giving it the capability of moving merchandise and troops down the river unimpeded. As with its annexation of Tashkent, its occupation did not prove to be merely temporary, despite earlier assurances. Some months later the khan did return, to sign a treaty making Khiva a Russian protectorate, while he became a vassal of the tsar.

The last piece of this geopolitical jigsaw fell into place in 1875, when Kaufman took the city of Khokand after a rebel uprising there. He maintained his troops were there only to help put down the disturbance, and restore order for the region's ruler. Once the rebels were overwhelmed in the surrounding towns as well, the whole area was consolidated into the new province of Ferghana, and the people duly became Russian subjects. This action marked the end of the three khanates of Western Turkestan, and the creation of Russian Turkestan. Within the space of a decade, Russia had annexed territory half the size of the United States and, short of going to war, there was little that Britain or any other European power could do about it.

The Second Afghan War

While the Russians were pushing into Central Asia, the world was witnessing many technological advances. Two, in particular, would go a long way towards dramatically reducing the communication and logistical problems between Britain and India. With the Suez Canal and faster steamers in operation, sailing times were reduced to two months. A telegraph link would soon follow, allowing messages to be relayed across the world in just a few hours. This meant Britain could exercise better control over its colony, and send troop reinforcements to the subcontinent faster if needed.

British India achieved another key defence initiative in 1876: first, by securing a permanent lease for the region around the Bolan Pass from the local khan; and then by occupying the town of Quetta, which sat twenty miles from the pass, guarding its entrance. Control of the area allowed the home army to launch an attack on the flank and rear of an invader entering via the more likely Khyber Pass. This move was a good example of forward policy in action, which the general in the area had been calling for: 'You wish the red line of England on the map to advance no further. But to enable this red line to retain its present position . . . it is absolutely necessary to occupy posts in advance of it.'

In contrast, the Khyber Pass remained a threat, as the emir of Afghanistan would not countenance British presence on his soil. Dost Mohammed had died a few years earlier, and Sher Ali succeeded his father after a six-year power struggle with his brother. For two decades following the First Afghan War, the relations between the neighbours remained uneasy, and there existed a phoney war which the governor-general described as 'sullen . . . without offence but without goodwill or intercourse'. This relationship started to falter sharply when reports began reaching Calcutta that General Kaufman, from his base in Tashkent, was courting the new emir.

At the same time, the wider relationship between Britain and Russia was also deteriorating. The previous growing disquiet had turned into a general consensus that another war between the two empires was inevitable, either in the Near East over Constantinople, or in Central Asia over Afghanistan. Talk of armed conflict was in all the newspapers; and influential military experts, analysing the regional interests of each side and their growing divide, wrote a number of books on the subject. One such Russian text, translated into English in 1876, was by Colonel M.A. Terentiev, titled *Russia and England in the Struggle for the Markets of Central Asia*. Its tone was strongly Anglophobic. Although this seemed at odds with Russia's official conciliatory stance, the fact that publication had been permitted at all showed it had tacit approval from Russian authorities, *and* reflected their current thinking. Terentiev painted a picture of India ripe for rebellion, arguing: 'Sick to death, the natives are now waiting for a physician from the north.'

Meanwhile, there were also several popular adventure books-cum-travelogues published in Britain. Captain Burnaby's *A Ride to Khiva*, released that same year, described his overland journey to Khiva, and quickly became a bestseller. With a strongly Russophobic flavour, it mentioned discussions with Russian officers he had met along the way, who seemed hungry for a decisive battle with Britain.

The flashpoint was not long in coming, and predictably centred on Turkey and its jewel, Constantinople. In 1878, the Russians were at its gates again, but Britain was determined the city would not be taken. With the Royal Navy strategically sailing into the Dardanelles, it was a clear signal to the Russian Army to proceed no further, or face the consequences: war seemed inevitable.

Across the other side of the continent, Kaufman was preparing to relieve British pressure in Turkey by applying counter-pressure in India. He was ready to strike once fighting broke out, by crossing through Afghanistan with a 30,000-strong force, plus whatever troops he could enlist from the emir in Kabul. His hope was that this invasion would spark another Indian revolt from within, forcing Britain into an unwinnable position while its home forces were tied up in Europe and Turkey.

After many tense months of military and diplomatic manoeuvring, war was finally averted, and a treaty signed by all the major European powers involved. For the Russian military, this was a particularly bitter moment: to be once more denied Constantinople, again because of the actions of its arch-rival.

Kaufman, for one, was not done with this matter yet. He had already dispatched three armed columns towards India when stand-down orders were received from St Petersburg. Although he did recall his troops, he let the mission to Kabul proceed. Its initial aim centred on securing the emir's support for the planned invasion but, with the attack called off, the emir saw no reason for its presence in Kabul now. Kaufman, however, was not about to back down. He bullied the emir into receiving the mission: on the one hand, he made threats of supporting a rival for the Afghan throne if he resisted; on the other, he promised the aid of Russian troops if the emir complied. Boxed into a corner, Sher Ali accepted the mission and its treaty of friendship, and in doing so sealed his own fate.

In the meantime, a harder attitude was emerging in Britain and India. Their earlier stance of masterly inactivity had been largely abandoned after the departure of its chief proponent, an earlier viceroy, Lord Lawrence. He had argued passionately that the security of India lay in the quality of British rule and the contentment of its subjects, rather than through territorial acquisitions or fighting expensive wars in faraway places. His parting warning was not to interfere in Afghanistan, but times had changed.

The current viceroy and great apostle of the forward policy, Lord Lytton, was not only itching for a decisive fight with the Russians in Central Asia, but also considering the outright annexation of Afghanistan. Soon after his arrival in 1876, he had written to London:

> The prospect of war with Russia immensely excites, but so far as India is concerned, does not at all alarm me. If it is to be— better now than later. We are twice as strong as Russia in this part of the world and have much better bases for attack and defence.

Lord Salisbury, then secretary of state for India, cautioned him when he continued in this aggressive manner: 'I think you listen too much to soldiers . . . if you believe the soldiers, nothing is safe.'

Lytton was incensed upon learning the Russians were being allowed into Kabul, when their own mission had been previously turned down twice. That his frustration was boiling over is apparent from his words: 'It is evident that the Ameer has been trifling with us . . . it must be made equally evident . . . that we will not be trifled with any longer . . . we have nothing further to say to the Ameer on any subject.'

By this stage, Lytton was receiving strong pushback from his superiors in London, who were patching up their differences with St Petersburg, and his aggressive stance angered them. They wanted a diplomatic solution in Afghanistan, without 'moving a single soldier', as Lytton had promised when he first set foot in India.

Not to be dissuaded, the viceroy pre-emptively dispatched his mission before obtaining permission from London, but it was refused entry by the emir and his troops at the border. Lytton then telegraphed London for approval to cross into Afghanistan by force if necessary and, despite serious misgivings, was given the green light to proceed. Sher Ali was now presented with an ultimatum: to 'welcome' the British mission into Kabul and apologize for his earlier discourtesy, or bear the consequences.

The emir was firmly trapped between 'the bear and the lion', with no room to wriggle free—all the while having to deal with a personal trauma following the death of his favourite son. When Lytton received no reply by the appointed hour, the stage was set for confrontation. Even though Sher Ali sent a belated letter agreeing to the mission, it arrived too late; and besides, it did not contain the apology Lytton demanded. In November 1878, three columns of redcoats began their march on Kabul; the Second Afghan War had begun.

* * *

With 35,000 British troops advancing on his country, the emir appealed to General Kaufman for the support he thought had been promised, only to be told this was not possible with winter now setting in. In desperation, he attempted to make his way to St Petersburg and appeal to the tsar in person, but was stopped at the frontier on Kaufman's orders. This was all too much for him: dispirited and overcome by sickness, he died a few months later.

His death allowed differences between Britain and Afghanistan to be patched up, at least for now. The new emir, Sher Ali's son Yakub Khan, soon gave in to Britain's demands, and signed the treaty thrust upon him. It gave London control over Afghanistan's foreign policy, and allowed its mission to be immediately established in Kabul. In return, Afghanistan was promised protection against any Russian or Persian incursions, as well as an annual payment of 60,000 pounds. As one English military correspondent later put it: 'We gave Afghanistan a stiff subsidy . . . but the condition was that it should have no windows looking on the outside world, except towards India.' Lytton and his superiors in London were delighted with the outcome; but local Afghans were infuriated, feeling they had been coerced into doing Britain's bidding once more.

The mission to Kabul was headed by Sir Louis Cavagnari, recently knighted for successfully concluding negotiations with the Afghans, and soon to be the first British Resident there. Many senior military and political staff had grave misgivings about sending another mission, recalling the fate met by the first one, but they were overruled. General Frederick Roberts hosted the departing group on the eve of their departure, and he later summed up the mood:

> After dinner I was asked to propose the health of Cavagnari and those with him, but somehow I did not feel equal to the task; I was so thoroughly depressed, and my mind was filled with such gloom and forebodings as to the fate of these fine fellows, that I could not utter a word.

Cavagnari and his small party reached the capital in late July 1879 and, after a warm welcome from the emir, settled into the residency located in the royal citadel, the Bala Hissar. All seemed to be going well, as Cavagnari's optimistic telegram to Calcutta on 2 September indicated, ironically ending with those words: 'All well.' That would be the last time anything was heard from them.

In piecing together what happened, it seems trouble first flared when a large body of returning Afghan troops arrived in Kabul. They were angry at not being paid their full wages, and further infuriated on finding the British there. Three mutinous regiments, spurred on by their mullahs, then marched on to the residency and, believing he had money stored there, demanded their outstanding wages from Cavagnari. When he refused, a skirmish erupted which quickly turned nasty. Despite sending pleas for assistance to Yakub Khan's palace nearby, where a large contingent of guards was stationed, no help was forthcoming. Cavagnari and his men, comprising two other staff, an officer and seventy-five soldiers, mounted a strong defence. During the ensuing twelve-hour pitched battle, they accounted for more than 600 of their 2000-odd attackers, before every last man was cut down.

News of their annihilation was received by stunned governments in London and Calcutta, and both were quick to seek retribution. A punitive force was hastily put together under the command of General Roberts. He would not be deterred by the emir's profuse apologies or pleas of innocence, replying: 'The Great British nation would not rest satisfied until a British army marches to Kabul and there assisted Your Highness to inflict such punishment as so terrible and dastardly act deserves.'

Once again, an 'army of retribution' forced its way into Kabul, meeting little resistance on the way. Roberts immediately held a commission of enquiry. Although it did not find Yakub Khan directly culpable, the emir chose to abdicate anyway, finding the pressures of being a ruler all too much for him. He pleaded with Roberts to be allowed to retire into self-imposed exile in India, saying he 'would rather be a grass cutter in the English camp than Ruler of Afghanistan'.

The commission did find many others guilty, and Roberts promptly had close to 100 Afghans hung. The gallows were erected inside the Bala Hissar, where Cavagnari and his men made their last stand. Those who were punished had in some way been found responsible for the demise of the mission; they included the ringleaders of the attack and the mayor, who reportedly carried Cavagnari's head around the city as a trophy. Some sections of both the British and Indian presses strongly criticized these executions as being unduly harsh; one newspaper warning that these actions were 'sowing a harvest of hate'. But Lytton had made it clear to Roberts that, in this case, strong measures were warranted, instructing him to 'strike terror and strike it swiftly and deeply'.

Inflamed by British presence on their home soil and their perceived heavy-handedness, the Afghan tribes rose in revolt and headed for Kabul, led by a ninety-year-old mullah who called for jihad. What followed was a classic fight between a small, well-disciplined military force up against a larger, uncoordinated and less well-armed group of tribesmen. Roberts had twenty pieces of field artillery, two Gatling machine guns and the latest breech-loading rifles. They allowed his garrison of 6500 to direct intense fire on their attackers, numbering more than 100,000. The battle lasted from sun up to noon; and after the Afghan attack broke, more than 3000 tribesmen lay dead, compared to only a handful of their enemy. It was a resounding British victory but, beyond preventing their own annihilation, what they had actually won was unclear.

For a second time, Britain was in possession of Kabul, only this time without a clear view of how it was to rule, or even of its next move. What it needed in short order was an exit strategy, with a compliant ruler on the throne as the army departed. The politicals looked to Abdur Rahman, Dost Mohammed's grandson, as their favoured candidate. The irony was he had been living in exile in Russian Turkestan for more than a decade, under Kaufman's watchful eye; and to many onlookers it seemed incredibly like a case of using a Russian sympathizer to forestall Russian influence. Not surprisingly, Kaufman supported his candidature for the throne as well, believing him to be pro-Russian. In fact, once he was installed as the new emir, Rahman proved himself to be overwhelmingly pro-Afghan, and an often-uncompromising ruler governing with a heavy hand, which earned him the nickname Iron Amir.

The war, however, was not over yet and, just as in the First Afghan War, British troops would suffer another terrible defeat in the second. The ruler of Herat, Ayub Khan, set out in June 1880 for the southern city of Kandahar, determined to at least drive the British out from that province. His initial force of 8000 infantries, supported by artillery, soon swelled to around 25,000 as more disgruntled tribesmen joined him. The British Army, characteristically undaunted by the superiority of its opposition's numbers and, in this instance, not appreciating the true strength of its enemy, advanced with a force of 2600 to engage them.

The two sides met in battle at the tiny village of Maiwand, forty miles west of Kandahar. This time the redcoats met their match in an able and experienced Afghan commander, who quickly seized the high ground and used his superior artillery with deadly effect. The outcome was a disaster for the British. By nightfall, they were forced to make a desperate retreat behind the city walls, leaving nearly 1000 of their men for dead, although taking account of perhaps five times that number of their enemy. Here, Ayub Khan's forces quickly surrounded them, and the situation looked grim for the besieged—but help was on its way.

In a forced march from Kabul, General Roberts arrived at the head of a 10,000-strong relieving army, covering over 300 miles in just twenty-two days. It was one of the most rapid marches made in military history—one that would earn him a hero's welcome back home, and the title Lord Roberts of Kandahar.* His troops quickly engaged Ayub Khan's forces and this time, in a more evenly matched fight, the outcome was different. By day's end, the Afghans were

---

* He describes this march in his autobiography, *Forty-one Years in India*. Roberts was awarded a Victoria Cross during the mutiny there, and went on to become a field marshal, and commander-in-chief of the British Army.

routed and Roberts's men, with minimal losses, had restored some semblance of British pride.

This battle effectively marked the end of hostilities, and the Second Afghan War. Yet it left many sceptics at home questioning what, if anything, Britain had achieved in waging either war: with hindsight, *both* seemed pointless and dishonourable. Roberts, writing a few years later, would reflect: '. . . I feel sure I am right when I say that the less the Afghans see of us, the less they will dislike us'.

Defining Borders

Back in Britain, following another general election, there was yet another change of government. In large part, the defeat of the previous Conservative Party was due to disapproval of its forward policy, seen as the root cause for the capitulation in Afghanistan. The incoming Liberals pledged to abandon this doctrine, and the enormous costs associated with it, believing the threat to India had been greatly exaggerated. They pointed out this line of thinking was self-defeating for Britain, as it provoked Russia into behaving in a like manner.

On the other side of the Pamir and Karakoram ranges, the question of sovereignty for Eastern Turkestan was being settled. The people of this vast and sparsely populated region, scattered around the dreaded Taklamakan, were mainly Muslim, such as those of Western Turkestan. However, they were decidedly less devout, as goes the saying that (perhaps unfairly) describes Chinese followers of Koranic law: 'Three Muslims are one Muslim; two Muslims are half a Muslim; and one Muslim is no Muslim.' Still, they had stronger ties with their western brethren and were ethnically similar to them, compared to their Han Chinese masters to the distant east.

Since the early 1860s, Yakub Beg had seized most of this province back from them, but Tsarist Russia was eyeing the territory closely as it continued to expand across Turkestan. In 1864, it concluded another favourable treaty with Manchu China, which realigned its borders to the gates of Eastern Turkestan. Worryingly for Britain, this move opened another possible invasion route into India, bypassing Afghanistan altogether.

Once Khokand had been annexed, Russia controlled the region all the way to the Pamirs, and only these mountains separated the two sides of Turkestan. But before the tsar could subsume the eastern half, the Chinese emperor acted. In 1877, his troops overran Yakub Beg's forces, although it took them two years to first reach Kashgaria; they halted at intervals along the way to sow and harvest crops as a means of provisioning their small army. After regaining this parched country dotted with oases, the emperor renamed the province Xinjiang (New Frontier), and this time China was to keep it forever.

Beaten to the punch in the east, the tsar's army began its final push to complete the conquest of Western Turkestan, moving troops from its base at Krasnovodsk to the Turcoman stronghold of Geok Tepe in 1881. Under the command of General Mikhail Skobelev, nicknamed Old Bloody Eyes on account of his cruelty, 7000 troops attacked the unruly Turcoman. Famed for their horses, and infamous for their lawlessness and trade in slaves, these tribesmen had inflicted a humiliating defeat on the tsar's forces just two years earlier, during his first attempt to bring the region to heel.

Now, as victors, the Russians took their revenge. A massacre followed and when it was over, reports suggest, no one was spared, not even the elderly, women or children. Skobelev's official report stated: 'The enemy's losses were enormous. After the capture of the fortress 6500 bodies were buried inside it. During the pursuit 8000 were killed.' He later declared: 'I hold it as a principle that the duration of peace is in direct proportion to the slaughter you inflict upon the enemy. The harder you hit them, the longer they remain quiet.' He claimed this to be a far more effective method than General Roberts's public hangings in Kabul, which only served to engender further hatred rather than fear. A fellow general's portrayal of him simply states: 'Skobelev was the god of War personified.'

East of Geok Tepe lay the Turcoman capital of Merv, and in 1884 it was the last city to be gobbled up. In this case it was a bloodless victory, as the Turcoman chiefs, having experienced the might and viciousness of the Russian Army, meekly agreed to becoming subjects of the tsar. Their acquiescence completed a redrawing of the loose political map of what was once Turkestan—with China regaining Eastern Turkestan, and Tsar Alexander III securing a 'united' Russian Turkestan.

* * *

Soon afterwards, Lord Curzon explored the region extensively, and was later awarded a gold medal by the RGS 'for travels and researches in Persia, French Indo-China, the Hindu Kush, and Pamirs'. He would regard this award as one of his most notable achievements, and one that gave him greater pleasure than becoming a minister of the Crown (this from a man who held the posts of viceroy of India and foreign secretary, and nearly became prime minister). He has been described as a bold and compulsive traveller—all the more since he suffered from a spinal injury that required the wearing of a metal corset to ease his continual pain.

After completing his travels, Lord Curzon published a book in 1889 titled *Russia in Central Asia*. Interestingly, its dedication begins: 'To the great army of Russophobes who mislead others, and Russophiles whom others mislead . . .' Within its pages, he conceded:

> First, then, it cannot be doubted that Russia has conferred great and substantial advantages upon the Central Asian regions which she has reduced to her sway . . . The Russian eagle may at first have alighted upon the eastern shores of the Caspian with murderous beak and sharpened talons, but, her appetite once satisfied, she has shown that she also came with healing in her wings.

Needless to say, it is unlikely the once-free people of Central Asia agreed wholeheartedly with his colourful assessment of their subjugation.

The fall of Merv greatly disturbed military strategists in London: it gave them an acute case of 'Mervousness' is how one British duke put it. The city offered Russia a closer base to India, and a clearer line of advance. Troops could now be moved south-east through Herat and Kandahar, then on to the Indus, without having to cross the Khyber or other passes to the north. General Roberts, soon to be commander-in-chief of India, was clearly concerned, assessing it as 'by far the most important step made by Russia on her march towards India'.

Following strong British protests, the two empires agreed the best way forward was to set up a boundary commission, and delineate a permanent border between Russian Turkestan and Afghanistan. For Britain, an unambiguous border would act as 'a line in the sand'. It reasoned that by virtue of already controlling Afghanistan's foreign policy, any Russian incursions would be tantamount to a hostile act. This logic, and their resolve, would soon be put to the test.

Before the boundary commission could complete its work, Russian troops seized the remote oasis of Pandjeh in northwestern Afghanistan in 1885 after intense fighting, killing most of the local garrison there. This skirmish—which came to be known as the Pandjeh Incident—created a flashpoint that would reverberate around the world. Military staff considered this settlement strategically important, as it lay between Merv and the approach to Herat. Britain believed the oasis belonged to Afghanistan, and being responsible for its foreign policy affirmed it would protect its neighbour's territorial integrity—by force if necessary. As the diplomatic and military manoeuvring between the two empires continued, it became evident that what had started out as a minor frontier incident was fast brewing into full-scale conflict.

In Britain, anti-Russian sentiment was again in overdrive, with sections of the press carrying dire warnings of the Russian menace to India. Troops were mobilized in readiness for a dash to Herat, and the Royal Navy was put on full alert as Britain initiated its largest preparation for war since Crimea. The *New York Times* grimly predicted on its front page, 'IT IS WAR', as a confrontation between the giants seemed inevitable. It took the dwarf in the middle, in the form of its able emir, to diffuse this volatile situation, and perhaps save his country from being crushed under the weight of two opposing armies.

Normally quick-tempered and eager for a fight, Abdur Rahman now behaved in a statesman-like manner. He refrained from pushing Britain into regaining the settlement immediately by force, or trying to avenge his fallen soldiers. Instead, by giving diplomacy a chance, he helped avoid armed conflict, as the viceroy later noted: 'But for . . . the fortunate fact of his being a prince of great capacity, experience and calm judgement, the incident at Pandjeh alone . . . might in itself have proved the occasion of a long and miserable war.' Later, a wider perspective of Rahman would emerge; according to historian Gerald Morgan: 'having finally thrown in his lot with India he remained staunch and thereby contributed more than any single man to the ending of the Game'.

After the powers had talked through their differences, they agreed the oasis be kept neutral until a boundary commission had completed its work. As it transpired, Russia did get to keep Pandjeh, although it had to concede the oasis in exchange of a strategic pass lying further west, which both Calcutta and Kabul were keen to possess. From Britain's standpoint, even with a Liberal government in power, which favoured masterly inactivity, it had demonstrated a firm resolve to defend its line in the sand and safeguard Afghanistan's sovereignty—although its real motive, of course, was to protect India.

10

The Final Years

With the Punjab and Sind under the Union Jack, and Russia 'warned off' Afghanistan, British India felt less vulnerable, particularly with the Khyber and Bolan passes secured to a large extent. Still, Britain's constant worry about protecting its jewel wasn't over just yet. Its focus now would shift to the no man's land where the three competing empires—Britain, Russia and China—came together. Here, a mountainous knot arises around the Pamirs, as some of the highest ranges in the world converge: the Hindu Kush, Himalayas, Karakorams, Kunlun and Tien Shan. This was a largely inaccessible and unexplored quarter, forming India's northern border.

Curzon, eloquent as ever, summed up the crucial role such lines on a map play: 'Frontiers are the razor's edge on which hang suspended the issue of war or peace and the life of nations.' The coming period would underscore how the ambiguity of these final frontiers between the Great Game empires shaped their rivalry.

The Northern Passes

The grey zone to India's north contained many high passes, some of which were known only to local hillmen and raiders. The fear of an invader locating and using these defiles was heightened by recent reports from the GTS and its Pundits, and by accounts of a few pioneers exploring the region, such as Robert Shaw and George

Hayward. Initial intelligence coming back to Calcutta indicated that these passes were more susceptible than first believed. There was a growing fear that an army, during a multi-pronged attack on India through either of the main passes, could also infiltrate via these lesser known ones. Furthermore, the recent defeat of Yakub Beg, who had nominally been Britain's ally in Chinese Turkestan, meant this flank too now became susceptible.

To counter any new threat while the boundary commission was completing its work in the Pamirs, the viceroy established a 20,000-strong defence force known as the Imperial Service Corps, made up of troops contributed by the Indian princes of the region. In the event of an invasion, the hope was that the maharaja of Kashmir would be able to defend the passes into his state, until help arrived either from Imperial Service troops or the Indian Army. All this tactical planning and speculation heightened the need to map these defiles thoroughly, and it rapidly became a key focus for British India's military.

For many experienced explorers and military personnel, however, the possibility of a serious invasion attempt through these passes was remote, even ridiculous, and they considered the mountainous knot around the Pamirs irrelevant to India's defence. For one thing, they pointed out that this thinly populated region was incapable of feeding and supporting a large number of troops. It was quite plausible, though, that Russian activity in this area was a deliberate attempt to distract British India from its more vulnerable western and northwestern frontiers, by diverting troops and resources towards the Pamirs. In concluding his detailed study of the region, historian Garry Alder commented: 'the belief in the feasibility of invasion by the northern frontier was directly proportional to the geographic ignorance of it'.*

Curzon and Roberts were far more concerned about the Trans-Caspian Railway, which was being built and run by Russia's Ministry

---

* Alder wrote *British India's Northern Frontier 1865–95* (and, later, the biography of William Moorcroft).

of War and steadily nearing completion. Starting from Krasnovodsk, through to its final stop in Tashkent, this rail link was changing the strategic balance in Central Asia. Mechanized transport overcame many of the difficulties an army faced in having to march large distances over unforgiving terrain, as the Russians had already learnt from bitter experience. It gave the tsar an ability to rapidly transport tens of thousands of his men to the Persian and Afghan frontiers. Prior to its construction, it would have taken troops two months to march from Orenburg to Tashkent, whereas now they could be railed from Krasnovodsk within a matter of days.

Nevertheless, these passes could not be discounted, as Britain could ill afford to leave any stone unturned in protecting its largest and most valuable colony.

Francis Younghusband

This shift of focus towards the north set the scene for a new officer to make his entrance. One who would go on to become one of the last and most famous players of the Great Game, and much more besides. Born in India and raised in England, a product of the elite Royal Military College at Sandhurst, Lieutenant Francis Younghusband had already made his mark as an explorer: he received the RGS's gold medal, after being elected its youngest ever Fellow at age twenty-four.*

This impressive achievement was the result of a seven-month journey on horseback across a large swathe of Asia, heading out from Peking in April 1887. Along the way he traversed China's bleak Gobi Desert, and then the mighty Karakoram Range, before making his way back to India. During winter, and with no mountaineering gear or previous climbing experience, he crossed the Karakorams using the treacherous 18,000-foot Mustagh Pass, with the K2 massif towering above. The lieutenant engaged a small party to accompany

---

*   Robert Shaw was his uncle from his mother's side.

him, including a guide who claimed to remember the location of the pass, even though he had last crossed it twenty-five years earlier. Still, he was full of confidence as Younghusband later related:

> He said he would show me the way, but only on the condition that I trusted him. He had heard that Englishmen trusted their maps and not their guides, and if I was going to trust my map I might, but he would not go with me as a guide—what was the use? I had no scruple in assuring him that I would not look at a map—because there was no map to look at.

Unfortunately, when they reached the vicinity of the pass, the guide's memory failed him, but the party managed to get through, although only by the skin of their teeth.

Some years later, Sven Hedin described this feat as 'the most difficult and dangerous achievement in these mountains so far'. Younghusband wrote about this epic journey, and his other travels through the Pamirs and Chitral soon afterwards, in his classic bestseller *The Heart of a Continent*.

Two years after his return, he was off to India's northern frontier on a mission to learn the whereabouts of a secret pass, the Shimshal, which led into the Hunza Valley. Local raiders were known to be using this defile, and his superiors wanted confirmation as to whether it could be used by an invader as well. Accompanied by an escort of six Gurkha soldiers, he soon located the pass and the fort guarding it. Younghusband spoke with the region's ruler Safdar Ali, warning him not to have any dealings with the Russians, who were thought to be making a reconnaissance of the area and seeking alliances with local chiefs. This turned out to be the case, and Younghusband soon ran into Captain Gromchevsky and his seven-man Cossack escort.

The pleasant dinner they shared high up in the Pamirs, discussing the relative merits of the position adopted by their respective empires in the Great Game, would mark the first time rival players eyeballed each other out in the field. Gromchevsky predicted his country would soon invade India, deploying an overwhelming number of troops on the subcontinent. Younghusband saw on the captain's map much of the unclaimed no man's land now marked in red, obviously intended to be absorbed by Russia at some stage in the near future.

When he reported back to his superiors, it was all the confirmation Britain needed to mobilize and plug this so-called Pamir Gap, extending some fifty miles deep within the mountains. Younghusband urged them to lose no time in exploring the rest of the region, and mapping the remaining unknown passes, some of which were relatively easy to cross as he had discovered. He also emphasized the importance of ensuring that local rulers in these areas, such as Hunza, kept allegiances only with India.

By July 1891, when rumours began reaching London that Russia was planning to seize the Pamirs, Younghusband was sent back to investigate. He quickly ascertained the truth of this, and it would bring the two empires close to conflict again, this time over a new buffer zone.

High in the mountains, 150 miles *south* of the Russian frontier in a region known as Bozai Gumbaz, he came face-to-face with a 400-strong Cossack force. Their commander Colonel Yanov wore the Cross of St George, his country's most coveted decoration. On challenging the Russians about their intentions, Yanov admitted without hesitation that his party was there to annex the Pamirs. He showed Younghusband a map that marked out this territory, including land that was clearly either Afghan or Chinese. They had also been making incursions into neighbouring Chitral, which India regarded as lying strictly in its own sphere of influence.

Although this revelation should have made the Russian an adversary, it didn't stop Younghusband from accepting an invitation to dinner, where he chatted long into the night with the colonel and his officers, just as he had done with Gromchevsky. This act of being cordial with his counterparts was a refreshing trait of Younghusband's, as his writings show: 'We and the Russians are rivals but I am sure that the individual Russian and English officer like each other a great deal better than do the individuals of nations with which they are not in rivalry. We are both playing at a big game . . .'

No doubt their camaraderie would have made it harder for Yanov to carry out what he was forced to next. The Russian reappeared three nights later, advising Younghusband in the politest manner that he had received orders to escort him off land that now belonged to the tsar. Despite vehemently pointing out that he was on Afghan territory, as he was out there on his own, Younghusband had little choice but to comply, although he did so under strong protest.

When news of his ejection reached Calcutta and London, there was immense outrage, especially after the *Times* incorrectly published a story that he had been killed during a skirmish with the Russians there. Obscure Bozai Gumbaz would quickly become a flashpoint in the far north, just as Pandjeh had been in the northwest six years earlier.* General Roberts mobilized a division of troops, eager to press home their advantage, while remarking to Younghusband: 'Now's the time to go for the Russians. We are ready and they are not.'

War between the empires loomed large, and once again over a scrap of countryside in the back of beyond, whose name had been barely known to either side until now. Faced with Britain's steely resolve and the real prospect of armed conflict, Russia backed down, much to its military's frustration. By way of explanation, St Petersburg conveniently made Colonel Yanov its scapegoat, claiming he had overstepped his orders in annexing the Pamirs. Soon afterwards, though, he was quietly congratulated by his tsar, presented with a gold ring, and promoted to the rank of general.

Younghusband, too, after a later expedition, would be censured by his government for exceeding his authority, but would also go on to win his monarch's approval and a knighthood.

---

* Younghusband had been present there too, although in a minor capacity on the Divisional Staff.

Locking the Door

Gradually, the military and political chiefs in British India came round to the view held by their experts: that the northern passes were, in fact, impractical as an invasion route. However, they still needed to 'lock the door' from their side and keep would-be intruders out, which meant securing these regions and aligning local rulers with India's interests.

Their first priority was the sparsely populated region of Hunza, supporting some 6000 inhabitants, and its somewhat larger neighbour Nagar, in the eastern Pamirs bordering China. This task was completed in 1891 using a force of nearly 1000 Gurkha and Kashmiri troops. First, they captured Safdar Ali's supposedly impregnable fort, and then the Hunza capital. With the ruler deposed, and a more amenable one in place, both areas were effectively subsumed.

Across from Hunza, in the western Pamirs bordering Afghanistan, lies the region of Chitral. In 1892, a new ruler, who was on friendly terms with British India, had taken command. All this changed three years later when he was assassinated by his half-brother, whom Calcutta would not recognize as the legitimate ruler. This forced the claimant to seek help from his southern neighbour, the ruler of Swat and his Pathan Army, even though he suspected they desired his land for themselves. Chitral was too important strategically to be left in unfriendly hands, prompting Calcutta to move quickly to unseat the new ruler, using a column of some 500 troops, before occupying his fortress.

At this point they ran into serious strife, but it would lead to one of the most memorable rescues of a besieged force in military history. By occupying the fort, which was the largest and most defendable building in Chitral, the garrison had gravely offended the locals, as it was the ancestral palace of their rulers and the harem. Fighting broke out and, with the arrival of the Pathans, the garrison was soon outnumbered and confined to defending themselves from within.

A long siege followed. As food supplies ran low, it looked as if the troops would have to surrender, although whether their lives would be spared afterwards was not at all certain. A relief column was hurriedly put together, commanded by an ageing Colonel James Kelly, with as many troops as he could muster: 400 from a regiment of the Punjab Pioneers (usually assigned to road building); 40 Kashmiri Sappers from neighbouring Gilgit; and 100 hardy irregulars offered by the Hunza and Nagar chiefs, who were gratefully accepted.

Kelly's ragtag army began its forced march in heavy snow, eventually covering over 200 miles in treacherous conditions. This included a three-day crossing of a 12,000-foot pass hauling two dismantled mountain guns, and with the men having to sleep out in the snow at night. The pass posed such a formidable barrier during winter that the tribesmen had thought it impossible to cross, and left it unguarded. After a pitched battle on the other side, with the mountain guns making a difference, the Chitralis fled before them. They fled again from the fort, once they heard Kelly's column had broken through. The siege, which had dragged on for six weeks, was finally over.

When the main relief column of 14,000 from Peshawar arrived, they found the garrison already liberated, although practically reduced to skeletons.* The British public, fearing the worst, was greatly relieved on hearing this news. Many who participated in the campaign won medals for bravery under fire, and all ranks were rewarded with an extra six months of pay and three months of leave. Kelly, in the twilight of an undistinguished career and nearing sixty, had fittingly discharged his most important command. It was the Punjabi Pioneers, though, men of the lowliest caste, who came in for special praise, having marched and fought exceptionally well.

The tussle for the northern frontier finally came to an end after London and St Petersburg reached an agreement on its demarcation, which effectively closed the Pamir Gap, and permanently separated

---

* Younghusband arrived with the troops from Peshawar, but this time as a special correspondent for the *Times*. He later co-authored a book describing *The Relief of Chitral*.

the two empires. This was achieved in 1873, by marking out the northern side of what would eventually become the Wakhan Corridor.* This agreement gave the Russians what they wanted, which was most of the territory in the Pamirs, but it at least provided Afghanistan with an official frontier that Britain could now enforce. Most importantly, it had diffused the potential for war, which had raised its ugly head again.

The Wakhan Corridor came to mark the limit of Russia's expansion towards British India, and the rivalry between the powers in Central Asia seemed to be heading towards closure. It had been played out in an arc around northern India, starting from the west and northwest, where Britain had secured Sind and the Punjab, together with the crucial Bolan and Khyber passes. Russia had completed its annexation of the three khanates of Western Turkestan to create Russian Turkestan. China had reclaimed its province of Eastern Turkestan. And now the uncertainty around Afghanistan and India's frontiers along the Pamirs was finally settled. The political map of the Great Game had been substantially redrawn; all that remained was Tibet to the east.

The Forward Thruster

An ancient poem, written over 1000 years ago, describes Tibet:

> The centre of high snowy mountains; the source of great rivers;
> a lofty country; a pure land.

Yet it was a land time had seemingly forgotten, at least in the eyes of many Westerners. The Chinese and Indians may have been using the wheel for thousands of years, but the Tibetans would have

---

* It was carved out over two decades, and became a part of Afghanistan. Looking much like a protruding tongue or a panhandle on a map, it is between 8 and 40 miles wide and some 220 miles long.

little to do with it: the kingdom was virtually devoid of vehicles, and seemed to work at the tempo of its yak. Although people were relatively poor, and peasants in their homespun clothes had an unkempt appearance, instances of destitution or starvation were rare. While they were often labelled 'filthy' by foreigners, this could be attributed to the lack of water for washing, in a land frozen hard for much of the year. A generally happy and contented race, Tibetans also accord a high position to women.

Initially, the new viceroy of India, Lord Curzon, had hoped to form a close alliance with his eastern neighbour: 'Tibet is, I think, much more likely in reality to look to us for protection than to look to Russia, and I cherish a secret hope that the communications which I am trying to open with the Dalai Lama may inaugurate some sort of relations between us.' Soon, however, British fears of Russian involvement in Tibet, and a growing friendship between them, were heightened by reports that an emissary from the Great Lama had been visiting St Petersburg.

This notable was a Russian subject who would play a salient role in this affair, but would remain a mysterious and elusive figure. The British believed him to be an agent of the tsar, despite Russian claims that he was only a monk. In fact, he was a Buryat Mongol named Aguan Dorjief, who had come to Lhasa twenty years earlier as a priest. After acquiring years of scholarship in the Tibetan religion, he became one of the young Dalai Lama's tutors and, later, one of his closest and trusted advisers.

Starting in 1898, he made several trips to St Petersburg, transiting through India without the knowledge of the British authorities, much to their chagrin. He is believed to have acted as the conduit between Tsar Nicholas II and the Dalai Lama, who had recently come of age. Dorjief returned from Russia with presents and offers of an alliance, which the Great Lama seems to have viewed favourably, emboldened by China's weak state at the time and its waning hold on his country. The physical distance separating the two capitals made it particularly difficult for the Chinese to exert effective control; a mission or an army travelling from Peking could take a year or more to reach Lhasa.

Curzon found this changing state of affairs unacceptable. He feared it was only a matter of time before Lhasa accepted a Russian envoy, and the country became a protectorate of the tsar. Like Afghanistan to its west, British India needed Tibet as a shield on its eastern front; but problems invariably arose because rival powers wanted buffer countries firmly under their own influence. Although the advice from his military staff indicated a Russian invasion through Tibet was near impossible, the viceroy still believed that if the Dalai Lama became aligned with the tsar, it would have grave implications for India's defence. He was supported in this view by General Roberts. Curzon seems to have been further piqued following rebuffs by the Great Lama, after trying to engage directly with him on two separate occasions, while Lhasa continued to be friendly towards St Petersburg.

Curzon was an avowed Russophobe. He had taken office in 1899 determined not to give in further to any territorial grab by the tsar, as some of his earlier writing suggests: 'As a student of Russian aspirations and methods for fifteen years, I assert with confidence— what I do not think her own statesmen would deny—that her ultimate ambition is the dominion of Asia . . . Each morsel but whets her appetite for more, and inflames the passion for pan-Asiatic domination.'

Frequently described as an inflexible and arrogant leader, Curzon had a brilliant mind, and was young and ambitious—not yet forty and already viceroy. He passionately believed, as did many other Englishmen of his day, that the British Empire was, as he put it, 'the greatest instrument for good that the world has seen'. By late 1902, Curzon's misgivings around St Petersburg's growing role in Lhasa had become a conviction: 'I am myself a firm believer in the existence of a secret understanding, if not a secret treaty between Russia and China about Tibet: and as I have before said, I regard it as a duty to frustrate this little game while there is yet time.'

Britain had signed an agreement with China some years earlier, permitting trade between India and Tibet, but the xenophobic

Tibetans refused to go along with this arrangement, not least because it had been made without their involvement.* They simply wanted to be left alone, without any foreign interference, and especially to prevent Westerners from setting foot in their holy capital.

This was a country ruled by religion and a god-king who was accepted by his people as their undisputed temporal and spiritual ruler. Every family willingly supplied at least one son to the priesthood as a matter of pride, and no separation existed between church and state. Lamas were a part of the social fabric, and there were as many attached to large monasteries in and around Lhasa as all its other inhabitants combined. However, many Chinese and foreign visitors felt that, from an economic standpoint, the lamas absorbed an unfair share of the wealth of this country from an already impoverished people with little arable land.

China, for its part, hadn't been able to maintain any real control over Tibet's affairs during the last few decades. On this issue, Curzon had stated Britain's position unambiguously: 'We regard Chinese suzerainty over Tibet as a constitutional fiction.' He was determined to bypass Peking and its powerless Amban, and deal with Lhasa directly. But, frustrated at being repeatedly snubbed, he described Tibet as 'a petty Power which only mistakes forbearance for weakness'. Although he insisted British India's dealings with its neighbour ought to be purely commercial, it was clear that these intentions were, first and foremost, political. Lord Hamilton, secretary of state for India, saw this for what it was: 'a gross exploitation and distortion of Britain's treaty relations with China for a purpose which went well beyond the original intent of the treaties'.

The viceroy was not to be deterred, as summed up by author John MacGregor†: 'the story of British initiatives in Tibet for the next two years is the story of Curzon riding rough-shod over domestic

---

*   Britain was granted concessions in Tibet by the Anglo-Chinese Convention of 1890 and the Trade Regulations of 1893.

†   This was the pen name used by a diplomat in the US Department of State to write *Tibet: A Chronicle of Exploration*.

opposition. The "forward thruster" would have his own way—for better or for worse.' Curzon would steadfastly pursue his conviction and prime objective: to ensure Russian influence was eliminated, by removing their presence from Lhasa. As to British India's 'purely commercial' goal, a former prime minister commented that it seemed the object 'was to make people drink Indian tea who did not like Indian tea and did not want Indian tea'. Nain Singh, too, had reported Tibetans preferred Chinese tea, in spite it being more expensive, and only poor folk drank the Indian variety.*

The Holy City

With much cajoling, the viceroy secured London's agreement to send a delegation into Tibet in 1903, although his masters insisted it penetrate only as far as Khamba Jong, just across the border from British-controlled Sikkim. After a careful study of this unfolding episode, which would quickly escalate into a mission forcing its way into Lhasa, author Charles Allen concluded: 'The official reasons for this invasion were almost entirely bogus . . .'

Curzon personally approached Major Francis Younghusband, by this stage a political himself, to command the mission. He had impressed the viceroy with his earlier feats. However, despite forays into journalism as a war correspondent for the *Times*, in far-flung places such as Chitral and South Africa, the major had been ignored by his government. When the call from Curzon came, Younghusband later recalled: 'Here indeed, I felt was the chance of my life. I was once more alive. The thrill of adventure once again ran through my veins.'

Accompanied by the Resident in Sikkim, and supported by army officers with an escort of 200 Indian troops, Younghusband

---

* The Company started tea cultivation in Assam during the first half of the nineteenth century in an attempt to break the Chinese monopoly, but it was only late in the century that India became a major grower.

crossed the border. The Tibetans, however, refused to negotiate on
their side of the frontier. After several wasted months the mission was
forced to return, having lost face and with Curzon feeling rebuffed
yet again. Younghusband now came to the conclusion that nothing
would be achieved unless negotiations took place in Lhasa—a view
which Curzon needed little convincing of. As a result, in December
of the same year, he was sent back. This time he was accompanied
by a larger expeditionary force, some 3000-strong, commanded by
Brigadier General James Macdonald.

Here was another pairing of the political with the military and,
as in Afghanistan, it came with a blurring of command that would
inevitably break down once conflict loomed. In Younghusband's
later estimation, Macdonald proved to be overly cautious at times
and ineffectual; even his troops would eventually refer to the ailing
commander as Retiring Mac.* Initially, though, there was no hint of
the command structure becoming a problem, as the two men set out
to deliver the outcome Curzon desired.

A column of over 7000 camp followers, and more than that
number of baggage animals, accompanied the troops; this severely
taxed the resources of the villagers along the way, not least in simply
trying to feed them. The pack animals used were an eclectic mix
of yaks, ponies, camels, bullocks, mules and *zebrules*—the latter an
experimental cross-breed that proved unruly, and were detested by
both men and other beasts. The accompanying *Daily Mail* staffer
described some of the others who made up the camp: 'There was
a man with a butterfly net and another who collected stones and
one with a trowel who collected weeds and a whole committee of
licensed curio-hunters for the British Museum. Then there were the
newspaper correspondents, devilish keen to be in on the show.' It was,
after all, in Curzon's words: 'The one mystery which the nineteenth
century has still left for the twentieth to explore.'

---

*   A nickname that was all the more offensive in playing on that of another
General Macdonald, famously known, for good reason, as Fighting Mac.

As they proceeded, the surveyors in the party carefully mapped the area with their latest instruments, confirming the route surveys made by the Pundits decades earlier. The expeditionary force carried Kishen Singh's plan-to-scale of Lhasa, and was accompanied by Kintup, who had visited the capital a number of times. The column marched across the border without being challenged, and continued on through the Chumbi Valley—the sliver of Tibetan territory running between Sikkim and Bhutan, marking the traditional trade route between India and Tibet.

Not a shot was fired until they neared the small village of Guru, on the road towards the fortress city of Gyantse. Here, their force of 1300 was confronted by around 1000 to 1500 Tibetan soldiers and militia, who had erected a stone wall to block their advance. They once again implored the mission to turn around and go back home. The lamas at the barrier solemnly pointed out to Younghusband that, to preserve their religion, no European was permitted on their land, and any negotiations could only be held back at the border. As much as *both* parties sincerely wished to avoid bloodshed, their irreconcilable positions soon became all too evident.

We are left with what happened. The Tibetans were armed mostly with swords and matchlocks: primitive muskets, loaded by ramming a charge down their long barrels before being ignited with a slow match or fuse. They possessed only a fraction of the firepower of the expeditionary force; yet each one wore a sacred charm bearing the Dalai Lama's own seal, which they faithfully believed would protect them from British bullets. Macdonald's troops and two Maxim machine guns (each capable of firing close to 700 rounds a minute) quickly surrounded them but, when commanded to disarm, the Tibetans resisted.

Reports of the ensuing confusion differ as to what occurred next. According to Younghusband, it was the Tibetan general who fired the first shot: 'he threw himself on a sepoy, drew a revolver, and shot him in the jaw. Not, as I think, with any deliberate intention, but from sheer inanity, the signal had now been given.'

In the boil-over, he and many of his men were dead within minutes. The final Tibetan toll amounted to 628 dead and 222 wounded, compared to only a dozen of the British injured. It was, as Younghusband penned to his father the next day, 'a pure massacre', and would long be remembered as a black day for Britain.

The captain commanding the Maxims later said, 'I got so sick of the slaughter that I ceased fire,' although Macdonald's order to the machine gunners had been to 'make as big a bag as possible'. Instead of running away from the murderous fire, the stunned Tibetans *walked off slowly* with heads bowed, looking bewildered, perhaps at being failed by their charms and their gods. Afterwards, Macdonald would report that his troops had discharged 1400 machine gun rounds and 14,351 rifle bullets during the incident.

Younghusband later labelled it the Guru Disaster. An improvised hospital was quickly set up for the wounded, which saved many. But even this action mystified the locals, as Younghusband noted: 'the Tibetans showed great gratitude for what we did, though they failed to understand why we should try to take their lives one day and try to save them the next'.

Contrary to British expectations that Tibetan resistance and morale would now be broken, they found the latter's resolve had instead stiffened. As a result, many hundreds more were killed in engagements all the way to the capital, while Macdonald and Younghusband lost only a handful of their men under fire. As they subdued the countryside, many monasteries were looted of rare cultural artefacts by officers and men alike, quite apart from the general plunder considered legitimate booty by the troops.

Within a few weeks, by August 1904, the column finally forced its way into Lhasa. Appearing splendid in full dress uniform, the troops marched behind their Gurkha band, thinking they were putting on a fine performance when the watching locals began to clap—not understanding that Tibetans do so in an attempt to drive out evil spirits.

Younghusband described the moment they first set eyes on the capital:

The goal of so many travellers' ambitions was actually in sight! The goal, to attain which we had endured and risked so much, and for which the best efforts of so many had been concentrated, had now been won. Every obstacle which nature and man combined could heap in our way had finally been overcome, and the sacred city, hidden so far and deep behind the Himalayan ramparts, and so jealously guarded from strangers, was full before our eyes.

The sight that impressed the visitors most was described by the correspondent for the *Times*:

Here . . . was no poor Oriental town arrogating to itself the dignity which mystery can in itself confer. From the first moment, the splendour of the Potala cannot be hidden, though, like all great monuments further acquaintance does but increase one's amazement and admiration . . . The Potala would dominate London—Lhasa it simply eclipses. By European standards it is impossible to judge this building; there is nothing there with which comparison can be made.

Yet despite the palace and the gilded halls of the monasteries, most British officers and their men were sorely disappointed by the capital, some describing it as dirty and squalid. Younghusband, too, was unimpressed in one particular regard: 'The religion of the Tibetans is grotesque, and is the most degraded, not the purest, form of Buddhism in existence.'

Contrary to expectation, the expeditionary force found few signs of Russian activity, or any real evidence of the suspected treaty between Tsar Nicholas II and the Great Lama—who had left the capital rather than be forced to receive the mission. The Amban posted a proclamation deposing the Dalai Lama, but this was defaced by the populace, who held the Chinese in contempt and threw stones at them. China's reaction to what amounted to an armed invasion of its country was interesting: as long as Britain continued to recognize its suzerainty over Tibet, this incident might teach the recalcitrant Tibetans a valuable lesson.

The Dalai Lama's representatives were strong-armed by Younghusband into signing an Anglo-Tibetan Convention, which set out a number of commercial and political provisions. The Chinese did not sign this document, but neither would the Tibetans accept their dictates in its internal affairs.* One article prohibited the Tibetans from having dealings with any foreign power without Britain's consent—obviously aimed at excluding Russia.

To add insult to injury, the 'agreement' forced the Tibetans to bear part of the expeditionary force's cost. This amounted to an indemnity of 7.5 million rupees (in excess of 500,000 pounds) to be paid over seventy-five years—a staggering burden for such an impoverished country. Since the convention entitled Britain to occupy the Chumbi Valley until the full amount was paid, Younghusband's secret aim was to keep this strategic route in British hands for decades by way of this indemnity. However, his masters in London were angered on learning of his aggressive initiatives, which were in defiance of their wishes and, as they well knew, would be offensive to Russia. They telegraphed back demanding he remain in Lhasa until these clauses were altered, but he ignored their orders and made haste to return.

After seven weeks of occupation, when the time came to leave, Younghusband did so proudly, claiming his mission had achieved its objectives. As he departed, he took a solitary walk in the mountains and, looking back on the holy city, experienced a moment that would change his life, as he later described:

---

*   An Anglo-Chinese Convention was signed two years later. According to Hugh Richardson, author of *Tibet and Its History,* this meant 'Chinese rights in Tibet were thus recognized to an extent to which the Chinese had recently been wholly unable to exercise them'.

... I was insensibly suffused with an almost intoxicating sense
of elation and good will. The exhilaration of the moment
grew and grew till it thrilled through me with overpowering
intensity. Never again could I think evil, or ever again be at
enmity with any man ... that single hour on leaving Lhasa was
worth all the rest of my lifetime.*

On his return, London officially censured Younghusband for
overstepping his authority by imposing such a harsh treaty, and
proceeded to dilute it considerably; the indemnity amount was
reduced by two-thirds, and occupation of the Chumbi Valley to only
three years.

A few weeks before he had entered Lhasa, Curzon had written
him complaining of the government's changed attitude towards
Tibet, which they now considered: 'a nuisance and an expense; and
all that they want to do is to get out of it in any way that does not
involve positive humiliation'. When the two met again, on greeting
him, Curzon wrung Younghusband's hands and, with tears in his
eyes, declared: 'If your Mission had been anything but the most
complete success it would have been the ruin of me. Remember,
throughout the rest of my life there is nothing I will not do for you.'

As far as his government was concerned, however, Younghusband's
perspective in Tibet had been too narrow, and without consideration
of its overall impact on 'the Great Game'. As Prime Minister Arthur
Balfour pointed out:

> The only chance of any permanent arrangement with . . .
> [Russia] in Central Asia depends on the mutual confidence
> that engagements will be adhered to; and if, as I fear, Colonel
> Younghusband in acting as he has done, wished to force the
> hand of the Government . . . he has inflicted upon us an injury

---

* This experience would turn him into a spiritualist, and founder of the
World Congress of Faiths in 1936.

compared with which any loss of material interest affected by
our Tibetan policy is absolutely insignificant.

Perhaps he had been made the scapegoat for an unpopular expedition,
as many officials and commentators firmly believed; nevertheless,
it effectively ended his public career. Still, Francis Younghusband
would be made a Knight Commander of the Indian Empire by year's
end, awarded the Star of India in 1917 and, two years later, elected
president of the RGS.

Britain's final imperial adventure left many at home wondering
what, if anything, had been accomplished, and about the damage
done to its international standing. What the mission had undoubtedly
resulted in, though, was the violation of a holy city and its largely
peace-loving people, who had only wanted to be left alone.

Epilogue

While Britain was engaged in Tibet, Russia had lost a disastrous war against Japan in 1905, considered its worst military defeat to date. A European superpower had been humiliated by an Asiatic country; in the eyes of its people, this was an irrecoverable setback for Imperial Russia. It signalled the approaching end of the monarchy and, with it, any dreams the tsars held of building a lasting empire in the East. At the same time, a growing military threat from Germany was driving Russia and Britain closer together as potential allies. Both powers wanted to settle all outstanding territorial questions in Central Asia and Tibet expeditiously; through this renewed cooperation, political tension seemed to dissipate from the region.

Historian Gerald Morgan ends his study of the Great Game with two important findings:

> The first of them is that Russia never had either the will or the ability to invade India. Whatever the hot-headed soldiers on both sides might threaten or expect, it was always the statesmen who prevented a war. The second conclusion is that contrary to Russian fears, India never had the military capacity to move into Central Asia . . . Trade not war was the Company's role.

And as for *that* evocative, yet euphemistic, phrase, he goes on to remark: 'it belittles what was a deadly serious affair marked by many

serious diplomatic and strategic blunders from which few emerge
with credit'.

On the last day of August 1907, the Anglo-Russian Convention
was signed in St Petersburg. But it was done in secrecy, as negotiations
had excluded participation by the other countries affected. This deal
formally recognized that Afghanistan lay in British India's sphere of
influence, and was not to be interfered with; while Britain undertook
not to change the country's political status, nor intrigue against
Russia in Central Asia. Both powers agreed to deal with Tibet only
through China, acknowledging the sovereignty of the latter over
the former. They also decided to maintain Persia's independence,
and worked out which of its parts were to fall into their respective
spheres. Of course, Afghanistan, Tibet and Persia were not consulted
in this 'carve-up', and were understandably dismayed and angered
when they finally learned of the deal.

So far as the Great Game's legacy for the region is concerned:
India and the arc of countries on its northern borders have fared
better or worse depending on one's viewpoint. In 1947, Indians
would wrest independence from the war-weary British, and the Raj
came to an abrupt end, but with Pakistan partitioned off and many
millions dead or displaced in the process. Within a few decades,
Bangladesh, too, would secure its sovereignty, but only after another
bloody struggle.

To west of the subcontinent, Persia would become the Islamic
Republic of Iran following a revolution in 1979. That same year,
lessons from the Anglo-Afghan wars would go unheeded as the
Soviet-Afghan War erupted, and would grind out for almost a
decade: Afghanistan seems doomed to suffer occupation by foreign
powers. In 2001, a United States-led coalition, with Britain included,
would put troops on the ground here, initially to drive out the
fundamentalist Taliban. But America remains bogged down there
today, in the longest military conflict it has ever participated in.

Russian Turkestan would revert to its former countries roughly
along ethnic lines, following the collapse of the Soviet Union in 1991

and the creation of new states, many of which still struggle with the newfound concept of democracy. Eastern Turkestan remains a part of China as the Xinjiang Uyghur Autonomous Region, although tensions between its ethnic communities and their Han rulers continue around what constitutes 'autonomous'.

Finally, to the east, Tibet has also changed irrevocably, after another Dalai Lama was forced to flee Lhasa. This time it was in 1959, before a brutal crackdown by Chinese authorities; his people remain subdued, yet praying for his return from exile.

Returning to *our* timeline of the Great Game: it officially concluded with the Anglo-Russian Convention of 1907. Despite its imperfections, this agreement brought down the curtain on a century-long rivalry—at least for the time being, as Europe would soon be engulfed by the winds of a great war.

Timeline of Key Events

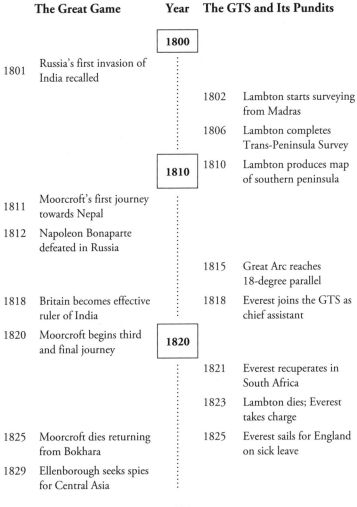

The Great Game		Year	The GTS and Its Pundits	
		1800		
1801	Russia's first invasion of India recalled			
			1802	Lambton starts surveying from Madras
			1806	Lambton completes Trans-Peninsula Survey
		1810	1810	Lambton produces map of southern peninsula
1811	Moorcroft's first journey towards Nepal			
1812	Napoleon Bonaparte defeated in Russia			
			1815	Great Arc reaches 18-degree parallel
1818	Britain becomes effective ruler of India		1818	Everest joins the GTS as chief assistant
1820	Moorcroft begins third and final journey	**1820**		
			1821	Everest recuperates in South Africa
			1823	Lambton dies; Everest takes charge
1825	Moorcroft dies returning from Bokhara		1825	Everest sails for England on sick leave
1829	Ellenborough seeks spies for Central Asia			

The Great Game	Year	The GTS and Its Pundits
1830 Conolly rides from Moscow to India	**1830**	**1830** Everest returns to India
1831 Burnes charts the Indus		
1832 Burnes visits Bokhara		**1832** Everest starts restructuring the GTS
		1836 Everest triangulates across the doab
1838 Persia fails in its bid to capture Herat		
	1840	
1841 Burnes hacked to death in Kabul		
1842 First Afghan War ends		
1843 Britain seizes Sind		**1843** Great Arc completed: Cape Comorin to Himalayas
		1844 Everest retires home to England (dies in 1861)
		1847 Everest publishes account of the Great Arc
1849 Britain takes the Punjab		
	1850	
1853 Crimean War begins		
		1855 Montgomerie starts surveying Kashmir
		1856 Mount Everest named
1857 Indian Mutiny/Rebellion		

1860

1863 Dost Mohammed dies	1863 Montgomerie launches native explorers
	1864 Abdul Hamid dies returning from Yarkand
1865 Russia takes Tashkent; Yakub Beg in Kashgar	
	1866 Nain Singh reaches Lhasa, his first mission
	1867 The Mirza journeys to Pamirs and Kashgar
1868 Russia seizes Bokhara, first of three khanates	

1870

	1870 The Havildar's first mission into Badakhshan
1873 Russia takes Khiva	1873 Montgomerie returns to England (dies in 1878)
	1873 Second Forsyth Mission to Chinese Turkestan
1875 Russian Turkestan created after Khokand falls	1875 Nain Singh returns from fourth and final mission
1877 China regains Eastern Turkestan	
	1878 Kishen Singh begins final four-year expedition

1880 Second Afghan War ends **1880**

	1883 The GTS completes triangulation of India
1884 Russia captures Merv without a fight	1884 Kintup returns after four years along Tsangpo
1888 Trans-Caspian railway reaches Bokhara	

	1890	
1891 Britain takes Hunza; Russia tries to annex Pamirs		
1893 Wakhan Corridor finally carved out		
1895 Britain overruns Chitral following siege		1895 Nain Singh dies (year of death disputed)
1899 Curzon becomes viceroy		
	1900	
1904 Younghusband Expedition enters Lhasa		
1907 Anglo-Russian Convention signed		

Glossary

Amban	Chinese high official
Bala Hissar	royal citadel
Bhotia	Indian of Tibetan origin
chu	river
dhoti	long loincloth worn by male native Indians
doab	area lying between the Ganges and Jumna rivers
dost	friend (an honorific title)
havildar	sergeant (infantry)
jemadar	lieutenant (infantry)
jihad	holy war
jong	fort
jongpon	fort master
kafir	unbeliever (to Muslims)
kangri	mountain
khalasi	native survey helper
la	mountain pass

mullah	religious Muslim leader, usually learned in religion and law
munshi	secretary, translator, or educated man
nor	lake
pundit	learned Hindu and/or schoolteacher
sepoy	native Indian soldier of the East India Company
shan	mountain range
tarjum	staging post
thok	goldfield or gold
tso	lake
zamindar	landowner

Note on Spellings

Names of people and places have been spelt or romanized in a way familiar to the general reader.

Bibliography

With the general reader in mind, only the primary books consulted are listed below, although a number of other books and journal references can be found in the body of the text.

Parts One and Four: The Great Game

Alder, Garry, *Beyond Bokhara: The Life of William Moorcroft, Asian Explorer and Pioneer Veterinary Surgeon, 1767–1825* (London: Century, 1985).

Allen, Charles, *Duel in the Snows: The True Story of the Younghusband Mission to Lhasa* (London: John Murray, 2004).

Dalrymple, William, *Return of a King: The Battle for Afghanistan* (London: Bloomsbury, 2013).

Edwardes, Michael, *Playing the Great Game: A Victorian Cold War* (London: Hamish Hamilton, 1975).

Hopkirk, Peter, *The Great Game: On Secret Service in High Asia* (London: John Murray, 1990).

Ingram, Edward, *In Defence of British India: Great Britain in the Middle East, 1775–1842* (London: Frank Cass, 1984).

Johnson, Robert, *Spying for Empire: The Great Game in Central and South Asia, 1757–1947* (London: Greenhill Books, 2006).

Meyer, Karl, and Shareen Brysac, *Tournament of Shadows: The Great Game and the Race for Empire in Central Asia* (Washington D.C.: Counterpoint, 1999).

Morgan, Gerald, *Anglo-Russian Rivalry in Central Asia: 1810–1895* (London: Frank Cass, 1981).

Seaver, George, *Francis Younghusband: Explorer and Mystic* (London: John Murray, 1952).

Yorke, Edmund, *Playing The Great Game: Britain, War and Politics in Afghanistan since 1839* (London: Robert Hale, 2012).

Part Two: The GTS of India

Edney, Matthew, *Mapping an Empire: The Geographical Construction of British India, 1765–1843* (Chicago: University of Chicago Press, 1997).

Hinks, Arthur, *Maps and Survey* (Cambridge: Cambridge University Press, 1913).

Keay, John, *The Great Arc: The Dramatic Tale of How India Was Mapped and Everest Was Named* (London: HarperCollins, 2000).

Markham, Clements, *A Memoir on the Indian Surveys* (2nd ed.) (London: W.H. Allen, 1878).

Phillimore, R.H., *Historical Records of the Survey of India*, Vols I–V (Dehra Dun: Survey of India, 1945–68).

Smith, J.R., *Everest: The Man and the Mountain* (Caithness: Whittles, 1999).

Styles, Showell, *The Forbidden Frontiers: The Survey of India from 1765 to 1949* (London: Hamish Hamilton, 1970).

Part Three: The Pundits

MacGregor, John, *Tibet: A Chronicle of Exploration* (London: Routledge & Kegan Paul, 1970).

Madan, P.L., *Tibet: Saga of Indian Explorers (1864–1894)* (New Delhi: Manohar, 2004).

Rawat, Indra Singh, *Indian Explorers of the 19th Century* (New Delhi: Government of India, 1973).

Stewart, Jules, *Spying for the Raj: The Pundits and the Mapping of the Himalaya* (Stroud: Sutton, 2006).

Waller, Derek, *The Pundits: British Exploration of Tibet and Central Asia* (Lexington: University of Kentucky, 1990).

Ward, Michael, 'The Survey of India and the Pundits', in *The Alpine Journal* (vol. 103, 1998), pp. 59–79.

General

Allen, Charles, *A Mountain in Tibet: The Search for Mount Kailas and the Sources of the Great Rivers of India* (London: Andre Deutsch, 1982).

Gardner, Brian, *The East India Company: A History* (London: Rupert Hart-Davis, 1971).

Keay, John, *Explorers of the Western Himalayas 1820–1895* (London: John Murray, 1997).

Kipling, Rudyard, *Kim* (London: Macmillan, 1901).

Mason, Kenneth, *Abode of Snow: A History of Himalayan Exploration and Mountaineering* (London: Rupert Hart-Davis, 1955).

Index